12 BOOKS
THAT CHANGED
THE WORLD

12 BOOKS
THAT CHANGED
THE WORLD

MELVYN BRAGG

HODDER &
STOUGHTON

Copyright © 2006 by Melvyn Bragg

First published in Great Britain in 2006 by Hodder & Stoughton
A division of Hodder Headline

The right of Melvyn Bragg to be identified as the Author
of the Work has been asserted by him in accordance with
the Copyright, Designs and Patents Act 1988.

A Hodder & Stoughton Book

1

A CIP catalogue record for this title is available from the British Library

Hardback ISBN 0 340 83980 5
Trade paperback ISBN 0 340 83981 3

Typeset in Garamond Three by Hewer Text UK Ltd, Edinburgh
Printed and bound by Clays Ltd, St Ives plc

Hodder Headline's policy is to use papers that are natural, renewable
and recyclable products and made from wood grown in sustainable forests.
The logging and manufacturing processes are expected to conform to
the environmental regulations of the country of origin.

Hodder & Stoughton Ltd
A division of Hodder Headline
338 Euston Road
London NW1 3BH

To
Vivien Green
a wonderful friend
and a great lover of books

CONTENTS

INTRODUCTION

The idea for this book came from a single image. About nine years ago, when I was reading about Isaac Newton, I imagined this awkward, unhappy, driven young man, sitting alone and in silence in his home, a farmhouse, forcing his mind to construct theories which eventually changed the world and changed it radically. Out of the unlikely context of that Lincolnshire farmhouse would come revolutions in thought whose force and consequences re-ordered human life. The juxtaposition of the solitary figure working to produce such a modest and harmless-looking object as a book and the explosion this caused in the minds of men and women then and since led me to look for others whose intense preoccupation posted in placid pages had seized the story of our species. That a mere book should have such power!

We think of the world changing 65 billion years ago when an asteroid hastened the death of the dinosaurs and allowed space for the growth of the mammals. We think of the upheavals in ancient ice ages and fear global warming to come. We know about the destructions of war and the inspirational energy which can bring about peace. There was the American Revolution, the French Revolution, perhaps most important of all the Industrial Revolution, the draining of populations from the countryside to the cities. There was the extension of the lifespan, the eruptive transformations brought by the advances of technology. The rise and rise of mass consumerism . . . A mere book seems a very unlikely contender as a world-changing catalyst.

Yet for those of us who love to read, the idea that a book can have an influence is not news. Our perceptions have been shaped through books, our store of information heaped up, our tastes extended, perhaps refined, our sense of humour tickled, our sense of well-being restored or reinforced; we have been excited, alerted, moved, consoled, felt less alone, even felt morally improved and inspired – at least for a while. We know that books can change us as individuals.

On a different level books have often been and still are the agents of creeds which have shaped and reshaped humanity. These generally religious books would, I think, have figured prominently in the reckoning for a list of the twelve most influential books in the world. At one stage I had a list dominated by the Ancient Greeks, books of God, Marx and Mao and two or three books of science. It felt unsatisfactory; too ambitious, and, despite the undoubted importance, not very lively as a selection. Out of the several lists that followed, I eventually saw that a number of books by British authors had a fair claim to have changed the world. Indeed it was difficult to cut down the number to twelve – James Clerk Maxwell, Tom Paine and Dr Johnson, for instance, were hard to omit. The British have produced and still do produce a high yield in key thoughts, inventions and proposals. By omitting the definite article – these are not *the* twelve books – I believed a case could be made for the twelve books from these islands and that is what I try to do. The British provide a surprisingly rich crop.

From the beginning I wanted to enjoy a range. Leisure and literature would, if I could make it work, figure alongside science and the constitution; changes in society as well as changes in technology would be addressed. This has meant taking a risk and, now and then, elasticating the strict meaning of the word 'book'.

For instance, I thought it essential, given its key constitutional importance, to include Magna Carta, which, though produced by the royal chancery in 1215 as a formal royal grant, became in effect a vital and enduring book of reference, the basic book of our constitution and that of many others, most importantly, of America and India.

Certain books suggested themselves, most especially Newton's *Principia Mathematica* (1687), Darwin's *The Origin of Species* (1859), Adam Smith's *The Wealth of Nations* (1776), Michael Faraday's *Experimental Researches in Electricity* (1855) and William Tyndale's massive contribution to the King James Bible (1611).

It was, I thought, impossible to ignore William Wilberforce's successful campaign for the abolition of slavery. True, it began as a four-hours-long speech in the House of Commons in 1789, but it was reproduced in print immediately afterwards and it is in its book form that its revolutionary and lasting influence resides. Nor could the emergence of women as equals in every respect be neglected and in different ways Mary Wollstonecraft's *A Vindication of the Rights of Woman* (1792) and Marie Stopes's *Married Love* (1918) spoke authoritatively and with far-reaching influence on that.

The arts could not be omitted, I thought, and nor could leisure. William Shakespeare's posthumously published First Folio in 1623 will be argued for as a book that has ever since changed and reshaped minds. The first Book of Rules of Association Football (1863) enabled the world to play a game which now commands a unique and previously uncharted, unimagined empire of followers, participants, fanatics and rich merchants.

Which leaves the Patent Specification for Arkwright's Spinning Machine (1769). I was being shown over his now-derelict mills in Derbyshire and learned then how crucially important this invention was to an industrial revolution which has never stopped. This was made possible by a patent cunningly and skilfully put on paper by Richard Arkwright. A patent, I thought, could be called an entrepreneur-inventor's book.

What I wanted these books to have in common was that they changed the world to that in which we now live. They could be reduced to plausible snapshots. You could walk into a pub or an airport, go on an outing or just stay in your house, and be aware of what these books had delivered to the lives you daily led and saw. Newton took us to the Moon; Faraday gave us electricity; Darwin took away God and the gods who had been there since civilisation began; Mary Wollstonecraft started the struggle for the equality of women and Marie Stopes for their right to control and enjoy their sex and family lives. After Wilberforce the equality of the races was on the march and Magna Carta is the keystone of opposition to the exercise of tyrannic power. Our markets operate through the laws of Adam Smith, our imaginations are most exercised by Shakespeare, our work organised by Arkwright, our language and religious thought by the King James Bible and our world-dominating sport by the FA Book of Rules. Of course, with 'our' I take a licence. This is the case in the whole book. Many authors know much more about individual writers and subjects than I do, which I acknowledge in the course of this book. I thought, however, that the juxtapositions, the chance to look around different fields in a single book might be as entertaining for you to read as it has been for me to write.

On much the same principle, I decided not to order the book chronologically. I thought it would imply an historical evolution which is only partly true. More importantly, though, as I had come across these books randomly I think the higgledy-piggledy is more honest and appropriate than the chronological.

It seems to me all but miraculous that amid the tumult of events and the mêlée of competing dramas, despite the uproars of wars and politics and all the bombast of the daily news, these British voices began, all of them, with the quiet strokes of a quill or a pen and were formed in seclusion to be sent out into the world, where a fuse was lit. There then followed a conceptual chain reaction, sometimes of awesome proportions, which changed the way all of us lead and experience our lives.

PRINCIPIA MATHEMATICA

1687

by

Isaac Newton

PHILOSOPHIÆ

NATURALIS

PRINCIPIA

MATHEMATICA.

Autore *JS. NEWTON,* *Trin. Coll. Cantab. Soc.* Matheseos
Professore *Lucasiano,* & Societatis Regalis Sodali.

IMPRIMATUR·
S. PEPYS, *Reg. Soc.* PRÆSES.
Julii 5. 1686.

LONDINI,

Jussu *Societatis Regiæ* ac Typis *Josephi Streater.* Prostat apud
plures Bibliopolas. *Anno* MDCLXXXVII.

'Nature, and Nature's Laws lay hid in night:/God said "Let Newton be!" and all was light.' In that brilliant couplet Alexander Pope, the supreme poet of his day, summed up the awe felt by everyone who could grasp what Newton had done. Voltaire, the most famous philosopher in Europe, witnessed Newton's state funeral in Westminster Abbey and praised an England which honoured a mathematician as other countries honoured a monarch. The great scholar Laplace, who was extremely sparing with his praise, makes Newton the one exception, and he laid out reasons still held to be valid which prove that Newton's most famous book *Principia Mathematica* will 'always have a pre-eminence above all the other works of human genius'.

There were those who were prepared to call Newton a god, and indeed, as well as bringing him, in his own lifetime and since, the support of the most accomplished minds in science, his work also gathered flocks of followers who saw him as the source of solutions to the meaning of life. It might be appropriate to note here that Newton, though an unorthodox Anglican, was a true believer. 'Gravity is God,' he said. Newton's fame and importance are still as strong today, and despite his disclaimer that 'if I have seen further it is by standing on the shoulders of giants', there are those, not least Einstein, whose ideas refined and extended but by no means

9

diminished the achievement of Newton, who still see him as unique. Einstein wrote, 'Nature to him was an open book. He stands before us, strong, certain and alone.'

And it was by thought alone that he achieved this pre-eminence. Newton made the most telling remark on the process of thought that I have ever encountered. It is also the simplest. When asked how he had come upon his theory of gravity, he said, 'By thinking on it continuously.'

Isaac Newton was the first man to reveal the true properties of light, just as he was the first to discover and examine the laws of motion. He discovered and proved mathematically the laws of gravity which frame and dictate our life on Earth. He defined space and time and unlocked the secrets of the planets and their movements. He gave man the knowledge that would enable him to leave our planet and explore the others. He enabled the establishment of new technologies that still shape and reshape our lives. He codified and exemplified the scientific method that is with us to this day. Even listed in that bare outline, this one man's achievement has something of the heroic about it. He did this by working in solitude. Through the inexplicable magnificence of the human brain he distilled his thought into a few books, most importantly *Philosophiae Naturalis Principia Mathematica* – usually known as the *Principia* – published in 1687.

I had the great good fortune to look closely at a first edition of *Principia* in the Wren Library in Trinity College, Newton's college, in Cambridge. It is an unprepossessing volume. While I looked around at the written splendour of ages on the shelves of that palatial room, I came across many grander, fatter, more gilded, more important-looking books. The *Principia* is about 6 by 8 inches. It is leather bound, weighs about 3 pounds, consists of 512 pages filled with mathematical problems, calculations and diagrams, and it is written in Latin. The material is arranged in three parts, and between the covers of the volume I was holding a scholar from Lincolnshire, only son of an illiterate farmer, figured out our world.

We are told that Newton had a difficult birth on the family farm at Woolsthorpe near Grantham. He was born on Christmas Day in 1642, three months after his father had died. When he was three his mother moved out to live with a wealthy rector in a parish near by and for the next eight years of his life he was brought up by Granny Ascough, his maternal grandmother. Very little is known about this period. It was believed that his mother was the only woman he ever loved. It is presumed that he hated his stepfather because at one stage he said he wanted to burn down his house with both his stepfather and his mother inside it. Later, in a written list of sins, he regrets having entertained such a thought.

Prompted by whatever impulse or guidance, this lonely, sickly boy began to make toys from a very young age. He made a working windmill driven by mice running around a treadmill; mice being easy to come by on a farm and windmills a feature of that part of the world. He made kites to which he attached lights which he flew at night, presumably scaring the wits out of the locals. Later he made clocks.

As a young adult, when it was intended that he become a farmer, he went, like a character in a Thomas Hardy novel, to Stourbridge Fair, a traditional English gathering of livestock, pedlars, young people on the gad, buyers and sellers of rare breeds and bargains, beer, an unusual concentration of noise and excitement in the silent, placid countryside; there, from a hawker of strange objects, he bought a rough-hewn glass prism. Back on the farm at Woolsthorpe Newton constructed an experiment which shone white light through the glass. The spectrum of colours on the wall was to set him off on his profound thoughts about the properties of light, a subject which had engaged natural philosophers for centuries and a study he pursued with outstanding success throughout his life.

He was also unafraid to use himself as an experiment, rather as painters use their own faces as a cheap and testing way to develop the skills of portraiture. He wanted to know what pictures could be made by the eye, and so in one experiment he pushed a bodkin, an ivory toothpick, underneath his eyeball almost right to the back of the socket. He wrote: 'I push a bodkin betwixt my eye and the bone as near to the backside of my eye as I can and pressing my eye with the end of it there appear several white, dark and coloured circles, which circles are plainest when I continue to rub my eye with the point of the bodkin.'

This is a most strange young man. After a few of these experiments he records that he was obliged to spend two weeks in bed with the curtains drawn.

There was an uncle educated at Cambridge who helped this clearly unusually clever, self-driven, solitary boy on his way by getting him, in his teens, to Grantham Grammar School, where the headmaster, Henry Stokes, was notable for raising the level of scholarship to that of a university. When Newton arrived at Trinity College, Cambridge, in 1661, he was well grounded in classics and mathematics. Despite the comfortable wealth of his mother and her second husband, he was poorly provided for. He was obliged to be a sub-sizar, that is to say a poor scholar who was forced to wait on other students and fellows and eat only after they had finished, his portion being their leavings.

The Cambridge that Newton came to in 1661 was not the dynamo of academic, especially scientific, enquiry and success it was to become – largely as a result of his *Principia,* which gave Cambridge its enduring reputation for high scholarship. It was here, very quickly, that he laid down his own laws of learning. In 1664 he wrote, 'Amicus Plato, amicus Aristotelis, magis amica veritas' (Plato is my friend, Aristotle is my friend, but my best friend is truth). His colours were nailed to the mast. It was as if he gave notice to himself that his great journey was begun.

At Cambridge Newton took up another study – that of alchemy – which he was to pursue as zealously as he pursued his physics. His writings on this ancient, occult and erudite subject are voluminous and, it is said even by experts, largely in code and impenetrable. For example, one entry reads, 'Today I made Jupiter fly on his eagle'. For long periods he had a furnace which burned continuously in which he developed, according to Dr Robert Iliffe, 'a whole series of amalgams and elements which we simply cannot replicate today. It is impossible', he goes on, 'to know whether various impurities entered the chemical material and made Newton develop various things that we will simply never be able to recover. Alchemy was . . . the province of adepts, gifted people touched by God. On a number of occasions in the 1670s and 1680s, he uses alchemical terms and language to shed light on aspects of what we would now call his science.'

As the influence of alchemy, called the Hermetic Tradition, grew stronger, Newton's concept of nature underwent a crucial change. He had been entirely what could be termed a mechanical philosopher in the accepted seventeenth-century style, one who explained natural phenomena by the motions of particles of matter. So, for instance, he held that the physical reality of light is a stream of tiny corpuscles diverted from its course by the presence of denser or rarer media.

Influenced by the Hermetic Tradition, he began to use the language of alchemists to describe puzzling phenomena such as chemical affinities. Unlikely as it seems, this combination proved fruitful: a match between the 'magical' and the mechanical. The words 'attractions and repulsions' and the ideas which flowed from them have been called 'direct transpositions of the occult sympathies and antipathies of Hermetic philosophy'. Newton ignored the protests of other mechanical philosophers and claimed an important place for these supplements to the merely mechanical theories.

By combining these two apparently irreconcilable states of knowledge and reconciling them through the concept of force, it has been said that Newton 'made his ultimate contribution to science'.

cedendo à Jove, & Sole decrescant eadem ratione ac lege, qua vis
gravitatis decrescit in recessu à Terra.

Corol. 1. Igitur gravitas datur in Planetas universos. Nam Ve-
nerem, Mercurium cæterosque esse corpora ejusdem generis cum
Jove, nemo dubitat. Certe Planeta Hugenianus, eodem argumento
quo Satellites Jovis gravitant in Jovem, gravis est in Saturnum.
Et cum attractio omnis (per motus legem tertiam) mutua sit, Sa-
turnus vicissim gravitabit in Planetam Hugenianum. Eodem argumento Jupiter in Satellites suos omnes, Terraque in Lunam, &
Sol in Planetas omnes primarios gravitabit.

Corol. 2. Gravitatem, quæ Planetam unumquemque respicit, esse
reciprocè ut quadratum distantiæ locorum ab ipsius centro,

Prop. VI. Theor. VI.

Corpora omnia in Planetas singulos gravitare, & pondera eorum in eun-
dem quemvis Planetam, paribus distantiis à centro Planetæ, proporti-
onalia esse quantitati materiæ in singulis.

Descensus gravium omnium in Terram (dempta saltem inæ-
quali retardatione quæ ex Aeris perexigua resistentia oritur) æqualibus temporibus fieri jamdudum observarunt alii; & accuratissi-
mè quidem notare licet æqualitatem temporum in Pendulis. Rem
tentavi in auro, argento, plumbo, vitro, arena, sale communi,
ligno, aqua, tritico. Comparabam pixides duas ligneas rotundas
& æquales. Unam implebam ligno, & idem auri pondus suspen-
debam (quàm potui exactè) in alterius centro oscillationis. Pixides ab æqualibus pedum undecim filis pendentes constituebant
Pendula, quoad pondus, figuram & aeris resistentiam omnino pa-
ria: Et paribus oscillationibus juxta positæ ibant unà & redibant
diutissimè. Proinde copia materiæ in auro (per Corol. 1. & 6. Prop.
XXIV. Lib. II.) erat ad copiam materiæ in ligno, ut vis motricis
actio in totum aurum ad ejusdem actionem in totum lignum; hoc
est

Newton's own corrections for the second edition of Principia

In order to stress the importance to Newton's mind and work of his alchemical studies, which for years were little known about and when first known little regarded, I have got ahead of myself in telling his story. What the pursuit of alchemy reveals to me, however, is that nothing intellectually demanding or mysterious was alien to him. He was rigorous in his examination of religious texts, especially those concerning the Trinity, in which, dangerously for his career, he did not believe; he was rigorous in the many branches of natural-philosophical or scientific enquiry that he inherited and developed and often reinvented; rigorous with Aristotle, with Plato, and equally with an antique study – alchemy – thought irrelevant and even rather ridiculous by gentleman scholars of the Enlightenment which Newton did so much to establish.

He sought out sources of knowledge everywhere he could. Robert Boyle, the seventeenth-century chemist, was to give Newton the basis for his work in chemistry. A study of Descartes set him off on the latest mathematics. He learned about algebraic techniques which could be applied to geometry. Typically he sought confirmation for the new geometry in classical geometry. Again and again Newton seems to be reaching out for a Theory of Everything. Perhaps this is a natural consequence of his belief in One God the Maker of All Things Visible and Invisible. Perhaps it is evidence of a mind incapable of accepting partial explanations and unafraid to seek out connections even when to others there appeared to be none at all.

In 1665 the plague came back to England in force. Those who could fled the towns and cities, seeking out isolated spots thought to be safest from the fatal infection. The University of Cambridge closed down and at the age of twenty-three Newton returned to his home, to Woolsthorpe. Out of the next two years grew the legend and to a certain extent a myth of the making of Newton's unique genius.

He himself said of that time: 'In the two plague years I was in the prime of my age for invention and minded mathematics and philosophy more than at any time since.' We also know that he said that he would sometimes work eighteen or even twenty hours a day. This gargantuan capacity for work continued for another quarter of a century.

There is often argument and unease about the word 'genius', especially when applied to scientists. A genius for centuries was a god or inspired by God or fed with the fire of that which had no name. In the nineteenth century Kant said that Goethe and Homer could be called men of genius but not Newton because Newton could explain how he arrived at his theories and conclusions. True genius came out of 'nothing' or out of total darkness. I think Kant was mistaken about Newton or genius or both. Goethe and Homer both came out of a tradition: as did Newton. All three transformed it.

In these two years at Woolsthorpe and for some time afterwards, with powers as gifted and strong as those of any artist, Newton imagined himself into the world as it is. He did it in the language of mathematics. There are those who believe that this language can bring us nearer to the truth of the world as it is than any other, that mathematics can describe the world more illuminatingly and comprehensively than any other method. Proofs are also offered and it is surely tendentious to assert that one form of thought – the literary, for example – is in its very nature capable of delivering greater riches of understanding than another because proofs are not offered. Are 'proofs' below the salt? It smacks a little of intellectual snobbery. It smacks even more of a mistaken understanding of an act of creativity. Cézanne could have explained his intentions and methods in discovering Mont St-Victoire during the course of making his seventy paintings of it. Shakespeare could have given reasons for the order and selection of words he used, the juxtaposition of phrases. To explain how you arrive at your conclusions is not a bar to being called a genius: if anything it is cause for additional admiration.

What Newton set about thinking on in the time of plague, when, for most of his days, he was locked away with his closest, most loyal and only true friend, solitude, was to result in revelations, in ideas, which had not been there before in those forms. I can see no distinction between Newton thinking on the consequences of the fall of an apple and Homer thinking on the consequences of the taking of Helen or Shakespeare thinking out the consequences of the witches prophesying to Macbeth. Imagination flows to wherever the intensity of a profoundly well-prepared mind beckons it. When Einstein was asked what was most important to him in his work, he said, 'Imagination. Above all else.' Newton's theories came every bit as much out of thin air as any of Goethe's lines.

In those two years in his early twenties he laid the groundwork for many of his great contributions to knowledge. It was at this time that he experimented with the prism and decided that white light was composed of different-coloured lights and different properties. It was not that he merely saw this rainbow spectrum, as many had done before him: he proved why it was so and what the consequences were for the study of light itself, and proved it by an early example of what is now cutting edge – particle physics.

He developed a new and extraordinarily powerful form of mathematics which would enable him to define, compute and predict the workings of the natural world. The Greeks had uncovered an arithmetic and geometry adequate to compute their world, and remarkably durable and useful it had been. The Arabs introduced algebra, which offered a dimension for more variables and a more extensive employment of mathematical formulae. Descartes had brilliantly combined algebra and geometry in a system which allowed the introduction of values like time and distance to be plotted and expressed in graphs. Leibniz, working at the same time as Newton and independently of him, was engaged with the same mathematical problems Newton set himself to solve, especially the calculus. Newton invented a system he called

The frontispiece of Volume II of Principia, *translated into English in 1729.*

'fluxions', a system which allowed him to treat a curve not as something fixed and static but as created by a moving point. He did this by chopping up the moving point into an enormous number of minute points along the way. We know this system as 'calculus', and it allowed him to apply his laws to complex situations such as the effect of force on a moving body.

And then there was the apple tree. Still there, at Grantham, the tree itself or its direct heir, propped up and gnarled but defiant, as if it is damned if it will give in until everyone takes a careful look and agrees to believe its story. It was put about by Newton himself that it was the simple fall of an apple, an apple almost as famous as the apple in the Garden of Eden, that set him off and directed his mind to the thought which led to his stupendous theory of the force of gravity. Why did the apple fall down? Not up. Not sideways. It fell, he concluded, but infinitely more importantly he proved, because the Earth was exerting force on it. Newton realised that all objects are attracted to one another; the bigger the object, the bigger the attraction. Then the years followed in which he sought out and built the proofs.

Newton did not call it gravity yet, and initially he only speculated about its operation on or near the Earth. It would entail twenty years of work before his ideas would be set out in the *Principia* and Newton would prove how the Universal Law of Gravity shaped the cosmos and kept the planets in their orbits.

Newton returned to Cambridge in 1667 and in the next twenty years, besides thinking through his law of gravity, he engaged in many other investigations, had titanic and virulent quarrels with those who dared challenge or criticise him, turned friends into enemies overnight, damned publication, grew to be a monster and a myth and had a truly terrible nervous breakdown, after which he did less and less science in Cambridge and became more and more a national monument in the capital and a figure of international wonder.

At the age of twenty-seven, he became a professor of mathematics. He continued his passion for optics but he was also applying his ideas to the movement of the planets. By 1680 he was persuaded that the laws of attraction and repulsion dictated planetary movements also and he quantified the force involved.

In 1684, the wealthy, enterprising and talented British astronomer Edmund Halley (he of the comet) went to see Newton in Cambridge with a problem about a planet's orbit. In response, Newton wrote a short tract, 'De Motu' – 'On the Motion of Bodies in Orbit' – which revealed how far he had got in quantifying the movements of the planets. Halley was so impressed and excited when he read this that he raced down to Cambridge and urged Newton to publish immediately, a publication for which he would pay.

But Newton was not ready. More than that, the writing of 'De Motu' had somehow nudged forward the progress of a Big Idea. 'De Motu' was just Book One. He put all other work aside, scarcely went out, barely ate and settled to it with that astonishing concentration and stamina that made him able to 'think on it continuously' for up to twenty hours a day. He covered hundreds of sheets of manuscript with new calculations, which became the *Principia* with a Book Two and a Book Three. The reservoir built up with so much application and genius and over such a span of work-time was now released into a river of verifiable proofs which was to sweep all before it.

By publication in 1687 it was all there in the book I had been allowed to pick up in the Wren Library: the Laws of Motion, the Observations on the Movement of the Moon and the Planets, and the force holding it all together known as gravitas or gravity.

The Universal Law of Gravity was now revealed. It defined how all bodies, terrestrial and celestial, heavy and light, of whatever materials, were bound together through the laws of repulsion and

A. absolute Gravity. B. Conatus against absolute Gravity. C. partial Gravity.
D. comparative Gravity E. horizontal, or good Sense. F. Wit. G. comparative Levity
or Coxcomb. H. partial Levity, or pert Fool. I. absolute Levity, or stark Fool.

A contemporary cartooon satirising Newton's theory of gravity.

attraction. Never before and never since had one mind discovered so much that was new and made such a profound and unending difference to our knowledge and to the way we would live our lives.

What was extraordinary enough was that these principles were expressed in geometrical form. What was most remarkable of all is that even though initially they may have been imagined, after twenty years of concentration, it could be seen by all who could understand, quite astonishingly to his contemporaries and to scientists ever since, that they were proved.

So how did the *Principia* change the world?

Perhaps we should begin with the world of Isaac Newton himself. He did not, like Byron, wake up to find himself famous, but when his fame rolled in it came from Mount Olympus, and it has rolled through the intellectual life of mankind ever since. Sir Edmund Halley, who had been a useful goad to Newton, said, in a poem he wrote as a kind of foreword to the *Principia*: 'No mortal may approach nearer to the gods', and that judgement, restated in the terms of the day, has never been overturned. Lord Rees, the Astronomer Royal, believes, as do the great majority of scientists and scientific historians today, that science is fundamentally an art of accretion rather than one of individuality, that scientists 'in the long run, if their ideas survive scrutiny . . . become just part of the corpus of public knowledge as it were, and their individuality fades'. But he felt compelled to add, 'I think most scientists would probably say that Newton may well be the most outstanding scientific intellect of all time.'

Initially only a few people could understand the book, but those who did, the savants of Europe (save France, which was reluctant to join in the acclaim and came in later, whipped into line by the authority and wit of Voltaire), began to spread the word and his reputation took wing. He was knighted, the first scientist (the word was not to be introduced until 1831, so more accurately 'natural philosopher') ever to be knighted. He became influential at court, first with Queen Anne, then with George I. He was made Warden of the Mint in 1696 (where he was the terror of all counterfeiters), then he became Master of the Bank of England. In 1703 he was elected president of the Royal Society.

Friendships came and went, with John Locke and Samuel Pepys and others on the metropolitan stage on which Newton, it seems rather clumsily, took his place, spending much of his time in London. Before his death he published *Opticks* and *Arithmetica Universalis*, seen once again as seminal in their fields, but the bulk and the truly great part of his work had been done before the end of the seventeenth century. The first quarter of the eighteenth century was a time of triumph. Rather like a Roman emperor, Newton inspired portraits, statues and poetry – especially by the most popular poet of the day, James Thomson, in his work *The Seasons* – influenced by the words Newton used as much as by the man he was. A whole generation of aspiring intelligences became Newtonians; mathematics, thanks to the *Principia* and the man who wrote it, became fashionable, its ideas socially exciting. Aristocrats were moved to build laboratories in their country houses, impoverished graduates gave lessons to refined young ladies on the wonders of Newton. He became a climate of opinion. In 1727 his death and burial were an occasion for official national mourning. Two years later the *Principia* was translated into English.

The chief way in which the *Principia* changed the world was to add so much and so majestically to our knowledge of the universe. 'Man is what he eats' is true; 'Man becomes what he knows' is another truth. Newton extended the boundaries of thought dramatically. Subsequently, often standing on his shoulders, almost three centuries of scientific investigation has been launched.

His fame and the excitement generated by his mind also made him an ideal to be followed by men and women, of the greatest intelligence. Newton was out there, he inspired and by the knock-on effect of history still does inspire young people to give their minds to science. He became the heroic example.

Professor Al Khalili, Head of the Theoretical Nuclear Physics group, University of Surrey, says that Volume One is the most important of the three because it is there that Newton virtually invented the calculus which is central to modern physics. This meant finding equations to describe the curve on a chart on the gradient of a line. It is absolutely central to understanding the world around you and all natural interactions that occur above the atomic level. To all intents and purposes 95 per cent of physics applied to daily life uses Newton's mechanics rather than Einstein's. Newton's equations, which Einstein refined, for instance on gravity, were accurate up to about the tenth decimal place, which was absolutely remarkable, Professor Khalili says, considering the paucity of research and equipment he had to rely on.

In terms of space, even after more than three centuries and the revelations of Einsteinian relativity and quantum mechanics, Newtonian physics continues to account for many of the phenomena in the observed world, and Newtonian celestial dynamics is used to determine the orbits of our space vehicles. In 1687 Newton laid out in mathematical terms the principles of time, force and motion that have guided the development of modern physics since. For instance, Newton regarded time as a kind of constant lying outside of space, which Einstein proved false, but in 99 per cent of instances it doesn't matter in practical terms and Newton's views hold.

In terms of scientific investigation, Newton's principles describe acceleration, deceleration and inertial movement, fluid dynamics and the motions of the Earth, Moon, planets and comets. The *Principia* also revolutionised the methods of scientific investigation.

With regard to light, ideas on which had moved on very little from Aristotle, Newton revised the notion that the separation of colours through a prism targeted with white light was due to the glass somehow modifying the beam and proved, yet again in mathematical terms, that the white light beam was made up of seven distinct types of moving particles, each with distinct properties that cannot be modified. These findings became the foundation of the science of physical optics.

The laws of motion seemed to be the critical issue in unlocking the secrets of 'natural law', and once again Aristotle's view still largely obtained before Newton. Galileo had challenged these ideas, for example that heavier objects fall faster than lighter ones. But it was Newton whose experiments uncovered the organising principle.

He introduced the notion that everything in the universe can be explained by mathematical laws. By the nineteenth century this idea had taken root to such an extent that 'scientific explanations' were, and largely still are, accepted as the best and liable to be the most accurate. Natural philosophers became 'the Priests of Nature'. To some natural philosophers, especially physicists, Newton's *Principia* stood not against but alongside the Bible, proving by the new scientific method what God had revealed in His words.

The scientific method, the acceptance of which is attributed to Newton, came to dominate most of scholarship. Notions could be floated as before, as in the golden age of the Greeks, but they were accounted worthless unless they followed the example of Newton and proved their case through experiments defined in the strictest terms. Science now stood for clarity, process and authority. You observed your experiments, and whatever the quality of your insights, they had to be substantiated in authenticated proofs.

As Newtonian methods gathered support, more former knowledge was dismissed as mere superstition. Comets had been seen as portents, supernatural agents. In the *Principia* Newton had calculated the orbit of a specific comet and predicted mathematically when it would reappear, as it duly did, by means of mathematics and not magic.

Through the *Principia*, people came to see the cosmos as an enormous machine, a colossal clock with God – if you followed Newton down that particular path – as the invisible clockmaker. The idea of the omnipotent power of the machine bit into culture. Soon the planet would groan with the sound of machines.

As you would expect there are varying emphases on the changes brought about by the *Principia*. I would suggest that while all scientists and scientific commentators agree on the importance and impact of Newton, shades in emphasis can be seen in the conclusions of John Gribbin, the distinguished historian of science, and Simon Schaffer, Professor of the History of Science at Cambridge.

John Gribbin does not believe in the 'genius' theory of the history of science, or that there are or were 'special persons' whose contribution was climactically transforming. Only for Newton does he make an exception.

Gribbin says:

> there are three Laws of Motion and the theory of gravity all in the *Principia*. They are laws which tell us the way things move, the way things bounce off each other, the way things respond to being pushed or pulled by forces and they underpin the whole of mechanics. They underpin everything from building the Forth Bridge so that it will not go down when a train goes across it to sending a spaceship to Jupiter and of course for that you also need the Law of Gravity.
>
> It is those laws which people use to build the everyday things in the world, even things as mundane as washing machines. The rate at which the spinning bits of the washing machine spin round depends on Newton's laws.
>
> Newton says that if you are rolling a ball down a plane, or if you are firing a cannon ball on a trajectory or working out how a sailing ship moves in accordance with the wind and the waves and the tides, all of these things come back to these very basic rules.

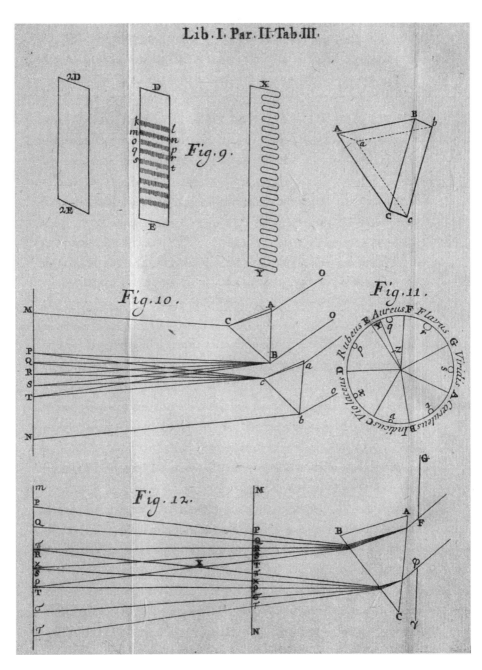

Newton's experiments into the nature of
colour, from Opticks *published in 1704.*

The first rule is that things keep moving in a straight line unless something pushes them or pulls them. This applies to the orbit of the moon. It tries to go in a straight line. Gravity stops it. The second, that action and reaction are equal and opposite. Things bang together, they bounce off with equal force and this applies with rockets – you make it move by throwing things backwards and that moves you forward. The third law tells you how fast things move when you apply a force. When we think we understand the Big Bang it can all be traced back to Newton's Laws.

It might be useful to present as practical a list as I can, not comprehensive but, I think, indicative of the bewilderingly profound impact of one man's book.

In the communications industry, Newton's orbital mechanics are behind the workings of satellites and the multi-billion-pound satellite industry, which includes not only entertainment but defence, intelligence gathering and measuring changes in weather, crops and water.

His work on the propagation of waves, in particular their application to determine the velocity of sound, gave us the supersonic aircraft. Another important technology relying on the wave principle includes ultrasound, also called ultrasonic scanning, to obtain images from inside the human body.

Newton's invention of the reflecting telescope led to the periscope and the principles behind the reflective telescope can be traced through to the laser industry. Again, from his study of light come optical fibres which carry light for extremely long distances.

His celestial dynamics still determine the orbit of our space vehicles.

The breadth, depth and success of such later developments, according to Gribbin, gave the British an intellectual confidence in themselves across the board.

Yet it is, I think, useful to look at it from a rather different perspective.

In Simon Schaffer's opinion you did not need the *Principia* in the early days of the Industrial Revolution to build bridges, mills, guns, steam engines or anything technological. That kicked in later. But if you claimed Newtonian authority you were much more likely to get the necessary and often hefty investment you needed. Newton's fame and reputation convinced people that mathematical formulae captured something real about the world. In the Stock Exchange, for instance, Newton's 'proofs' were claimed for the structure of capitalism, and members of the Royal Society would give lectures to financiers in the London coffee houses in which the market took shape.

So the early Industrial Revolution did not need the theories of Newton, according to Schaffer, but by the end of the nineteenth century technology had advanced to a state where it had, as it were, caught up with Newton's theories. It was then that his great direct influence began to bite, taking the intellectual community on a journey which continues today.

Schaffer, incidentally, is not pleased that Dava Sobel, in her book *Longitude*, gave the credit for the discovery to John Harrison and cast Newton as 'the villain'. This he describes as 'absurd, ridiculous'. The main method of finding out where you were at sea was, he says, a method drawn from the *Principia*; the system they used depended on a book containing 'lunar distances'. Basically in this book was information about the time at, say, Greenwich when the Moon was in front of a certain star. If you knew the local time then, by observing the location of the moon and consulting the book, you would be able to determine the time at Greenwich and work out where you were longitudinally. Newton designed that method and, Schaffer says, he was given a prize for it under the 1714 Longitude Act.

Schaffer's broad point is that, initially and crucially, Newton issued a kind of promissory note to society: there was going to be nothing weird in the sky, certainly nothing we could not explain; you could spend money on machines and feel secure about doing so; you could work out exactly where you were in a ship. The effect of this on the eighteenth-century mind was enormous and, according to Schaffer, stimulated the rise of capitalism, industrialism and international trade.

Finally, from Schaffer, comes the observation he makes on the very title of the book itself. A strange one, he maintains, even bizarre by the standards of the time. It was a time when there was a long and well-established division of labour between mathematics and 'natural philosophy', between what Schaffer calls 'sums and inquiries into causes'. Newton declared them to be one and the same in his provocative title *The Mathematical Principles of Natural Philosophy*.

Despite the intellectual contributions of others, most notably Einstein, over the last three hundred years, the new world created by the *Principia* still works, still explains the world, and the later contributions are more refinements than refutations of a work still acknowledged as supreme.

Newton reinforced – indeed he may have invented – the popular notion of the absent-minded genius. His concentration on his work was so fierce that the world as it was could seem remote. There are stories of one or two Cambridge colleagues being invited to his rooms for dinner and waiting for a long time while Newton searched for wine in another room, only to find him back at his desk, dinner, wine and guests forgotten. His rages were those of a solitary beast disturbed. He was a recluse, but after *Principia*, as if he knew his great work was done, he based himself in London and in his own way and on his own terms became part of society, lionised, feared, wondered at.

It is not always sensible to trust comments that people make about themselves, but this sentence by Newton, written at the end of his life, seems to me to capture the spirit of that lonely, curious boy on the Lincolnshire farm whose appetite for learning was to change so much. 'I do not know what I may appear to the world,' he wrote, 'but to myself I seem to have been only like a boy playing on the sea-shore, and diverting myself now and then finding a smoother pebble or a prettier shell than ordinary, whilst the great ocean of truth lay all unknown before me.'

TIMELINE
PRINCIPIA MATHEMATICA

1687   Isaac Newton's *Philosophiae Naturalis Principia Mathematica* is published

1708   Claude Boutet's painter's circle is the first to be based on Newton's *Opticks* of 1704

1727   Isaac Newton's death becomes an occasion for national mourning

1729   Newton's *Principia* is translated from Latin into English

1758   Joseph Louis Lagrange finds the complete general solution to Newtonian equations of motion for a vibrating string

1783   John Michell writes a paper in which the concept of a Newtonian 'black hole' is discussed for the first time

1798   Henry Cavendish makes the first recorded laboratory observation of the force of gravity between pairs of objects and determines the mass of the Earth

1800   Sir William Herschel discovers infrared light

1801   Johann von Soldner predicts Newtonian bending of light by the Sun

Thomas Young discovers interference of light

Johann Wilhelm Ritter discovers ultraviolet light

1808   Modern atomic theory is put forward by John Dalton

1814   Joseph Nicéphore Niépce achieves first photographic image

1816   Augustin Fresnel explains the refraction of light

1825   Pierre Laplace completes his five-volume survey of the solar system, *Mécanique Céleste*

1842   Chritian Doppler discovers the 'Doppler effect'

1847   Hermann von Helmholtz discovers the principle of the conservation of energy

1856   James Clerk Maxwell demonstrates that a solid ring around Saturn would be torn apart by gravitational forces and argues that Saturn's rings consist of a multitude of tiny satellites

1883   Konstantin Tsiolkovsky shows that a rocket would function in a vacuum due to Newton's 'action-reaction' laws of motion

1888   Heinrich Hertz discovers radio waves

1900   Max Planck puts forward his quantum theory

1901   Marconi transmits radio waves that are detected across the Atlantic Ocean

1902   Sir Howard Grubb designs the first periscope based on principles of the Newtonian reflecting telescope

1905   Albert Einstein puts forward his Special Theory of Relativity

        Einstein introduces the idea of discrete portions of energy, later called 'photons'

1912   Einstein explains the curvature of space-time

1916   Einstein's General Theory of Relativity is published

1922   The possibility of an expanding universe is predicted by general relativity

1929   Edwin Hubble provides an observational basis for the Big Bang theory

1932   Ernst Ruska and Max Knoll build the first electron microscope

1941   The first production rocket-powered aircraft (Me 163) is launched

1946   The first American-built rocket to leave the Earth's atmosphere (the WAC) is launched

1947   US Air Force pilot Captain Charles 'Chuck' Yeager breaks the sound barrier

1957   Russia places the first satellite, Sputnik, into space, based on the mathematics of orbital mechanics

1958   Explorer 1 becomes the first US satellite to orbit the Earth

1959   The Russians launch Luna 1, the first probe to go near the Moon

1960   The first operable laser is invented

1961   Yuri Gagarin becomes the first man in space

1962   John Glenn pilots Mercury 6, the first American orbital flight by NASA

1969   Apollo 11 adjusts its orbital velocity to land on the Moon

1977   Telephone companies begin trials with fibre-optic links carrying live telephone traffic

1985   An American probe reaches a comet

1987   The Russian space station MIR becomes the first permanently occupied space station

1988   The first transatlantic fibre-optic cables are laid

        Stephen Hawking publishes *A Brief History of Time*, a best-selling introduction to astrophysics, astronomy and cosmology

1992   The Vatican admits that the Catholic Church erred in condemning Galileo's work proving that the planets circle the Sun and not the Earth

1997   The fibre-optic link around the globe (FLAG) provides the infrastructure for the next generation of internet applications

2000   The American space shuttle, Endeavour, makes a detailed global map of Earth

MARRIED LOVE

———

1918

by

Marie Stopes

MARRIED LOVE

A New Contribution to the
Solution of Sex Difficulties

BY

MARIE CARMICHAEL STOPES

*Doctor of Science, London; Doctor of Philosophy, Munich; Fellow
of University College, London; Fellow of the Royal Society of
Literature, and the Linnean Society, London*

*With a Preface by Dr. JESSIE MURRAY
and LETTERS from PROFESSOR E. H. STARLING, F.R.S.,
and FATHER STANISLAUS ST. JOHN, S.J.*

London: A. C. Fifield
13, Clifford's Inn, E.C.4.
1918

'In my own marriage,' Marie Stopes wrote in the preface to *Married Love*, 'I paid such a terrible price for sex-ignorance that I feel that knowledge gained at such a cost should be placed at the service of humanity.'

A more seductive advertisement for the content of such a book at such a time can scarcely be imagined. Here was an evidently educated woman prepared to put her life's most guarded and humiliating secret into the marketplace of common knowledge. Here was a teacher who would lead from experience. In the final chapter she wrote: 'In my own life, comparatively short and therefore lacking in experience though it may be, I have known both personally and vicariously so much anguish that may have been prevented by knowledge. Hence I conclude this little book, for though incomplete, it contains some of the vital things you should be told.'

There was urgency there, the promise of precious knowledge, and a modesty which was deeply reassuring at the time. The time was Marie Stopes's greatest ally. The ideas of Mary Wollstonecraft had worked their way through the nineteenth century; the suffragettes had stormed the barricades of masculine superiority and the armies of the growing feminism – embracing both women and men – were winning the intellectual argument. Writers, especially novelists –

D. H. Lawrence, for instance, was writing his sexually driven novels at the time – were unveiling the subject of women's sexual restrictions and rights, and the complexity of modern cities was leading to the creation of more possibilities for more people for more varied and unrestricted sexual encounters.

All this was dynamised by the explosion in society after the fall-out of the First World War. If ever a time had come for a book to rip away the curtain of sexual convention once and for all in a language the educated and the opinion formers would accept, it was 1918: came the time, came *Married Love*. Its impact was instant, profound and lasting. Today Marie Stopes International provides sexual and reproductive health information and services to 4.3 million people worldwide in thirty-nine countries across Asia, Africa, Australia, Europe, Latin America and the Middle East. It provides advice and help on abortion, contraception, female sterilisation, health screening and vasectomy.

'Seldom, if ever,' wrote the journalist Mary Stocks, 'has a book brought more happiness to more people.' Sam Roddick, the owner of Coco de Mer, a shop in London specialising in erotic female lingerie, says, 'Female sexual pleasure is big business and men understand what women like nowadays.' It all started with Marie Stopes and her book on married love. Her book not only legitimised female sexual pleasure, it encouraged it and set out instructions on how to obtain it. Yet it was couched in such terms and with such political guile as to appear wholly respectable. Its tone was level and flattering; its message was sharp and unequivocal. 'The English and American peoples, who lead the world in so many ways, have an almost unprecedentedly high proportion of married women who get no satisfaction from physical union with their husbands, though they bear children, and may in every other respect appear to be happily married.'

It was one educated middle-class woman telling it like it was to a reader who was her own kind. Like Mary Wollstonecraft before her,

Marie Stopes spoke of what she knew to those she knew well, and found that she could ignite a revolution in what must then have been thought the most unlikely location – the homes of married, comfortably-off, apparently contented middle-class Anglo-Saxon families. She wrote for and to married women. Pre-marital sex was not on the agenda. Nor was abortion. Nor was homosexuality. There was enough tinder inside the married establishment. She was well aware of her ambition. In 1915 she told Margaret Sanger, the American advocate of birth control, that she was finalising a book 'which will probably electrify this country'. It did. In its first two weeks of publication, it sold 2,000 copies – a huge number for those days – and by the end of the year it had been reprinted six times.

Marie Stopes was born in Edinburgh in 1880 and educated in Scotland until she was fourteen, when her parents moved to London. She went, as few women of the day managed, to University College, London, from which she graduated in 1902 with honours in both botany and geology. She continued her education abroad, making her even more rare in her day, and in 1904 gained a PhD from the University of Munich, where she met a Japanese botanist, Kenjiro Fugii, and fell in love with him. In 1904 she moved to Manchester University, at which she taught until 1910. During that period, in 1907, she went to Japan to be with Kenjiro Fugii, but the love affair ended. In 1910 Marie Stopes moved to Canada and met a Canadian geneticist, Reginald Ruggles Gates, whom she married. They returned to England in 1911. It was this unhappy marriage which stimulated the first sketches for what became *Married Love*. In 1916, in order to end the marriage, she had to prove that she was still a virgin, as this was the only ground for annulment. There is a body of opinion which doubts her declaration of sexual naivety and her unviolated condition, but the divorce was obtained.

The book was originally planned as a series of short novels, and there is some proof in the prose – that reaching out for metaphors of sexuality which marked most erotic fiction before the mid-twentieth century. 'When knowledge and love go together to the making of each marriage,' she wrote, 'the joy of that new unit the pair will reach from the physical foundations of its bodies to the heavens where its head is crowned with stars.' Elsewhere in the book she wrote, 'one might compare two human beings to two bodies charged with electricity of different potentials. Isolated from each other the electric forces within them are invisible, but if they come into the right juxtaposition the force is transmitted, and a spark, a glow of burning light arises between them. Such is love." What's interesting here is that Marie Stopes is using a scientific metaphor and using it with a deftness which her readers would recognise, as they would her musical metaphor: 'only by learning to hold a bow correctly can one draw music from a violin: only by obedience to the laws of the lower plane can one step up to the plane above'. Sex was put in its place but seen as inextricable from 'the heavens', which was, for many readers, a revelation and a relief.

The novelettish tone is by no means dominant. The outbreak of the First World War seems to have been a catalyst: fiction was not the way. 'Then came the war,' she wrote in 1914, at that time living in a tent on the Northumbrian coast trying to get through the unhappy end to her marriage. She had written several drafts of a novel called *They Twain* but, as she wrote, there came the war. 'As it progressed, I saw more and more clearly that what the world wanted was not the themes diluted into novels, which might or might not be interesting, but help in some form direct, swift and simple.' One of Stopes's biographers, Jack Coldrick, wrote that *Married Love* 'not only represents a landmark in the progress of liberal sexual values and women's rights; it also represents an important document of the First World War, and can only be understood in that context'.

Married Love came out eight months before the First World War ended. It was a war that had given women far more opportunities, one of which was to mix more freely and wide-rangingly with men.

*The First World War had brought more middle class women
into paid work and into the struggle for female suffrage.*

The book also appeared a month after certain women had been given the vote – householders, wives and women over thirty. The war had brought more working-class women into the struggle for female suffrage. It had taken the protected, closeted and cosseted Victorian women, middle-class women (working-class women had been part of the workforce, though unrecognised, for centuries), into paid work and into some degree of competition with men. It is, however, worth noting that another biographer of Marie Stopes, Ross McKibbin, argues that although Stopes says the war was crucial to the direction taken by the book, there is no reference to the effect of the Great War on the European middle classes.

The fact is, however, that the war reflected movements in society, particularly among women, which made the publication of *Married Love* supremely well timed.

Publication, though, was not easy. The subject scared off respectable publishers. Again and again Stopes is characterised as a woman with a very forceful personality – she dressed flamboyantly, modelling herself on the extravagantly scarved and Hellenistically garbed American dancer Isadora Duncan; she was forever quarrelling, later in life, with organisations set up in her name. And she was – which many men at the time disliked intensely – intellectually very sure of herself and very sure of her purpose. 'I have read, I think, everything written in all the leading languages', she wrote, 'on the subject of sex relations, but I found that they dealt with abnormalities, some of those leading books with the most horrible abnormalities, but there was nothing that gave guidance to the morally healthy pair who started with love and desire to maintain a happy home.' In Havelock Ellis's *Studies in the Psychology of Sex*, for instance, the emphasis was on sexual dysfunction, impotence and perversions such as bestiality. Cassell's sex manual, one of several 'Questions of Sex' published to educate the soldiers, was packed with information about how to avoid incurable diseases associated with sex. And this was a time when some women still thought that a kiss could make you pregnant. Marie Stopes saw her book as a gospel.

Her first step was the publisher Blackie, who had taken on her first two books. She sent in a copy in February 1915. Five months later she received this reply:

Dear Dr Stopes,

Thanks. But the theme does not please me. I think there is far too much talking and writing about these things already. The world is suffering from too many psychologists and it's not me that will lend a hand . . . Pray excuse the suggestion, but don't you think you should wait publication until after the war at least? There will be few enough men for the girls to marry and a book would frighten off the few.

Her answer was immediate.

Dear Mr Blackie,

I shall send you a copy of the book when it is out. *What* an idea of marriage you must have if you think the truth about it will frighten people off.

 Yours sincerely,
 Marie Stopes

Other publishers followed Mr Blackie, and she began to seek other routes. She sent the manuscript to a great number of the leading intellectuals to build up a body of favourable opinion. Edward Carpenter suggested that she might adopt a strategy employed for other dangerous books of the day. 'I don't want it to hasten your end (professionally) . . .,' he wrote; 'is it possible you might like first to publish it in French . . . and after a year or two in English?'

Professor Wheeler, a respected colleague, responded to her

manuscript in words which may have characterised even the most enlightened and benign of her contemporaries: 'Some of the writing must lie among the finest in the English language,' he wrote.

> You can understand then how it is so appalling to be suddenly knocked down by a grisly word or a brutal sentence . . . The point, you seem to hammer home, is the '*medical* necessity for sex relations' . . . This is to reduce what has always been to me . . . a mystery of love to a business-like arrangement for keeping fit. And it is a tribute to the power of your writing that you have almost convinced me that man should model himself on other 'mammals' – and so have disgusted me with the whole idea of marriage relations. My fear is that as it stands . . . your book would . . . establish among Englishmen that abominable calculating condition of mind where women are concerned that is characteristic of Frenchmen.

She also sent the book to organisations such as the Cinema Commission of Inquiry where, improbably, she seemed at first to strike lucky. Her contact there, the Reverend James Marchand, secretary of the National Council of Public Morals, suggested she try the publisher Stanley Unwin, who saw the sales possibilities but was overruled by his colleague C. A. Reynolds. Calculating, correctly, that support from the Church of England would be of weight, she sent it to Dean Inge, the Dean of St Paul's, the idol of the progressives, but even he told her that she would find it impossible to get any clergyman to associate himself with such a book. For a book which, when eventually published and for ever since, has been described as one 'whose time had come' – which it had – and a voice for which the public mood was ripe and ready – which it was – it proved to be a very protracted birth.

In 1916 Marie tried but failed to get funds from the Royal Society. Her marital status as well as her gender told against her, although the Natural History Department of the British Museum and the Royal Society itself had both published her works in the past. After many rejections and letters of support which did not gather sufficient momentum, she fell in with Dr Binnie Dunlop at the Malthusian League. He favoured contraception for economic reasons. She lent the doctor, a sixty-year-old virgin, a copy of her manuscript in autumn 1917. At about the same time she discovered a small publishing firm, Fifield and Co., who said they would publish it if she could produce the financial backing. Back to Dr Dunlop, who came up with a philanthropist, Humphrey Roe, who was anxious to help impoverished mothers overburdened by bearing too many children. The three of them had lunch. Humphrey Roe agreed to back the book and sent a cheque for £200 the next day. The book would be published thanks to Mr Roe. And, reader, she married him.

The book cost two shillings and was 120 pages long. From Chapter 1, 'The Heart's Desire', to Chapter 11, 'The Glorious Unfolding', Stopes gave clear advice on all aspects of marriage. A basic prerequisite for a happy marriage was that men and women should treat each other as equals. Children should be planned, birth control practised, men should know how to satisfy their wives' sexual desires by learning about menstruation, the sensitivity of the clitoris and other matters – most shocking of all to many readers, women should admit to feeling sexual desire and seeking sexual satisfaction.

Marie Stopes was sniffed at and patronised as the years went by for what is seen as an over-flowery, over-gushy style. There's no doubt it is. But I would suggest that the passion of the work and the urgency of its message to the readership of that era were well served by a style more often associated with romantic Edwardian fiction than the prose of the Edwardian classification of facts. She found the apt medium for her message. I have quoted two or three passages to illustrate this; the following passages demonstrate, I think, how effective her prose style could be:

In Chapter 2, 'The Broken Joy', she writes with great insight, 'the woman is slower to realise disappointment and more often by the sex life of marriage is of the two more profoundly wounded with the slow corrosive wound that eats into her very being'. While all generalisations are suspect, this seems to carry authority and prepares the way for the more open suggestions which follow. First, though, she dispels prevailing masculine-favouring myths.

In Chapter 3, 'Women's Contrariness', she writes, 'woman is not essentially capricious; some of the laws of her being might have been discovered long ago had the existence of law been suspected. But it has suited the general structure of society much better for men to shrug their shoulders and smile that woman is an irrational and capricious creature.'

In the same chapter she writes, 'prudish or careless husbands, content with their own satisfaction, little know the pent-up aching, or even resentment, which may eat into a wife's heart and ultimately affect her whole health'. The seamless way in which the most powerful metaphor for the seat of love, 'the heart', is woven into a practical guide ('affect her whole health') might be one of the reasons why the book provoked such a positive, vivid and widespread reaction.

There is nothing prudish or unworldly in Marie Stopes. If there are those who will murmur Lawrence as well as Freud, so there are other passages which evoke de Maupassant as much as any brimstone clergyman. A final statement from that chapter reads, 'many men who enter marriage sincerely and tenderly may yet have some experience of 'bought' love. It is then not unlikely that they may fall into the error of explaining their wife's experience in terms of the reaction of the prostitute. They argue that because the prostitute shows physical excitement and pleasure in union, if the bride or wife does not do so, then she is 'cold' or "undersexed".'

In Chapter 4, 'The Fundamental Pulse', she has the enemy firmly in her sights. 'By the majority of 'nice' people,' she begins,

C.B.C.

CONSTRUCTIVE

BIRTH CONTROL
SOCIETY AND FREE CLINIC

Founded by

DR. MARIE STOPES.

The Free Clinic is under the patronage of a distinguished Committee, staffed with qualified Lady Doctors and Certified Midwives.

The C.B.C. Headquarters are the Pioneer Centre for advice, instruction, and help.

108, Whitfield Street, W.1.   **Telephone: Museum 9528**

READ THE
BIRTH CONTROL NEWS

SIXPENCE MONTHLY.

Ask for it at the Railway Bookstalls

The 'Mother's Clinic' offered free advice to married women.

'woman is supposed to have no spontaneous sex impulses . . . so widespread in our century is the view that it is only depraved women who have such feelings that most women would rather die than own that they do at times feel a physical yearning indescribable, but as profound as a hunger for food.' This was a call to arms, all the more effective, I believe, for being phrased so politely and underpinned by an experienced voice of frustrated passion – 'would rather die . . .', 'as profound as a hunger for food'.

She aligns the emotional with the practical most openly of all, I think, when she writes: 'When the man tries to enter a woman who he has not wooed to the point of stimulating her natural physical reactions of preparation, he is endeavouring to force his entry through a dry walled opening too small for it. He may thus cause the woman actual pain, apart from the mental revolt and loathing she is likely to feel for a man who so regardlessly uses her.' The phrase 'to force his entry through a dry walled opening too small for it' is a superlative example of Stopes's accuracy; and it teaches a specific and essential lesson.

In Chapter 5, 'Mutual Adjustment', she switches the tone and becomes the model for the future army of sex manuals: 'It should never be forgotten that without the discipline of control there is no lasting delight in erotic feeling. The fullest delight, even in a purely physical sense, can only be attained by those who curb and direct their natural impulses.'

There is, in Chapter 7, a good example of her understanding that this is very much a partnership. Woman, she writes, 'has been so thoroughly "domesticated" by man that she feels too readily that after marriage she is all his. And by her very docility to his perpetual demands, she destroys for him the elation, the palpitating thrills and surprises of the chase.' This, it seems to me, still reads as a bold recognition of the realities of coupling and of difference. The idea not only of interdependence but of individually distinctive demands is beyond merely 'blaming the man' and admits him into the argument on terms he will understand.

Nor does she entertain a sentimental view of perpetual cohabitation. 'Whenever the finances allow,' she writes, wisely proffering the suggestion in economic terms, 'the husband and wife should have separate bedrooms. No soul can grow to full stature without spells of solitude.' That last sentence gives the reader a glimpse of something greater, in Stopes's view, than even the finest sexual relationship, and this, I think, helped the book strike such a very deep chord. It is the soul of the individual which is at the centre of life. She develops this, however, in what many might think a rather too mechanical way. 'The profound truth which is perceived by the ascetics is that the creative energising of sex can be transformed into other activities. This truth should never be lost sight of in marriage, where between the times of natural, happy and also stimulating exercise of the sex function, the periods of complete abstinence should be opportunities for transmuting the healthy sex power into work of every sort.'

When she comes to an aspect of sex and marriage which for tactical or personal reasons she wishes to pass by, she says so. In Chapter 9, 'Children', she writes, 'of the innumerable problems which touch upon the qualities transmitted to children by their parents, the study of which may be covered by the general term Eugenics, I shall here say nothing; nor shall I deal with the problems of birth or child rearing.' And yet . . . in the same chapter she does show her colours. 'Even when a child is allowed to grow into its mother, all those hundreds of millions of sperms are inevitably and naturally destroyed every time the man has an emission, and to add one more to those millions sacrificed by nature is surely no crime!' And, 'To those that point out that we have no right to interfere with the course of Nature, one must point out that the whole of civilization, everything that separates man from animals, is an interference with what people commonly call "Nature".'

Equality is at the core of it, most plainly stated, I think, in Chapter 10, 'Society': 'Marriage can never reveal its full stature until women possess as much intellectual freedom and freedom of opportunity within it as their partners.'

In the final chapter, 'The Glorious Unfolding', she returns again, as I quoted on the opening page, to her mission.

She added this subtitle to her book: 'A new contribution to the subject of sex difference', a little more explicit than the harmless-looking title but still well within the bounds of respectability. Part of the project was to make her views respectable, even though she must have known by the time of publication that to do that she had to overthrow a phalanx of prejudice. She appealed over the heads of the establishment: and the response could be called phenomenal.

The great and the good now rallied to her cause: Havelock Ellis, Arnold Bennett, George Bernard Shaw, H. G. Wells and others – intellectual opinion-formers in an era when the opinions of such people counted for sales as well as for support. These put their hands to the pump, and the book which had taken more years to find a publisher than it had to write marched across the land. By the end of 1918, after reprinting the book six times, the little publishing house was in uproar, faced with the overwhelming task of responding to literally thousands of letters. At first Marie answered each one personally, but soon it became impossible. They enquired about sexual satisfaction, frigidity, impotence, premature ejaculation, masturbation and, most of all, birth control. She refused to answer questions about abortion.

Several who wrote to her were clergymen and their wives. A vicar from Newark wrote about his premature ejaculation and his wife's coldness towards his sexual advances. This, one of hundreds of examples, perfectly illustrates the way in which her book had broken through the traditional reserve of her countrymen and women and hit a nerve in what appears, from the volume and heartache of the correspondence, to have been a sad, depleting ignorance and fear, which drained life out of so many marriages. It was the style, I think, the nature of the address of Dr Stopes, clearly an educated woman, which reassured them and released their despair. There are many thousands of letters in the Wellcome Library from readers all over the UK, Canada, Australia, India, America and Europe. She even attained the status of a children's skipping song:

> Jeanie, Jeanie, full of hopes
> Read a book by Marie Stopes
> But to judge by her condition
> She must have read the wrong edition.

Here are a handful of examples from these letters, evidence that this book worked with extraordinary effect on a strictly personal level right across society.

In 1924, the twenty-seven-year-old wife of a farm labourer wrote to her asking advice on how to stop having children. The woman was expecting her fourth and the family had an income of £1 7s. a week.

My children do not have enough to eat and I cannot buy boots for them to wear . . . I have got into trouble with the school because my boy did not go, as I had no boots for him to wear. I wrote and told my mother but she cannot help me because my father has died and left her with three children still going to school. She says I must stop having children . . . Do you think it would be best if I leave my children and go into the workhouse . . . so we don't have any more children? I have gone without food and have tried to win money but everything I try fails. If you can kindly advise me I would be very grateful.

CHIMES OF THE TIMES

Oranges and Lemons
Say the bells of Saint Clements.

When shall I grow rich ?
Say the bells of Shoreditch.

I'm sure I don't know
Say Big Ben and Old Bow.

I can tell you to-day
Hear our Saint Marie say :—

When the People will breed
No more mouths than they feed,

When the mothers will bear
No more babes than they rear.

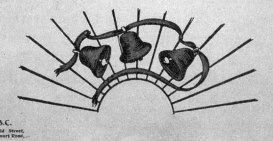

C.B.C.
108, Whitfield Street,
Tottenham Court Road.

A poster issued by Marie Stopes's Society for Constructive Birth Control.

This Dickensian cry is from the heart of darkness in one of the richest, best-educated and in some ways most enlightened countries in the world.

Forty per cent of her correspondents were men. Mr. H. from the Carlton Club in Pall Mall wrote: 'I did not know that a woman either required or was capable of having any decided orgasm on having connection and when my wife had them which she did freely when aroused, I was frightened and thought it was some sort of fit . . .'

Naomi Mitchison, who was herself to become a widely admired writer, married in 1916. She bought a copy immediately it came out, read it and bought another to send to her husband, a liaison officer with the French serving in Italy. She attached a note: 'Read this before we meet again.' Apparently it made all the difference.

Many were simply grateful. A Mrs B. of Felixstowe wrote: 'Will you let me thank you from the bottom of my heart for your book and congratulate you in putting into words so beautifully the great message of help and hope to us poor mortals who strive to make married life a success and to place love in its right position . . .'

In the same vein: 'I feel most bound to thank you for a large share of the happiness of our blissful wedding night and of the many happy unions which have succeeded it . . . Can a man's life hold any experience so sweet as the occasion when he first feels a woman – his beloved wife – in his arms – shaken to the depths of her being in the ecstasy of physical union with him?'

From India: 'The widespread sympathy and knowledge contained in these books were a great help to us.' From Shanghai: 'My mother died when I was a tiny child and I have no one I can come to for advice.' From South Africa: 'We think it's just perfectly beautiful of you to give the world such information, and we can never thank you enough for all you have taught us.' From Puerto Rico: 'My appreciation and gratitude for a contribution of far reaching importance towards the progress, better understanding and happiness of mankind.' From Philadelphia: 'You are doing magnificent work. Some of us Yankees trust that our English cousins will charge up the narrow minded bigotry one sees in America.'

That was and continues to be the good news. Apart from much else, Marie Stopes became a prototype marriage counsellor, a universal guide to unravel sexual problems, the begetter of the agony aunt whose columns now flourish in print and on radio the world over. But unsurprisingly there were negative reactions. The book was, wrote Dr Blacker of the Eugenics Society, simply 'a practical handbook of prostitution'. It described, wrote Lord Hewart, 'copulation without consequences'. In 1919, Father Zulueta, a Catholic priest, wrote a letter to the author, part of which reads: 'Madam . . . I consider it most useful to pray God that your writings may not do as much injury to morals – the ignorant poor especially – which they are calculated to do . . . I had hopes that no woman would write such books.'

The churches stood four square against Stopes and it was decades before the Anglican Church admitted that the instructions contained in the book could be accepted as Christian. One correspondent, Sydney Clift, gives us a useful example of the letters of protest she received. He objected to the suggestion that a married couple should consider the use of contraception. 'Do you really think that my wife and I and our poverty stricken friends (though none of us can afford to have more than two or three children) are sadly in need of such dirty advice as you offer? Is it a desire to put bank notes in your pocket that you write such stuff as *Married Love?*'

The book was banned in America and declared 'obscene'. It would have been banned on the same grounds in Britain had it not been so carefully aimed at married couples. This allowed it to enter into the public domain. The Welsh Education Board even asked the author to give schoolchildren advice on sex.

There was a famous court case, *Stopes* v. *Sutherland*, which was an

Isaac Newton: 'Nature and Nature's laws lay hid in night,
God said "Let Newton be!" And there was light!'

Newton's Laws of Motion revealed that to any action there is always an opposite and equal motion.

The Apollo 11 mission and all other space flights depend on the application of Newton's Laws of Gravity, as defined in his *Principia Mathematica* of 1686.

Newtonian maths is still used to fix the paths of orbiting satellites.

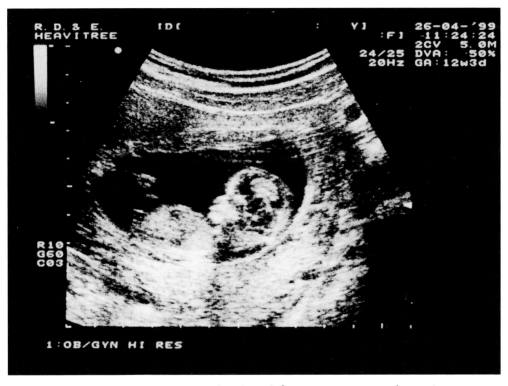

Ultrasonic scanning was developed from Newton's work on the
propagation of waves.

Dr Marie Stopes: 'What chains of slavery are, or have been, or ever could be so intimate a horror as the shackles on evey limb, on every thought, on the very soul of an unwilling pregnant woman?'

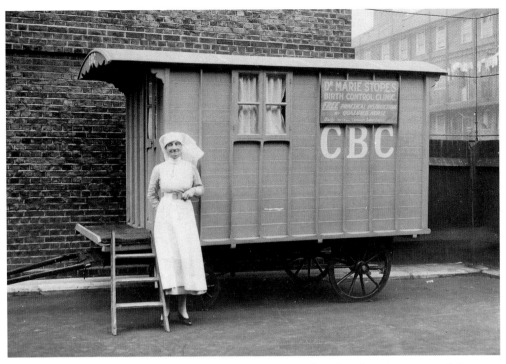

Mobile birth control clinics made advice on family planning accessible to millions for the first time.

Marie Stopes clinics have helped women all over the world: this clinic is in Bangladesh

King John (below), who met the barons at Runnymede, was nicknamed 'Soft Sword', in contrast to his brother Richard 'the Lionheart' (top).

The clearest influence of Magna Carta on the American constitution is in the famous Fifth Amendment: here Humphrey Bogart and Lauren Bacall lead other actors in protest at the Un-American Activites committee hearings on communism, October 1947.

The memorial at Runnymede erected by the American Bar Association bears the inscription 'To commemorate Magna Carta, symbol of freedom under the law'.

The United Nations Universal Declaration of Human Rights was called 'A Magna Carta for all humanity' by Eleanor Roosevelt: this is a graphic representation of Article 9.

attempt to restrict her support for birth control. For the defence, Dr Agnes Forbes Saville claimed that *Married Love* caused ill health. She alleged that a twenty-five-year-old woman had suffered sleeplessness, become a nervous wreck, thin, lost her health and become prone to self-abuse because of reading *Married Love*. It had been a 'horrible revelation'.

Q: In what way a horrible revelation?
A: She had been brought up in a nice, clean home: this is not a nice, clean book.

But the main charge was that Stopes's book would increase immorality by encouraging 'copulation without consequences', as Lord Hewart put it in his summing-up. George Bernard Shaw wrote to her at the end of the third hearing, when Marie Stopes was forced to pay the defendant's costs as well as her own (the total costs came to £12,000). 'The decision is scandalous,' he wrote in 1924, 'but I am not surprised at it . . . the opposition can always fall back on simple taboo. The subject is obscene . . .' The case is a good illustration of the determination of the establishment, the Church, the law, to destroy or at least defuse the power of her book.

The press reaction was better than she could have hoped for.

The *Medical Times* suggested: 'All medical men and women should read this. They can't fail to glean valuable information.' *The Lancet*: 'An extremely sensible little book.' *The English Review*: 'The great revolution in women's position and attitude is shown in the frank physiological statement.' The *Book Monthly*: 'Frank, straightforward truth finds no greater admirers than in the heart of Mayfair and this is the real reason for the success of Dr Stopes' book.' The author relished all this and particularly rejoiced in the establishment hypocrisy of *The Times*. She wrote to Humphrey Roe, then her fiancé: 'The Times Book Club has ordered over 50 copies!!! All sorts of papers are now bothering the publisher for

"Marie Stopes, lady !—we ain't never 'eard of 'er !"

By the 1930s Marie Stopes's work had become the subject of satirical comment.

review copies, also the Times newspaper has definitely, finally and absolutely refused an advertisement for the book, which seems rather comic, doesn't it?'

By 1927, the book had been translated into twelve languages – including Afrikaans, Arabic and Hindi – and had gone into eighteen editions in Britain. In 1931, Judge John M. Woolsey declared the book legal in the United States, and three years later a group of American academics listed *Married Love* as one of the most influential twenty-five books of the last fifty years.

It added to the force of feminism, and took momentum from the remoulding of society owing to the First World War. The excitement given it by its notoriety, the blessing given it by its insistence on monogamy and its absorption of ideas potent then (suspect now), such as Stopes's commitment to eugenics, also helped it reach a mass audience. The lure of the romantic prose which disarmed and enticed the common reader, and the light it brought to what, from the correspondence, can now be seen as a worldwide dungeon of ignorance, despair and pain, together with its insistence on the pleasure of sex lovingly entered into, sped it on its way not only into the hearts and lives of its many readers but into the bloodstream of society. It became a touchstone, a point of reference which could not be ignored, a mould-maker.

For Marie Stopes, the publication of *Married Love* was the beginning, not the end of her campaign for equal rights for women. She continued to proselytise and, as importantly, make practical progress. She was not only an intellectual champion but a hands-on leader, someone who set up clinics and encouraged the extension of her ideas into working practice, institutions which would become, and are still today, schools for day-to-day explanation of her thoughts.

Nor did she cease to address the powerful. She wrote this to President Wilson, for instance:

What chains of slavery are, have been or ever could be so intimate a horror as the shackles on every limb, on every thought, on the very soul of an unwilling pregnant woman? And you have thousands of such slaves in your 'free' United States, many of them 'honoured' wives, forced to stumble through nine months of nightmare for want of the scientific knowledge which every grown man or woman has a right to know.

Through highly publicised letters such as this, she made birth control a worldwide issue for which fact alone her book would have a fair claim to have changed the world. She was active in domestic politics and, owing to her book, her clinics and her public declarations, a mere six years after the publication of *Married Love* both the Labour Party and, to a lesser extent, the Liberal Party began to press for advice to be given to women at local authority maternity and welfare centres.

During the rest of her long life – she lived until 1958 – Stopes continued with her mission. She was not successful in her second marriage, she virtually disowned her son, she is reported to have been difficult to work with and seceded from the National Birth Control Association (now the Family Planning Association) which she had inspired, and she did not find it easy working with other strong women. Perhaps the time when she fought alone had branded itself too deeply on her character for that. Yet her importance only grew. In 1999, for example, she was voted Woman of the Millennium by readers of the *Guardian*.

The modern organisation which bears Marie Stopes's name was re-established in 1976 after years of difficulty. Since then the Marie Stopes International Global Partnership has been set up in thirty-eight countries and has offices in London, Brussels, Melbourne, Tokyo and Washington, DC. Today, in some, possibly even in great part owing to Marie Stopes, there is sex education in schools, contraceptive pills at chemists', and hundreds of birth control clinics around the world.

'Far too often', she wrote in *Married Love*, 'marriage puts an end to woman's intellectual life.' Not in the case Marie Stopes. A desperately unhappy marriage spurred her on to think about the problems of sex in marriage with a tenacity and effectiveness wholly exceptional and liberating for men and women the world over.

TIMELINE
MARRIED LOVE

1918   Marie Stopes publishes *Married Love*

       2,000 copies are sold within a fortnight and by the end of the year it has been reprinted six times

       The US Customs Service bans the book as being obscene

1919   Magnus Hirschfeld opens the Institute for Sexual Science in Berlin, designed to further the study of sexuality and promote understanding

1920   Marie sends a copy of *Married Love* to Queen Mary with an accompanying letter but receives no reply

       Marie Stopes's *Radiant Motherhood* and *The Control of Parenthood* are published

1921   Marie founds Holloway Clinic, the first birth control clinic in Britain

1923   Catholic doctor Halliday Sutherland criticises Stopes in a book, *Birth Control*

       Marie Stopes sues Sutherland for libel, loses, wins at appeal, then loses in the House of Lords, but the case generates a huge amount of publicity, just as she had planned

       Margaret Sanger opens the first permanent birth control clinic in the United States to protect women from life-threatening pregancies

1927   *Married Love* goes into its eighteenth edition; it has been translated into twelve languages, including Afrikaans, Arabic and Hindi

1930   The Labour Party and the Liberal Party begin to press for advice to be given to women at Local Authority maternity and welfare centres

Married Love

1930s The National Birth Control Association is founded

1931 American Judge John M. Woolsey declares *Married Love* welcome in the USA

1934 A group of American academics list *Married Love* as sixteenth in a list of the twenty-five most influential books, of the previous fifty years, ahead of Einstein's *General Theory of Relativity*, Freud's *Interpretation of Dreams* and Hitler's *Mein Kampf*

1938 Marie Stopes secedes from the National Birth Control Association over her inability to work collectively with the other strong-minded women in the movement

1939 The National Birth Control Association is renamed the Family Planning Association

1948 Marie sends a copy of *Married Love* to Princess Elizabeth and Prince Philip as a wedding gift and receives a thank-you from the lady-in-waiting, Margaret Plymouth

1952 Marie sends a nurse, trained at her Mother's Clinic, to Bombay to teach the technique of birth control

1957 The first lubricated condom is launched in the UK by Durex

1958 The Anglican bishops' Lambeth Conference finally acknowledges the need for birth control, accepting that procreation was not the sole purpose of marriage

Marie dissolves her Society for Constructive Birth Control

Marie Stopes dies

1960 The Searle drug company receives US Food and Drug Administration (FDA) approval for the first birth control pill, revolutionising contraception

1965 The US Supreme Court strikes down the Comstock laws that banned contraception

1971 *Cosmopolitan* magazine is launched in Britain, remaining at the forefront of women's rapidly changing lives throughout the 1970s and 1980s

1974   Family planning clinics finally become part of the NHS

1976   Marie Stopes International (MSI) is established in London

1977   MSI sets up its first overseas centre in Ireland and, a year later, a programme in India

1980s   The modern, low-dose, two and three-phase birth control pills become available

        Condoms become available in pubs, bars and supermarkets

1992   The female condom becomes available in Europe

1993   The female condom is approved by the FDA

1994   The world's first polyurethane condom for men was launched in the US

        Coloured and flavoured condoms begin to appear

1999   Marie Stopes is voted 'Woman of the Millennium' by readers of the *Guardian*

2003   The first continuous birth control pill, which women take every day to suppress their periods and provide birth control, is approved by the FDA

2004   MSI in the UK are now providing services to over 84,000 clients

2005   The MSI Global Partnership is providing sexual and reproductive health information and services to 4.3 million people worldwide in thirty-nine countries across Africa, Asia, Australia, Europe, Latin America and the Middle East

MAGNA CARTA

—

June 1215

by

Members of the English Ruling Classes

It has sixty-three clauses, sometimes called chapters, and inside the thicket of references strictly related to its own time it embodies one of the great ideas in the world – that government and society, liberties and rights, can be organised around a document and made to hold not by an individual, a despot, an emperor, or even a benevolent king, but by a piece of writing. In 1956, Winston Churchill wrote, 'Here is a law which is above the King and which he must not break. This reaffirmation of a supreme law and its expression in a general charter is the great work of Magna Carta: and this alone justifies the respect in which men have held it.'

It is a respect which has endured for almost eight hundred years, a respect which has led to the foundation of a democratic and freedom-seeking constitution not only in the United Kingdom but in the United States of America, in India, in Australia, New Zealand, Canada, and in other countries wanting to shake off tyranny and found their state on a basis of laws and liberties equal to all. If there is one written text which through its long legal testing and its powerful mythic influence has shaped the world that free men and women aspire to, then it is Magna Carta. Its resonance is extraordinary.

I am writing – more accurately, rewriting – this in November 2005 in London. There has just been a fierce debate in the House of

Commons over the length of time terrorist suspects can be detained without charge or trial. The headline on the leader page of the *Guardian* blazes out in capital letters: 'PROTECTING MAGNA CARTA'. Similarly, in these months, in arguments about the legitimacy of holding suspects in Guantanamo Bay and in Belmarsh, in the rights of protesters and those who march against the government, the appeal is to Magna Carta. It is in the bloodstream of our politics; it *is* the bloodstream. In the centuries after its rough and violent conception, Magna Carta has become deeply integrated into our national life. So when Tony Hancock at his comic best was playing Henry Fonda's role in *Twelve Angry Men* and berating his fellow jurors for their lack of legal knowledge and understanding of the vital importance of the rights and liberties of the individual, he could turn to them with the widely appreciated plea: 'Does Magna Carta mean nothing to you? Did she die in vain?'

Magna Carta, which shines so brightly still, which has guided men and women in their pursuit of the highest ideals and inspired their loyalty to ideals sometimes unto death, was born of what could be called a desperate gamble by warlords to chain down a leader who had ceased to meet their needs. It was a case of document or death. Out of the bloody battlefields of the Middle Ages came this lasting constitutional principle – that the power of a king could be and henceforth would be limited by a written grant.

It was an attempt to codify the relationships between three forces – the king, the Church and the barons. It was a deal to solve the deepening crisis of confidence in the state. One of the many ironic riches in Magna Carta is that what could be called a stitch-up by the ruling classes of the day has become an authority for democracy, a cornerstone of liberty, and the chief defence against arbitrary and unjust rule. As the authors Danziger and Gillingham point out, Magna Carta's promise of the people's liberty under the law depended on popular participation in law-making, and this in turn led to the formation of our democratic government subject to law. The law of unexpected consequences is here apparent in its fullest glory: had any one of the participants at Runnymede in 1215 even dreamt that would happen . . . ?

Moreover, this most brutal of settlements between men blood-steeped in the *realpolitik* of medieval battle and butchery has achieved pacific iconic and mythic status all over the world. It is, for instance, probable that those opposed to overweening authority are very likely to defend their right to protest by referring to Magna Carta. Yet there is nothing in the document about the right to protest. But the protesters are right in the deeper sense that the whole charter represents a protest, arrived at by way of a rebellion; its force is primal in that it legitimises the challenge to any power which claims to be unaccountably supreme. This is what made it so potent in the seventeenth-century civil wars and from there, as said, to the United States, India, Australia, New Zealand, Canada . . . and more to come. It has become the book of the foundation words of the free world.

Magna Carta came out of the failings of King John. It was demanded owing to his weakness. It survived because of his death. King John never actually signed Magna Carta (there is no evidence that he could write) but he did seal it, and in the presence of the barons. Strenuous efforts have been made recently to redeem or at least soften the caricature of King John, known for many years as 'the worst English King', though admittedly those words are taken from a 1936 cigarette card which reads in full, 'John was cruel and completely selfish; he has been termed "the worst English King"'. Nor does the contrast with his popular enemy, the bold and virtuous Robin Hood, do him any favours.

In an age of unspeakable cruelty, John's alleged cruelty seems unexceptional. (For instance, at the time the Holy Crusade against the Cathars, an idealistic religious sect in the south of France, was stained by the decision to slaughter all, men, women and children regardless, on the grounds that 'God would know His own'). King

John had no luck, losing his navy to a storm at a crucial moment, and finding himself opposed by a particularly ruthless cluster of barons. Their idea of loyalty to the King of England was so corrupted that when John turned his face against them they instantly pledged their allegiance to Prince Louis of France and were happy to bring him over and help him conquer the land that gave them their wealth.

Yet there were real charges against him. He was an over-enthusiastic tax collector. This is an under-appreciated factor in disturbing the English, as can be seen from the tax resisted by John Hampden, which helped start the avalanche which brought about the Civil War, to the much lesser but significant poll tax of Mrs Thatcher, which brought about the downfall of an apparently invulnerable prime minister. King John needed the funds to fight wars on the Continent to defend and if possible extend the huge dominion in France that he had inherited from his parents: the golden couple of Europe in their day, Henry Plantagenet and Eleanor of Aquitaine.

Those wars would have been fine if he had won and brought all the plunder safely back across the Channel. But John did not have the talent or the fortune of his brother, Richard 'the Lionheart'. His nickname was 'Soft Sword' and he was thought to be a coward on the field of battle. This, in a warrior society, meant shame. Moreover the barons were also disaffected because King John preferred mercenaries or men who had come up through the ranks. They were being cut out of what they believed to be the prime purpose of aristocratic existence: making war, leading in battle, seizing land and loot after victory.

The barons were determined to depose him or tie him down.

The chronicler Roger of Wendover offers an account of the initial meeting which led to Magna Carta. He writes:

In November 1214, the earls and barons of England assembled at St Edmund's as if for religious duties, although it was from some other

A thirteenth-century map of Britain.

reason; for after they had discussed together secretly for some time, there was placed before them the Charter of King Henry I which they had received in the City of London from Stephen, Archbishop of Canterbury. This charter contained certain liberties and laws granted to the holy church as well as the nobles of the kingdom, besides some liberties which the king added of his own accord.

It is significant, I think, that the Church also needed its liberties enshrined in print. The savagery of the autocracy imposed by William the Conqueror and his direct heirs was clearly seen to be too harsh and tyrannical, even by those Norman barons (some of whose successors were to be present at Runnymede) who had benefited so massively in land and wealth from the Conquest.

The chronicler goes on:

All therefore assembled in the church of St Edmund, the King and Martyr, and commencing from those of the highest rank, they all swore on the great altar that, if the King refused to grant these liberties and laws, they themselves would withdraw from their allegiance to him, and make war on him, till he should, by a charter under his own seal, confirm to them everything they required: and finally it was unanimously agreed that, after Christmas, they should all go together to the King and demand the confirmation of the aforesaid difficulties to them, and they should in the meantime provide themselves with horses and arms so that if the King should endeavour to depart from his oath, they might by taking his castles, compel him to satisfy their demands, and having arranged this, each man returned home.

I have quoted from this remarkable document at some length, not only because it reads with such a vivid sense of the time and the place, but because it lays bare the literal force of arms behind the decision to move towards what was intended as a peace agreement.

Magna Carta came out of a sense of grievance and a belief in ancient rights which some commentators used to believe leapt back in history to precede the Normans, and finds its truer roots in Anglo-Saxon law and practice. But it finally came from an ultimatum backed by force of arms.

In the winter of 1214/15, the scribes gathered to copy out the Coronation Charters of previous kings, documents always sworn by on Coronation Day and often abandoned by nightfall. They used the charter of Henry I, the charter of King Stephen and the charter of Henry II. All were translated from Latin into Anglo-Norman so that the classically illiterate barons could read them.

Impatient, battle hungry or to prove their strength by arms, the barons, having had their demands rejected by the king in January, captured London in May 1215. Had there been a logical native successor to King John at that point, then civil war would certainly have broken out; there was not, and so jaw-jaw replaced war-war and the barons met the king beside the River Thames in a meadow at Runnymede, which was halfway between their headquarters at Staines and the king's force at Windsor. There were twenty-five barons led by Robert Fitzwalter, a bully and an unsavoury character, who held a series of grudges against King John. They also included English barons whose titles flaunted their Norman origins: Eustace de Verci, Saer de Quincy and William d'Aubigny of Belvoir. The Archbishop of Canterbury, Stephen Langton, assisted in the writing, anxious as he was to see a settlement between these two glowering parties and to include the voice of the Church. King John had no option but to comply. The barons rallied to the charter as to a rival prince.

The baronial observer of the day would have read Magna Carta's sixty-three clauses and seen the nub of it as a demand to redress grievances over feudal tenures; provisions regarding heirs, wards and tenants-in-chief. But other clauses were inserted which were to have great significance – on the marriage of widows for instance, which can be seen as a founding document for the rights of women; on the declaration of the inviolability of the liberties of the City of London and other ports and towns; on freedom of commerce for foreign merchants, an imaginative law for what was to become a great trading nation; the strict administration of justice; the permanent abode of the Court of Common Pleas at Westminster; the holding of assizes in different counties; the abolition of extraordinary taxation; the protection of life, liberty and property; one standard of weights and measures; no banishment or imprisonment save by judgement of peers. It was not only specific to the time, but it had in it, as we can see and as time has proved, a remarkably universal reach and in many of these clauses the seeds for growth and adaptation which have made it relevant across the spectrum century after century up until today. There has never been anything like it before or since. Each clause, each chapter has bred a library of laws.

The concessions made by King John were outlined in a document called 'Articles of the Barons' to which the King's Great Seal was attached. Nine days later the barons renewed their oath of allegiance to the king. Soon afterwards the Royal Chancery produced a final royal grant, based on Runnymede, first called 'The Charter of Liberties': it became known as Magna Carta (Latin for Great Charter). It was written in abbreviated Latin and four copies survive, two in the British Library, one each in the cathedral archives of Lincoln and Salisbury.

It was written on vellum, a fine parchment made from calfskin. The ink was made from gall – a liquid that comes from the mounds on oak trees formed when the gall wasp lays its eggs on the bark. It appears as a practical document: the scribes must have decided that its seriousness did not need to be emphasised by exotic capital letters or illuminations. When soot or iron salts were added to the gall-based ink it turned a rich dark brown colour which has been retained in all four surviving copies. The scribes would have made their own materials and used goose or swan feathers to make their quills, retrimming the nibs with a penknife every ten lines or so.

A Victorian artist's impression of the ceremony at Runnymede.

It was signed and sealed but not delivered. Not then. Not for years. King John saw it as a delaying act. The barons reneged on their promise to surrender London. Its initial period of effectiveness was less than three months. By November 1215, King John had won back the key castle of Rochester and was well placed to strike at London. Which he failed to do, preferring to ravage the heartland of the rebels, who now invited Prince Louis of France to be their leader. John's outer London rampage enabled Louis to raise an army which he landed in May 1216 at Sandwich.

John's navy had been prepared for this but his ships were scattered by a storm and he withdrew to head northwards and earn himself a curious niche in history when he lost his treasure in the Wash. Meanwhile the army of Louis was swollen by barons who thought they could see the winning side. It looked set to be a rerun of the Conquest when a bout of dysentery ended John's life in October 1216 and left his nine-year-old son to be declared Henry III by a regency council led by William Marshall. Magna Carta was reissued. The rebel barons were stumped. The old king was dead, long live the new, and especially a malleable nine-year-old. The loyal corps of barons not only abandoned Louis but fought against him and defeated him by land and sea at London and Sandwich.

John's life had inspired Magna Carta. His death secured it. From now on Magna Carta would be part of the English agreement to crown their king. England, which had the first vernacular publishing house in Europe – in Winchester under Alfred – could now boast the first written constitution in European history.

In 1225, the charter was reissued again, and it was this version that entered the statute books. It was, significantly, translated not only into Norman French but also into English so that, like Henry V's subsequent letters home from the wars in France, it could be read in the shires to those who had stuck to the English language despite the overwhelming temptations and coercions of the Norman tongue, which at that time dominated the power levels in English life.

In 1265, when Simon de Montfort was attempting to give more shape and influence to Parliament, it was decreed that the Great Charter should be proclaimed twice a year so that no one in the land could be ignorant of it. It was branded on the minds of the people as firmly as parts of the Bible: it could be called the fifth gospel, the gospel according to good government. Whenever a king over-stepped the mark, the cry went up: 'Magna Carta!' – every bit as confident and insistent as any appeal to Saints Matthew, Mark, Luke or John. Edward I was compelled to confirm the charter in 1297: it was the First Statute of the Realm.

Lord Woolf, in his speech 'Magna Carta: A Precedent for Constitutional Change', on 15 June 2005, called it 'the cornerstone of liberty in the English-speaking world'. To this day, he said, the first petition presented by the Commons to the monarch is a request that the Great Charter be kept.

In 1770, William Pitt the Elder called it 'the Bible of the English Constitution'. It remained on the statute book in its entirety until the Law Reform Act of 1863, wherein its essential principles were preserved for the future in a necessary upgrading and enlargement of the laws. Lord Denning called it 'the greatest constitutional document of all times – the foundation of freedom of the individual against the arbitrary authority of the despot'.

Its influence has spread across oceans, most notably to the biggest democracy in the world, India, and the most powerful, the United States of America, which see it as fundamental to their own constitutions.

This owes much to the constitutional arguments before and during the English Civil War in the seventeenth century. Magna Carta was constantly invoked in legal battles which often masked an otherwise naked struggle for power between the king and Parlia-

An early draft of what became known as the Bill of Rights.
The Fifth Amendment to the United States constitution directly echoes Magna Carta.

ment. In 2005 Geoffrey Robertson, a civil rights lawyer, quoted in the *Guardian* leader headlined 'Protecting Magna Carta', wrote: 'It was forged in the crucible of a civil war that cost one Englishman in ten his life, culminating in the trial for treason of a head of state who intimidated judges and refused political and religious freedom.' I agree with that, save that instead of 'forged' I would write 'forged anew'. Its success in the thirteenth century cannot be underestimated.

Yet Robertson points up a truth, which is that in the hands of the seventeenth-century lawyer Sir Edward Coke, Magna Carta became a voice and a force for liberty. It was, said Sir Edward Coke, 'the fountain of all the fundamental laws of the realm . . . a confirmation or resolution of the common law'. This appeal to the common law once again points back, this time more surely, to what many considered the pre-Norman Anglo-Saxon birthright of Englishmen. By tying the two together Coke appealed to ancient immemorial rights and the relatively recent imposition by the barons of restraints on any ruling power.

The use of Magna Carta in a ferocious debate in the seventeenth century came at a time when the American colonies were being settled, when, increasingly, they were turning to the King James Bible as their book of unifying religion and when the English language was pushing itself forward as the American tongue. The clearest influence in the American Constitution can be seen in the crucial Fifth Amendment: the words 'Nor shall any person be deprived of life, liberty or property, without due process of law' directly echo Magna Carta's Clause 39: 'No free man shall be seized or imprisoned or stripped of his rights or possessions except by the lawful judgement of his peers.' This is still on our statute books, as is 'To no one will we sell, to no one deny or delay right or justice'. This is the basis of the Sixth Amendment in the American Constitution.

There are two memorials at Runnymede. The place is still a beautiful meadow which has escaped the attentions of the tourist and the heritage industries: there is not even a visitors' centre. But there are those two memorials. The John F. Kennedy Memorial is Britain's tribute to the assassinated president. The inscription is from his inaugural address in January 1961, in which the writers, in my view, clearly and not unsuccessfully sought to live up to what has proved the lasting prose and the enduring effectiveness of Magna Carta. It reads: 'Let every nation know, whether it wishes us well or ill, that we shall pay any price, bear any burden, meet any hardship, support any friend, or oppose any foe, in order to assure the survival and success of liberty.' It is Magna Carta on the offensive. If the great declaration of Magna Carta can be seen in the context of the defence of the domestic liberties and rights of individuals, this great declaration of J. F. Kennedy can be seen as the ethos of a nation which has assimilated the ideals of Magna Carta, turning its energies outwards, to attack, and aid, those in the world, wherever they are, whose liberties are threatened. Liberty is now seen as seamlessly global and memorialised at Runnymede.

The second memorial is a rotunda, and it is also American. It was built by the American Bar Association as 'a tribute to Magna Carta, symbol of freedom under law'. The Bar Association came in 1971, 1985 and 2000, each time 'to celebrate Magna Carta, foundation of the rule of law for ages past and for the new millennium'.

The myth of Magna Carta comes either from what can be assumed between the lines or, more usually, because of the spirit which imbues it. I have emphasised the infighting, the less than idealistic nature of some of the rebel barons, the opportunism of the monarch and to a certain extent the archbishop. Yet it is also possible to see it as a charter won by liberty-hungry barons determined to preserve and put in writing their rights, which became the rights of others and – just as importantly – prepared to fight and to die for them. It is that dual origin, the idealistic and the force of arms, which has again and again made it such an influence.

In the mid-seventeenth century the Leveller John Lilburne proclaimed his rights as an Englishman: 'I am a freeman, yea a freeborn denizen of England . . . and I conceive I have as true a right to all the privileges that do belong to a freeman as the greatest man in England, whoever he be . . . and the ground of my freedom, I build upon the grand Charter of England.' When arrested in 1648, he wrote that the arresting officer had 'stabbed Magna Carta . . . to the very heart and soul'.

Even more graphic are the words of another Leveller and pamphleteer, Richard Overton, who described how he was arrested and dragged to Newgate gaol by his head, yet all the while holding on to his copy of Sir Edward Coke on Magna Carta. "I clasped it in my arms, and I laid myself upon my belly, but by force they violently turned me upon my back, then smote me . . . to make me let go my hold . . . thus by an assault they got the great Charter of England's Liberties and Freedoms from me, which I laboured to the utmost of power in me to preserve and defend, and ever to the death shall maintain.'

It continues to be a source of inspiration and Runnymede a site to be honoured. Vaclav Havel is one of the recent visitors from eastern Europe. Anglo-American legal associations are constantly working with citizens of the former Soviet bloc countries to encourage the reception of the precepts of Magna Carta in eastern Europe. When the prime minister of India, Mr P. V. Narasimha Rao, visited Runnymede he spoke of it as 'a source of inspiration throughout the world, an affirmation of the values of Freedom, Democracy and the Rule of Law, which the people of India cherish and have enshrined in their constitution'.

In Australia, the Chief Justice, the Hon. Sir Gerrard Brennan, AC, KBE, spoke of Magna Carta in October 1957. It is a statement, all encompassing and wise to the way in which the Great Charter was so fundamentally right that it was able to adapt, is able to adapt to the landscape of rights and liberties down the centuries:

Magna Carta has lived in the hearts and minds of our people. It is an incantation to the spirit of liberty. Whatever its text or meaning, it has become the talisman of a society in which tolerance and democracy reside, a society in which each man and woman has and is accorded his or her unique dignity, a society in which power and privilege do not produce tyranny and oppression. It matters not that this is the myth of Magna Carta, for the myth is the reality that continues to infuse the deepest aspirations of the Australian people. These aspirations are our surest guarantee of a free and confident society.

As a piece of writing, as a book of law, it has, as the previous few instances prove, a most profound resonance. It was written at a time of the birth of the great selfless mendicant orders of St Francis and St Dominic, but also in an age of the unspeakable cruelty and religious fundamentalism of the Crusades. It was a time when cities were beginning to assume the stake in the land which was to make them hubs of an ever more richly embroidered civilisation, a time of movement towards writing in vernacular tongues and the renewing of the Greek masters. In this age the men of Runnymede arrived at a document which has become the noblest adversary of a barbarism which has continued unabated since the Middle Ages. They wrote down a declaration whose longevity and continued importance show that the truest and most profound insights and calls to aspiration can come out of what appears an unlikely combination of forces. It shows also that the written word can, did and does masterfully affect history.

In 1939, the Lincoln Cathedral copy of Magna Carta was sent to America for safe-keeping during the war. It became a sensational attraction at the World's Fair, and 14 million people queued to see the parchment before it was locked away in the world's most secure vault in Fort Knox.

After the Second World War, the United Nations adopted the

Universal Declaration of Human Rights. With phrases like 'No one shall be subjected to arbitrary arrest, detention or exile' it reaffirms the demands of the twenty-five barons in 1215. Eleanor Roosevelt called it 'a Magna Carta for all humanity'.

Rudyard Kipling wrote a poem which is I think a truly graceful and romantic memorial:

> And still when Mob or Monarch lays
> Too rude a hand on English ways,
> The whisper wakes, the shudder plays,
> Across the reeds at Runnymede.
> And Thames, that knows the mood of kings,
> And crowds and priests and suchlike things,
> Rolls deep and dreadful as he brings
> Their warning down from Runnymede!

TIMELINE
MAGNA CARTA

1215   Magna Carta establishes for the first time that the power of the king can be limited by a written grant

1216   The first of three charters based on Magna Carta is issued by supporters of King John's son, Henry III

1217   The second of these charters appears

1225   The third charter enters the statute books; three of its chapters stand today

        The text is translated into French and English and read out at meetings of shire courts throughout the realm

1265   With the government of England in the hands of Simon de Montfort, it is decreed that the charter should be proclaimed twice a year so that no one could be ignorant of it

1297   Edward I is forced to confirm the charter and Magna Carta is formally recognised as the law

1610   Lawyers during the Civil War, such as Sir Edmund Coke, cite the charter repeatedly in order to claim that the king's power to alter ancient customs could be limited

1641   Magna Carta is used by lawyers in the struggle between Parliament and Charles I

1642   Throughout the English Civil War the Levellers appeal to Magna Carta to justify their resistance to Charles I, the Long Parliament and eventually to Oliver Cromwell

1770   William Pitt the Elder refers to Magna Carta as 'the Bible of the English Constitution'

1787   The unamended American Constitution already contains a number of prohibitions on the national government and protections of the rights of the citizen

1791   Two clauses of Magna Carta become the fifth and sixth amendments of the American Constitution

1948   The Universal Declaration of Human Rights is presented to the United Nations as 'a Magna Carta for the future'

1956   The English judge, Lord Denning, describes Magna Carta as 'the greatest constitutional document of all times – the foundation of freedom of the individual against the arbitrary authority of the despot'

Senior representatives from the judiciary, Church, various county and district councils, the English-Speaking Union, the Pilgrims Society of Great Britain, the Royal Empire Society, the Victoria League, the Over-Seas League, the National Trust and all the High Commissioners come together to plan the Magna Carta Trust as successor to the Magna Carta Soceity

1965   The John F. Kennedy Memorial is unveiled in Runnymede; the site was chosen for this tribute due to its association with freedom, justice and human liberty

1971   The American Bar Association visit the Magna Carta Memorial in Runnymede, built as 'a tribute to Magna Carta, symbol of freedom under law', pledging their adherence to the principles of the Great Charter

1985 and 2000   The American Bar Association return again to celebrate Magna Carta, 'foundation of the rule of law for ages past and for the new millennium'

THE RULE BOOK OF ASSOCIATION FOOTBALL

———

1863

by

A Group of Former
English Public School Men

THE
FOOTBALL
ASSOCIATION
LAWS

1863

The game of football has, over the last century, totally changed the worlds of sport, the media and leisure. It was able to do that solely because of a book of laws – more commonly called rules – written by a group of former public school men in 1863 in London. Without that book, 'the beautiful game' as the great Brazilian footballer, Pelé, called it, would not have kicked off. Because of that book and the proselytising enthusiasm of British sailors and merchants and adventurers on their expeditions around the planet, it is now estimated that this year – 2006 – eight out of ten people *in the world* are expected to watch something of the World Cup being held in Germany.

Football is played worldwide by more than one and a half million teams and three hundred thousand clubs. This does not include the hundreds and thousands of schools and youth clubs. There are over 5 million officials involved in the game. More than 20 million women play the game and their numbers are growing.

It has become part of the national consciousness of almost every country in the world. It would be fair to say that it has become more than just a game: it attracts tribal followings, it produces icons, it provokes passions sometimes not too far removed from extreme politics and a devotion which has religious connotations. It is a colossal money-spinner and money-eater on an ever increasing scale.

It drives television channels and radio stations and newspapers national, local and specialised. It is a form of universal language, perhaps the most effective form. It has caused at least one war and many battles, often tragic, off the pitch. It has always triggered outbursts of local and national joy, pride, unity. It is colour blind and its influence on breaking down racial prejudice has been strong and widely noted. And all this flowed from the meeting of a few Victorian Oxbridge graduates in a pub in Lincoln's Inn Fields in London in 1863. Before the afternoon was out they had called themselves 'The Football Association' and the Rule Book was on its way.

This short book made it possible for everyone everywhere to play the same game. Before 1863, football had been a riotous confusion.

There are several versions of how the game began. One is that it has its origin in the Roman city of Chester where, half a millennium after the Romans departed from Britain, the Anglo-Saxons played a sort of football with the heads of the conquered Danes. Some scholars push it back farther, into the time of the Roman occupation, and claim it was a way of celebrating occasional British or Celtic victories against the imperial occupiers, this time a Roman head doing the honours. Religion appears in another early version where we have the football (or blown-up bladder) symbolising the sun. It was punted around the fields to ensure a rich harvest. But Professor James Walvin, author of *The People's Game*, has little truck with any of this. 'Games of football', he writes, 'were ubiquitous, spontaneous and traditional . . . The killing of animals provided people with bladders, unsuitable for most other purposes but ideal to inflate and play with.'

Football emerges more substantially in the written records in the Middle Ages. In the same book Professor Walvin writes, 'The game was simply an ill-defined contest between indeterminate crowds of youths, often played in riotous fashion, often in tightly restricted city streets, provoking uproar and damage to property and attracting to the fray anyone with an inclination to violence.'

It is complained of regularly in medieval chronicles. Between 1314 and 1410 new banning orders had to be passed about every twenty years. Yet it would not be put down. One criticism was that it distracted young men from their real business in leisure hours which was to practise with the bow, to maintain the fearsome reputation of the British archers in the French wars. In 1477 a law was passed banning football outright on the grounds that 'Every strong and able-bodied man shall practice with the bow, for the reason that the national defence depends on bowmen'. In Scotland they were more direct. A law issued from the court of King James I stated, 'Nae man shall play at fute-ball.' It is not stretching a point too much, I think, to see these bans still with us in the many 'No Ball Games' signs on estates.

But the bladder would not be denied. Sometimes it was allowed on Shrove Tuesday, a Saturnalian festival before the start of Christian Lent, and a day on which order was deliberately allowed to be, even encouraged to be, overturned. Football was good at that. In his pamphlet 'The Anatomy of Abuses' in 1583, Philip Stubbs wrote, "Football playing is a devilish pastime.'

He continued:

... it may rather be called a friendly kinde of fight than a play or recreation, a bloody and murthering practice than a felowly sport or pastime. For dooth not everyone lye in wayht for his adversarie, seeking to overthrow him and picke him on his nose though it be upon hard stones? ... So that by these means ... sometimes their necks are broken, sometimes their backs, sometime their legs, sometime their arms; sometime one part is thrust out of joint, sometime another ... Sometime the noses gush out with blood, sometimes their eyes start out and sometimes hurt in one place, sometimes in another.

A few lines from the eighteenth century indicate that the game had not changed despite all the censures:

> I spy the Forces of the Football War:
> The Prentice quits his shop, to join the Crew,
> Increasing crowds the flying Game pursue.

It was land enclosures in the countryside and heavy industrial building in the towns and cities which began to do what the authorities had failed to do – squeeze football off the national agenda. An article in *The Times* in 1842 says, 'The Poor have been dispossessed of their games, the amusements and their mirth.' Football, when played at all, became much toned down, the number of players and even the space involved limited.

Help and eventually salvation came from the English public schools. They were not, in the first half of the nineteenth century, well ordered preserves designed to serve and lead a country and an empire. They were often freewheeling, rambunctious pens into which the sons of the rich were herded while they wreaked the havoc of adolescence. In 1797 at Rugby a revolt among the pupils was quelled only by the arrival of the army and the reading of the Riot Act. In 1808 the young Byron led a mutiny at Harrow against an unpopular master. In 1818 at Winchester the militia with fixed bayonets came in to put down another schoolboy rebellion. This was rich soil for the growth of football. Sometimes they were encouraged by the school authorities: better football, it was thought, than rebellion.

What happened at these schools was that the game took on not one but several shapes. In Charterhouse School, for instance, which was then housed in an old Carthusian monastery in London, a very confined space, the art or craft of 'dribbling' the ball was developed. On the vast playing fields of Eton the ball could be kicked high and long, and it was. At Rugby, between the 1820s and the 1840s, the

Before 1863, football had been 'played in riotous fashion'.

boys caught and ran with the ball and began to develop what would become a separate game but was then called, as they all were, football.

We are moving into a period of muscular Christianity. As Hunter Davies writes in *Boots, Balls and Haircuts*, headmasters came to see football as 'a way of instilling order and discipline and also providing a healthy activity for adolescent boys, distracting them from probably more controversial or even disgusting personal activities'. Two of the key men in this respect were Dr Thomas Arnold at Rugby and, more importantly, Edward Thring, the headmaster of Uppingham School from 1853 to 1887.

At Uppingham, Thring developed the idea of an education for the full man, in body and in mind: 'mens sana in corpore sano'. Thring wrote the 'Simplest Rules of Football' in which he emphasised fair play, equal numbers in each team, team spirit and discipline. All this has been seen as part of the preparation of these boys for their imperial role, when all over the globe a few handfuls of young British males from a damp and underpopulated island were almost accidentally dragooned into world governance. Discipline, cohesion, team spirit – as the empire grew so these characteristics had to be put in order and mass produced. Headmasters like Thring and Arnold saw team games, classical learning and no-nonsense Anglicanism as the three pillars of Imperial Wisdom.

There's a passage in the *Labour Force Survey Quarterly* of 1863 which reads: 'the fascination of this gentle pastime is its mimic war, and it is waged with the individual prowess of the Homeric conflicts . . . The play is played out by boys with that dogged determination to win, that endurance of pain, that bravery of combative spirit, by which the adult is trained to face the cannon-ball with equal alacrity.'

Football had come a long way since medieval times. What was once disorder, mayhem, a threat to public peace is now the way to train the gilded youth who will lead and expand a nation. And where once football was seen as, among other things, a distraction from the much more vital honing of the arts of war, it is now seen as an influential factor in the essential, dangerous disciplines of world domination.

Football, then, was up and running in the public schools but struggling to gain space in the big industrial cities, especially in the North and the Midlands. It was the public school men who pushed it forward.

The problems arose when the boys from different schools went to Oxford and Cambridge, wanted to continue to play football and found that because different schools followed different rules, all hell broke loose. This is from the description of a match played in Cambridge in 1848: '. . . The result was dire confusion, as every man played the rules he had been accustomed to at his public school. I remember how the Eton man howled at the Rugby man for handling the ball.'

There was no difference at that stage between what we now call football and rugby. It became common practice to play half a match by one side's rules, the second half by the other's. That's how half-time evolved.

It was not satisfactory, however, and the public school men who were putting the world in order turned their minds to the game they had come to love with a passion. They beat a path through the jungle and finally arrived at a Book of Laws. The beginning of the process may be claimed by Cambridge where, in the middle of the century, it was agreed that fourteen players from different schools should frame a set of rules: these took the game towards football. These were codified in 1863 as 'the Cambridge Rules' by nine Cambridge men representing Shrewsbury, Eton, Harrow, Rugby, Marlborough and Westminster.

But these were almost immediately superseded, only a few days later, on 26 October 1863, in a pub, The Freemasons' Tavern, in

Lincoln's Inn Fields in London. There will be those who say that the finalising of the rules of the most influential game in the world in a pub is deeply satisfying; others might say, 'Typical'. In Britain, at any rate, discussions and disputes on the rules of football have been a feature of our pubs ever since.

On that Monday, representatives, public school men still, from a dozen London and suburban clubs met to sort it out once and for all. This was a book written by a committee – men from a team later to become the Wanderers (a mix of Oxford and Cambridge men), N. N. Kilburn (N. N. standing for No Names), as well as Barnes, War Office, Crusaders, Furnival House, Blackheath, Kingston School, Surbiton, Blackheath School and Charterhouse School. By the end of the afternoon it was announced that 'the clubs represented at this meeting now form themselves into an association to be called The Football Association'. The process was launched but it took another half-dozen meetings to classify and codify what became The Football Association Laws.

The central problem was whether a player could pick up the ball and run with it. Blackheath insisted on two clauses: that 'a player may be entitled to run with the ball towards his adversaries' goal if he makes a fair catch' and, second, that 'if any player still run with the ball towards his adversaries' goal, any player on the opposite side shall be at liberty to charge, hold, trip or hack him, or wrest the ball from him'.

At what proved to be the final meeting on 8 December, the Blackheath motion was defeated by thirteen votes to four. Blackheath withdrew from the Association. The laws of the game, which were foreshadowed in the Cambridge Rules, were formally accepted and Association football was born.

So, soon afterwards, was Rugby football, often preferred by headmasters of public schools as it more obviously encouraged the courageous and aggressive traits. A few decades later, when the industrial teams moved in, there appeared this distinction: 'Football is a game for gentlemen played by ruffians. Rugby is a game for ruffians played by gentlemen.'

There were, originally, thirteen rules. A few more were added as experience demanded, but those thirteen were all that was necessary to set alight what became the world's favourite game.

This is the original list:

The Football Association Laws of 1863

1. The maximum length of the ground shall be 200 yards, the maximum breadth shall be 100 yards, the length and breadth shall be marked off with flags; and the goal shall be defined by two upright posts, eight yards apart, without any tape or bar across them.

2. A toss for goals shall take place, and the game shall be commenced by a place kick from the centre of the ground by the side losing the toss for goals; the other side shall not approach within 10 yards of the ball until it is kicked off.

3. After a goal is won, the losing side shall be entitled to kick off, and the two sides shall change goals after each goal is won.

4. A goal shall be won when the ball passes between the goal-posts or over the space between the goal-posts (at whatever height), not being thrown, knocked on, or carried.

5. When the ball is in touch, the first player who touches it shall throw it from the point on the boundary line where it left the ground in a direction at right angles with the boundary line, and the ball shall not be in play until it has touched the ground.

6. When a player has kicked the ball, any one of the same side who is nearer to the opponent's goal line is out of play and may not touch the ball himself, nor in any way whatever prevent any other player from doing so, until he is in play; but no player is out of play when the ball is kicked off from behind the goal line.

7. In case the ball goes behind the goal line, if a player on the side to whom the goal belongs first touches the ball, one of his side shall be entitled to a free kick from the goal line at the point opposite the place where the ball shall be touched. If a player of the opposite side first touches the ball, one of his side shall be entitled to a free kick at the goal only from a point 15 yards outside the goal line, opposite the place where the ball is touched, the opposing side standing within their goal line until he has had his kick.

8. If a player makes a fair catch, he shall be entitled to a free kick, providing he claims it by making a mark with his heel at once; and in order to take such a kick he may go back as far as he pleases, and no player on the opposite side shall advance beyond his mark until he has kicked.

9. No player shall run with the ball.

10. Neither tripping nor hacking shall be allowed, and no player shall use his hands to hold or push his adversary.

11. A player shall not be allowed to throw the ball or pass it to another with his hands.

12. No player shall be allowed to take the ball from the ground with his hands under any pretext whatever while it is in play.

13. No player shall be allowed to wear projecting nails, iron plates, or gutta percha on the soles or heels of his boots.

Rule thirteen can be read as a throwback to earlier, rougher times.

A few more rules were soon added: in 1865 it was agreed that tape should be stretched across the goalposts at a height of eight feet; in 1866 the offside rule was introduced; goal kicks were introduced in 1869, the game limited to ninety minutes in 1877 and a year later referees were allowed to use whistles. But the basis was well and truly laid in 1863. The game could travel. In 1865, for instance, Buenos Aires FC was formed by British residents.

The first game to be played by the Association rules – the word 'soccer' was already in use, derived from 'Association' – was between Barnes and Richmond. *The Field* reported: 'Very little difficulty was experienced on either side in playing the new rules, and the game was characterised by great good temper, the rules being so simple and easy of observance that it was difficult for disputes to arise.'

The score was 0–0. In 2005, in a television recreation of that game with the same teams and on the same field, the score was 3–3. The game itself was very fast, non-stop (no referee) and, the Victorian-clad participants declared, exhausting.

Although rugby was favoured by headmasters, it soon became apparent that football was much more favoured by pupils. It could be played by anyone of any size and weight and still today men of slight build and average height can dominate a game through their skills. It could be played anywhere – and it came to be played in cobbled yards, under street lights, in parks, on any odd scrap of clear ground. Some sort of game could be hacked out with any size of ball, with jackets for goalposts, with no special gear, and it could last any length of time.

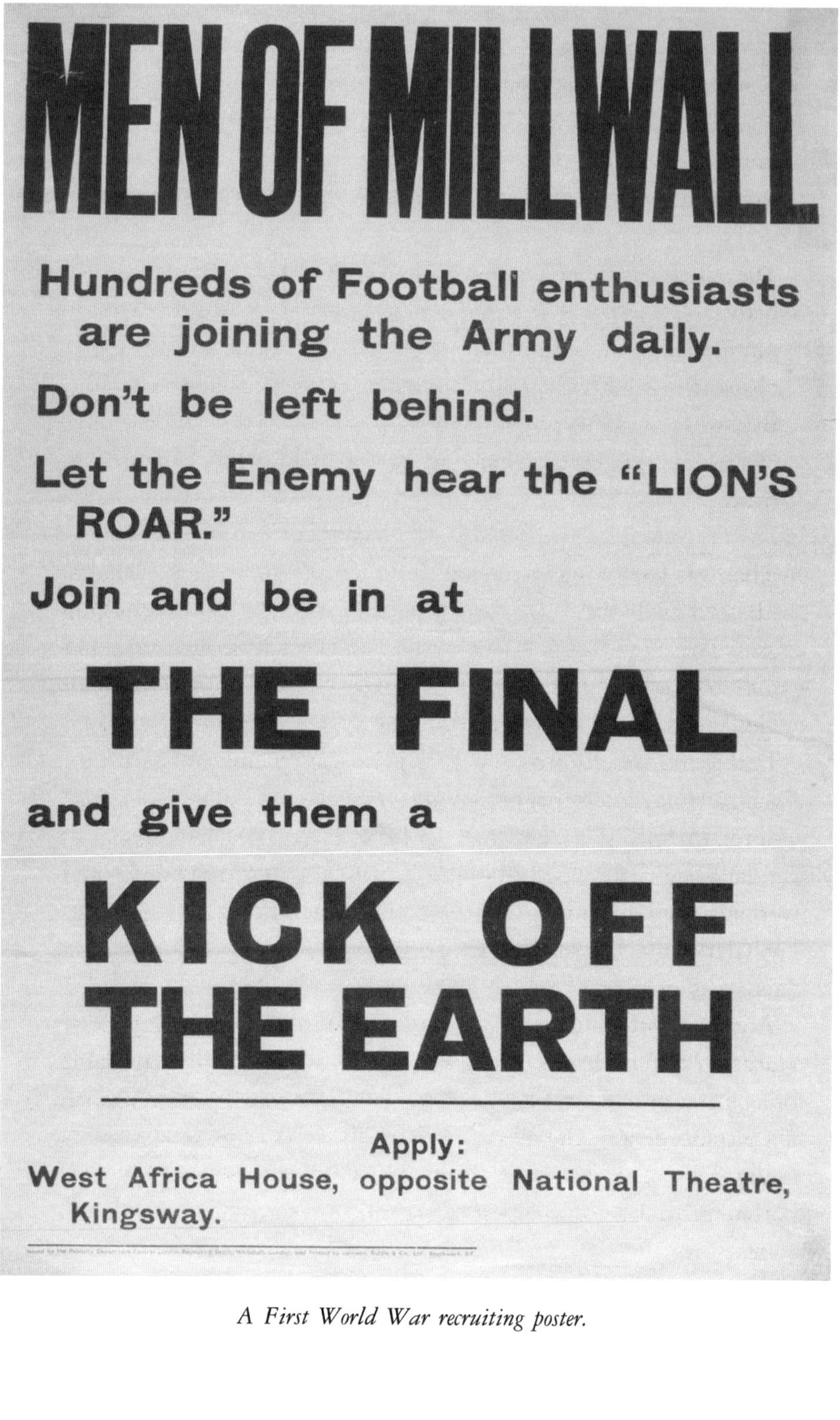

A First World War recruiting poster.

Some public school men of the day saw it as their duty to take this game to the working classes, whose blighted state moved them to concern and to action.

Professor Walvin writes:

The Victorian preoccupation with the healthy (and beautiful) body . . . and more served to draw attention to the wretched physical condition of millions of people. To public school men, obsessed with fitness and athleticism, it seemed clear enough that what working people needed was exposure to the benefits of the sporting culture from which they themselves had benefited.

That was one prong of the attack which was to bring the rules of football to its first and key mass of participants, the British working classes. These public school men were pioneers whose passion for the game and whose proselytising zeal took it from Lincoln's Inn Fields to fields of sand, dust, lush grass and stone around the world.

In the mid-nineteenth century, textile workers in the North were given Saturday afternoon off. By the 1860s, several other trades had adopted this practice. And some, as in Sheffield, gave Wednesday as the half-day. It helped the big industries because they could overhaul their machines with a skeleton workforce on that half-day. Clerks and shop assistants had to wait longer for this privilege. There was now time for the game.

Another rather unexpected boost was the burgeoning state education system. It was difficult to pull in all the children available for a cluster of reasons – the need to bring in a wage, however much of a pittance it was, the need to help in the house and, in the case of young boys, a simple lack of interest. Giving time and space for football proved one of the best carrots for the reluctant boys. Walvin writes:

the new emphasis on football in state schools was perhaps *the* most important factor in guaranteeing the fortune of football as a mass game and was undoubtedly a fact in making football a national game . . . It also helped to lay a basis for the mass readership of new-style national and local popular magazines. There was an enormous appetite for publications covering football and increasing prominence came to be given to the sport in all sorts of supplements, cheap weekly editions and local papers . . . learning to read about football was one of the major incentives (among boys), of learning to read in general.

The Law of Unexpected Consequences strikes again. Football makes you read.

Now football began what became a pandemic. Factory teams sprang up in Britain as did pub teams, police teams, church teams, town teams, schoolboy teams, village teams. Spectators began to organise themselves around their local teams. Out of the old playing fields with carts and wagons drawn around them to provide better views for the better-off, came new stadiums with cheap tickets. Much of the money was put back into the clubs by the early gentlemanly owners still motivated by philanthropy. Early commercial developments included turnstiles, numbered tickets, telegraphic terminals for posting results to pubs, and changing rooms. There were rewards, money prizes and payments to players who were losing paid work by turning out for a local team. Travel had to be paid for. The day of the professional came upon football.

For almost thirty years after the Book was written, the gentleman amateurs to whom it owed so much continued to dominate the game. The FA Cup was usually won by the Old Etonians or by the Wanderers. Spectators would as often as not turn up to watch the renowned expertise of a particular player as to support a team. The game itself was the thing, the taking part, the honest effort, the demonstrable skills.

There is a theory that not only were the working classes more besotted with the sport than their social 'superiors' and not only was the idea of winning more urgent for them, but they took factory practices into the game – Adam Smith, if you like, or Richard Arkwright – and the notion of the division of labour. Previously the players had roamed the field and the individual of greatest prowess was ubiquitous. Now there were nominated defenders, split into full-backs and half-backs, there were forwards and wingmen. Inside lefts and inside rights were developed, as were centre-halfs. This changed the game for ever.

If we are looking for a critical turning point, 1891 is a good candidate. In that year, the professional Blackburn Rovers defeated the Old Etonians in the FA Cup. By 1914 teams such as the Etonian-educated Corinthians were the last remaining exception in a game which they had passed on to the now dominant working-class professionals.

And also by 1914 football was being used for recruitment by the government, whose predecessors had condemned it as weakening the readiness for war. In pre-conscription days, the government decided to use the football ground as a recruiting ground. An FA agreement with the War Office stated, 'Where football matches are played, arrangements are to be made for well-known public figures to address the players and spectators, urging men who are physically fit, and otherwise able, to enlist at once.' Posters went up. One, rather carelessly phrased, reads, 'Do you want to be a Chelsea Diehard? If so, join the 17th Battalion Middlesex Regiment ("the Old Diehards") and follow the lead given by your favourite football players.'

By November 1914, according to *The Times*, more than 100,000 men had volunteered through football organisations. Two thousand out of the 5,000 professional footballers had joined up. And football was played up to the front lines – employed as a cheap and effective way to keep the men fit.

The first football International was England v. Scotland from The Graphic, *1872.*

There are several stories of football in the First World War. They appear as tiny dabs of light in the Stygian slaughterhouse of trench warfare. A Captain Nevill used to lead his men over the top with the rather obvious but suitably sporting signal of kicking a football towards the German trenches. There's a painting by John Singer Sargent, *Gassed*, which shows a number of injured soldiers approaching a dressing station. Behind them other soldiers are playing football: the contrast and the connection could not be more clear.

Most famous, however, are the 'Christmas Truces' between the German and the British soldiers. Some are apocryphal, others undoubtedly happened.

Kurt Zehmisch of the 134th Saxons recorded in his diary: 'The English brought a soccer ball from the trenches and pretty soon a lively game ensued. How marvellously wonderful yet how strange it was. The English officers felt the same way about it.' It is doubtful whether the English had more than a few words of German even though a Germanic dialect was and remains the backbone of the English language. But football, to use an appropriate even though hackneyed word, transcends language.

In 1872, the first international took place, England v. Scotland, result 5–2. In that same year, France was introduced to the game by English sailors playing in Le Havre where a club was formed. It was also in 1872 that the circumference of the ball was fixed. France early became a major force and in 1904 formed the Fédération Internationale de Football Association (FIFA) in Paris. Seven European countries joined FIFA and agreed to play by the FA rules. Britain was at first reluctant to join, thinking perhaps that this should have been their initiative. Sulking stopped a few years afterwards. Today FIFA has more member countries (204) than the United Nations (191). None of this could have happened without that simple Rule Book. When you played football and wherever you played football, you played by the rules and that was that.

In 1876, in Canada, the Carlton Cricket Club set up a football section. The game was being spread both by visitors to Britain, who took it back with them, and British workers who took it abroad with them. Sweden was introduced to the game by British embassy officials in Stockholm and Scottish textile workers in Göteborg. An English professor at Montevideo University formed the first club in Uruguay in 1882 and British railway workers formed another soon afterwards.

It is interesting that India took to cricket, not to football. Perhaps the preferred team game of the upper classes with its elegant dress code and multiple opportunities for finesse had more appeal. America rejected it early on, possibly in the mood of rejecting as much association with Britain, especially England, as it could, wanting, as to some extent it has done ever since, to downplay the crucial role the English played in setting up the USA. Australia also preferred the rougher versions – rugby, the Celtic or Gaelic version, Australian rules, and cricket of course. But now football is on the way in Australia too. It's a great shame that America in particular does not join in – but it never will, fully, until the game is as popular and as well promoted in schools there as it is in the rest of the world. American women, though, are currently world-beaters.

In Africa and South America the game was usually introduced by British sailors who knew their Rule Book and passed it on complete. In Brazil, for instance, the Santos Club, later to be Pelé's club, was inaugurated at the instigation of British sailors.

Back in England the game had moved on royally from the start. In 1888 the Football League was formed with twelve teams: Aston Villa, Derby County, Notts County, Stoke, West Bromwich Albion, Wolverhampton Wanderers, Accrington, Blackburn Rovers, Bolton Wanderers, Burnley, Everton and Preston North End, all from the North or the Midlands.

In 1889 the Boldspil League, the oldest association outside Britain, was formed in Denmark. Three years later, Argentina was the first country outside Britain to have a national champion-ship. A year after that, the movement hit Italy, with Genoa the first club. And just before the end of the century, in 1898, the number of official laws reached the grand total of seventeen – still the modern number.

So it went on, so it goes on. In 1920 the first football pools coupon was introduced, in 1927 the first league match was broad-cast on radio, in 1930 there was the first World Cup (Uruguay 4, Argentina 2).

Football drove out other games which was often a cause for anxiety and even mourning. In Tsarist Russia, for example, where the game was introduced by Lancastrian mill engineers, the game was by the 1890s already attracting crowds of 30,000 and it all but eliminated traditional peasant sports. British influence on what became the Russian national game later disturbed the communist authorities and history was rewritten to demonstrate that its growth was inextricably linked to the triumph of the Russian proletariat.

It has been linked to more than that. The war between El Salvador and Honduras in 1969 is known throughout South America as the 'Football War', and led to about six thousand deaths in a series of three World Cup qualifying matches. Sup-porters who travelled into the rival country with their home team were lucky to get out alive. The pitch at one of the games was surrounded by soldiers with sub-machine guns. Armoured cars took the teams to the airports. When Honduras lost in El Salvador 3–0, their coach said, 'We're awfully lucky to have lost.'

Soon afterwards El Salvador invaded Honduras.

It happened nearer home during the break-up of Yugoslavia. In front of the ground of Dynamo Zagreb (now known as Croatia Zagreb) there's a statue of heroic soldiers. The inscription reads, 'To the fans of this club who started the war with Serbia at this ground on May 13 1990'. Though not precisely true, this now has the binding force of an unchallengeable myth. What is true is that the

The first World Cup competition in 1930 was won by the host nation, Uruguay.

original Croatian army was largely made up of Dynamo supporters around which Croatian nationalism gathered its force. On the Serbian side, it was the Red Star supporters who helped activate Serbian coherence. Arkan, the Serbian war criminal, was the head of the Red Star fan club.

In this respect, and faced by evidence time and again of violent behaviour between competing fans, football must stand fairly accused still of enabling the sort of medieval mayhem which has tarnished its reputation for centuries. There is a sound case to be made that football teams, local and national, foment and deepen differences and trigger unacceptable violence.

There is, however, and I think this a prevailing view, an opinion well if rather euphorically presented by Simon Kuper, writing before the 1994 World Cup in his book *Football Against the Enemy*:

> The World Cup will be what it always is: a carnival of peoples, the one place where Swedes, Russians and Tunisians will hug and kiss and swap shirts on neutral soil. Even Americans will be allowed to join the party. If US forward Clint Mathis scores a beautiful goal, Iranians, Iraqis and Libyans will rave about it. Soccer has many uses, and one of them, fleeting as it may be, is universal love.

It is also big enough to accommodate vice. In the 1986 World Cup, Diego Maradona's key goal for Argentina against England was punched in with his fist. This foul, which he got away with, he claimed to be 'the hand of God'. All Argentina and much of the rest of the world let him get away with it and laughed at a man who had the cheek of the Devil and brought it into play. Breaking the rules with God on your side is OK, especially if you are as great a player as Maradona. In that same game he scored a second goal described (without irony) by the England manager Bobby Robson as 'a bloody miracle'.

Football has been used and still is used to bring nations together.

At its most effective the success of a national team brings a sense of national coherence in nations both old – for instance, England when it won the World Cup – and new – Brazil for example. Much more importantly in Brazil, in Peru and in many other countries, a football team bridges or ignores the race divides. When, for instance, in the 1970s, the Brazilian military government attempted to 'whiten' the national team, there was a huge popular and successful demand for the return of the black players who had been and were soon again selected on merit.

The love of football can become a madness. In his book, Simon Kuper writes:

> In the early days of a World Cup, while the Brazilian team are still winning, life in Brazil is a party. Cars honk on the street and everyone sings and dances. Then Brazil lose and are knocked out. The mood suddenly changes, and people who suffer most are the nation's manic-depressives. Carried along by the general euphoria they cannot bear its end. Their 'high' becomes a 'low' and they commit suicide.

The extreme reaction can be quite funny. Kapuscinski Ryszard, in his book *The Soccer War*, writes:

> After Mexico beat Belgium one-nil, Aynto Mariaga, the warden of a maximum security prison . . . became delirious with joy and ran around firing a pistol in the air and shouting 'Viva Mexico!' He opened all the cells, releasing 142 dangerous hardened criminals . . . A court acquitted him . . . he had acted in a patriotic fashion.

Football now rakes in billions of pounds. The huge success of Sky Television in Britain was driven by football. Rupert Murdoch saw its power and bought key rights at what seemed exorbitant costs, but football drove what had until then appeared a sick enterprise to compete with and outgun the leaders of British broadcasting. Advertisers assert that only sex beats football in shifting products. American companies – Coca-Cola, MasterCard, McDonald's – bid for space in football games with advertisements never seen back in the USA. Stadiums are built for hundreds of thousands of pounds, players paid £50,000, even £90,000 a week, ticket costs soar. Tabloid newspapers make their profits through football coverage. Football merchandise is big business even in countries where football is not yet strong on the international scene.

It is claimed, I think rightly, that football has been more effective than anything else in Britain in combating racism. As Simon Kuper wrote in the *Financial Times*, football's gift was 'to make racism seem unpatriotic. Whenever England's black players were abused during a match abroad, in Spain or Slovakia, their white team mates complained to the media . . . they were defining racism as a foreign custom . . .'

Jay Scott, an official in football's Charity Street League, said, 'Football is more than a game – it is a tool for personal development, a model for social change and an international language. Involvement in football can help build a better future. Football can have a powerful and positive influence on people in all aspects of society.'

It is there in the surest test of all – the language. A football: *el fútbol*, in Spanish, *o futebol* in Portuguese, *le football* in French, *der Fussball* in German. Goal: *un gol* in Spanish and Portuguese and Italian. The captain: *el capitán* in Spanish, *o capitão* in Portuguese, *le capitaine* in French, *der Kapitan* in German, *il capitano* in Italian.

As Mark Ives, the Football Association's vice-president, said after taking a football mission to children in Botswana, 'All you need is a ball and some kids and they all start speaking the international language of football.'

Provided they play by the rules.

Footballers are now compared to Greek gods. Football stadiums are often called the cathedrals of our day. Football is routinely described as an art, its theatricality, its human triumphs and tragedies thought by some far to surpass the dramatic feasts available on the stage. It can obsess children, as I know, and continue to obsess them when, as apprehensive adults, they turn up to watch their team and are mesmerised by a game of such simplicity and yet such complicated possibilities, of such dynamism confined to such a small space and of such a power to affect thousands and move them to roars of rage, of delight, even of ecstasy, that they can only wonder once again at the irradiating impact of a book, and such a small book, a book of laws put together in a pub in London by a dozen English gentleman enthusiasts in 1863.

TIMELINE
THE RULE BOOK
OF ASSOCIATION FOOTBALL

1863   At the Freemasons' Tavern, Great Queen Street, Lincoln's Inn Fields, London, the Football Association (FA) is formed; a month later, the FA meets again to consider a set of rules for its members to follow

1865   Buenos Aires FC is formed by British residents

1866   The first game to be played by FA rules, between Barnes and Richmond

1869   Goal kicks are introduced

1871   The first FA Cup competition (Wanderers v. Royal Engineers 1–0 at Kennington Oval)

1872   The first International game (England v. Scotland 5–2)
       France is introduced to football by English sailors playing in Le Havre
       The circumference of the football is fixed

1875   Oxford University tour Germany and a number of German universities take up the game
       Football introduced in Sweden

1876   In Canada, Carlton Cricket Club forms a football section

1877   Game limited to ninety minutes

1880   Clubs charge for admission and players (still part time) are paid lost wages and expenses

1882   Uruguay's first club is formed
       Two-handed throw-in is introduced

1885   Professional players are allowed

1887   The British introduce football to Russia

1888   The Football League is formed with twelve teams

1889   In Denmark, the Boldspil League is formed – probably the oldest association outside Britain
       Football is introduced in Brazil

1890   Goal nets used for the first time

1891   Penalty kicks introduced. Referee and two linesmen replace umpires

1892   Argentina becomes the first country outside Britain to inaugurate a
        national championship

1893   Italy forms its first club in Genoa

1894   Referee is placed in complete control of game

1898   The number of official laws reaches the modern total of seventeen
        Athletico Bilbao becomes the first club formed in Spain

1899   First club is formed in Iceland

1904   The Fédération Internationale de Football Association (FIFA) is formed
        in Paris with seven European founder countries

1905   Goalkeepers are ordered to stay on their line for penalty kick
        England belatedly joins FIFA

1907   In December, the Professional Footballers' Association (PFA) is formed

1912   Goalkeepers are not allowed to handle the ball outside the penalty area

1913   Opposing players are to stand at least ten yards from free kick

1914   Football organisations encourage members to enlist for war service

1923   The first FA Cup is played at Wembley

1924   Goals may be scored direct from the corner

1927   The first League match is broadcast on radio

1930   The first World Cup – Uruguay beat Argentina 4–2 in the final

1938   First live TV transmission of FA Cup Final

1955   First European Cup

1960   League Cup is launched
        First European Cup Winners' Cup

1981   Points system is changed so that three points are awarded for a win
        and one point for a draw

1985   In May, the Heysel Stadium disaster claims the live of thirty-nine
        people in the European Cup Final in Brussels. English clubs are
        subsequently banned from European competition for five years

1989   The disaster at Sheffield Wednesday FC's Hillsborough ground
        ultimately takes the lives of ninety-six people, with 766 fans receiving
        injuries
        The Government introduces the Football Spectators Act calling for the
        carrying of identity cards at football matches but it is quietly dropped

1992   Formation of the FA Premier League in which the former First
        Division became the Premiership and old leagues 2, 3 and 4 became
        divisions 1, 2 and 3 respectively

2004   Division 1 is renamed the Championship with Divisions 2 and 3
        becoming 1 and 2 respectively

ON THE ORIGIN OF SPECIES

—

1859

by

Charles Darwin

ON

THE ORIGIN OF SPECIES

BY MEANS OF NATURAL SELECTION,

OR THE

PRESERVATION OF FAVOURED RACES IN THE STRUGGLE
FOR LIFE.

By CHARLES DARWIN, M.A.,

FELLOW OF THE ROYAL, GEOLOGICAL, LINNÆAN, ETC., SOCIETIES;
AUTHOR OF 'JOURNAL OF RESEARCHES DURING H. M. S. BEAGLE'S VOYAGE
ROUND THE WORLD.'

LONDON:
JOHN MURRAY, ALBEMARLE STREET.
1859.

'In the beginning God created heaven and earth . . .'

Today there are still millions of Christians who believe, literally, in the Old Testament account, in Genesis, of the Creation. The human race was made once and whole by God in His image and it remains the summit of His creation. Any other explanation is false, blasphemous and unthinkable. About 150 fifty years ago, when Christianity was far stronger in Britain and Europe than it is now, when its churches colonised much of the world and its armies and traders encircled the globe in what seemed a divinely ordained command, Christianity, among the masses and among a substantial number of their leaders, was a fortress of certainty, a source of essential truths. It legitimised the Western empires, seemed to guarantee Western morality and preached Western superiority.

Although, as in every case in this volume, there was a movement which preceded the key publication from which so much is said to have flowed, there are few who would doubt that the greatest challenge to the Christian monopoly came from a book published in 1859 which deals almost exclusively with the genealogy of several plants and animals. Yet for this, the author, Charles Darwin, was called among much else 'the most dangerous man in Britain'.

In great detail, Darwin laid out the evidence for evolution as an undeniable process, with natural selection as its driving force. In doing so the book demolished beliefs in the fixity of the species and seriously challenged, and some claimed wholly undermined, views and convictions about both the nature of man and the presence of God in the natural world.

The core of it is Darwin's theory of natural selection. This, encapsulated, is based on three observations. First that organisms produce far more offspring than could possibly survive. Darwin pointed out that if the millions of eggs produced by the cod all survived it would not be long before cod filled up the oceans and piled up on the land. The second observation is that all organisms vary — the human species is a readily observed case in point with individual fingerprints just one of the proofs. Third, the sum of the variation is inherited, i.e. you do not produce clones but new individuals genetically derived from ancestors but different each one from the other. Add these three together and the inference is that only some can survive and therefore, on average, those that survive will be the ones that are better adapted, better suited for their environment and this will be determined by the individual differences.

The late Professor Stephen Jay Gould gave a simple but striking example: 'a ridiculous caricature', he called it. 'Say there is a population of ordinary elephants in Siberia when it is warm and then the ice age starts. Well, there is natural variation in the amount of hair of those elephants on average . . . [and they] will do better and have more offspring and a hundred generations down the line you get a woolly mammoth.' It does not seem, on the surface, very earth-shattering now. But at the time Darwin's book caused a conceptual earthquake.

It wholly decries all ideas, from whatever religion or none, which up to that time had taken it for granted that humankind was special, superior and apart. In the course of doing this, in a book of striking clarity and easy access, Darwin forced a profound rethink of the workings of life, just as Newton's discoveries forced a rethink of the workings of the universe. It exerted and still exerts a radical impact on scholarship and on all the ramifications of the information society we now acknowledge to be so important. It has had a great influence on political philosophies ever since, often, through wilful but not altogether blind misunderstanding, for the worse. And it has been seen as the destroyer of the Christian, even the humanitarian and atheistic, justification for morality and ethics.

According to Daniel Dennett, Professor of Arts and Sciences at Tufts University, Massachusetts: 'If I could give an award for the single best idea anybody ever had, I would give it to Darwin, because his idea just unifies in a stroke those two completely disparate worlds, until then, of the meaningless mechanical physical sciences, astronomy, physics and chemistry on the one side and the world of meaning, culture, art and of course the world of biology. One stroke shows how to unify all the sciences.' Richard Dawkins, the Charles Simonyi Professor of the Public Understanding of Science at Oxford University, says, '[Darwin] discovered a principle which with hindsight seems enormously simple; it is hard to believe that anybody did not think of it before and yet nobody did, not really.'

Darwin's discovery came out of decades of close observation, classification and study; it came at the end of a very long line of 'evolutionists', many of whom he acknowledged with scrupulous generosity in his book, but none of whom arrived at his unassailable truths; it owed something to his deep reading in the sciences and his wide reading in world literature. Perhaps, though, it owed most to two strokes of good luck. First, his appointment at twenty-two, though wholly untrained, as naturalist on the voyage of the *Beagle*, and second, the fortune of his birth which gave him sufficient wealth to lead the opulent life of the English country gentleman of his day without needing to stir to earn a living.

Charles Darwin, born in 1809, went first to Edinburgh to study medicine and then to Cambridge where he studied, in his time left over from gambling, ratting, shooting and stuffing animals, to be a clergyman. His father was a wealthy doctor and he was a direct descendant of the philosopher, naturalist and poet, Erasmus Darwin; his mother was the daughter of Josiah Wedgwood, another rich intellectual, and it has been pointed out that his early life with its balls and picnics, its country sports and rolling acres of privilege and leisure was not unlike that to be found among the richer young men in Jane Austen's novels.

Darwin's father objected strongly to his young and as he saw it idle son's attempt to escape the responsibilities of the Church by joining the crew of the *Beagle*, but Charles enlisted the support of a sympathetic uncle, drew up a persuasive list of points to fortify himself against his father's arguments, won the day and set off on a voyage into the future of intellectual life. The expedition would take five years, some of it agony for Darwin, who was a poor sailor and often seasick.

He began collecting specimens and making notes at the *Beagle*'s first landing in the Cape Verde Islands, 300 miles off the African coast. In Brazil he collected beetles and flowers and shot lizards and saw his first monkey. After three and a half years on the *Beagle*, he had seen earthquakes, volcanic eruptions and gigantic fossils.

In 1831, the *Beagle* landed in the Galapagos. Darwin found the animals oddly docile. They had not met predatory man. He poked a hawk with his gun barrel. After five weeks they put out to sea, Darwin glad of it, writing that the place was 'extremely useless to man or the larger animals'.

But he began to think more about those sixty-one islands, with their own Edenic mini-climate, home, it transpired, to 607 species of plants, twenty-nine species of land birds, nineteen species of seabirds, and 484 species of fish. It was the visit to these islands which persuaded him to study nature and abandon what would have been a secure career in those easy pastures of the Anglican Church preserved for men of Darwin's class.

He had collected some birds, mostly finches and mockingbirds, and a number of turtles which the crew of the *Beagle* ate. Perhaps because he had been particularly seasick, he was slapdash at recording which animal came from which island; yet he arrived home with immense booty, the treasure chest of a naturalist.

One of the first things he did was to consult one of England's most experienced ornithologists, John Gould of the Geological Society, about the taxonomy of a number of mockingbirds. Gould pointed out that he had misclassified some of the birds because it was difficult for him to tell the species apart from the subspecies: they blended into each other. It was probably the first clue. This meant to Darwin that the criteria he had been trained to use in determining 'the fixity of species' were a useful guide but prone to untested assumptions. Logically, therefore, if species were not a series of perfect individual replications, then the 'transmutation' of one species into another was a possibility if, say, one subspecies had become isolated on another island.

The hunt was on.

Clue number two came from fossils collected in Argentina – gigantic armour-plated creatures, megatheres, apparently unlike anything else in the world, save for the armadillos Darwin had also seen in South America – the one extinct, the other still living, but so alike they might both be part of a large South American group which had evolved body armour. Just as the mockingbirds of the Galapagos nudged him into consideration of biological change by comparing living animals, so the armour-plated beasts from South America allowed him to compare the extinct and the living and brought in the dimension of time.

Darwin immediately realised that he had not enough specimens nor had he classified well enough those he had. He then did what he was to do for the rest of his life: he wrote letters to request help, on

A page from Darwin's notebook, showing the 'family tree'.

this occasion from fellow crew members, specifying that they try to remember which species they had collected from which islands. He had heard, for example, that Spanish sailors could tell which finch belonged to which island. He consulted experts, writing thousands of letters. For the next twenty years this gentleman scholar would use his inherited leisure to work and think his way through to a theory based on minute, exact and mountainously accreted observations.

'The distribution of tenants of this archipelago', he wrote,

> would not be nearly so wonderful if, for instance, one island has a mocking thrush and a second island some other quite distinct species . . . But it is the circumstance that several of the islands possess their own species of tortoise, mocking thrush, finches and numerous plants, these species having the same general habits, occupying analogous situations and obviously filling the same place in the natural economy of this archipelago that strikes me with wonder.

Different species, in short, could evolve from a common ancestor. In his notebooks he drew a diagram of a family tree by way of illustration. He wrote: 'The affinities of all the beings of the same class have sometimes been represented by a great tree. I believe this simile largely speaks the truth. The green and budding twigs may represent existing species; and those produced during each former year may represent the long succession of extinct species.'

This brilliant flash of insight was to be reinforced over the next two decades by home-based research.

In 1842 Darwin and his wife moved into Down House in Kent. He had become a maker of lists. The matter of a wife would not escape the usual treatment. Under a column 'Marry', he wrote:

Children – (if it please God) – constant companion (and friend in old age) who will feel interested in one – object to be beloved and played with. Better than a dog anyhow – Home and someone to take care of house – charms of music and female chit-chat – those things good for one's health – but terrible loss of time.

My God it is intolerable to think of spending one's whole life like a neuter bee working, working and nothing after all – No, no won't do – Imagine living all one's day solitary in a smoky dirty London house. Only picture to yourself a nice soft wife on a sofa with a good fire and books and music perhaps – compare this vision with the dingy reality of Grt. Marlbro' St. Marry, marry, marry. [Q.E.D.]

He married his cousin Emma Wedgwood of the same Wedgwood family that supported William Wilberforce. She had been taught the piano by Chopin and in the drawing room at Down House her fine grand piano still sits (and so he had his music), a large marble fireplace (he had his 'good fire'), deeply comfortable chairs and even a 'sofa'. Some of his books, classics of literature and learning, are beautifully displayed in fine bookshelves along one wall, and Emma does indeed seem to have been a 'nice soft wife' who provided him with a loving and large Victorian family and took good care of their ample, comfortable though not particularly stylish residence a few miles to the south-east of London. Darwin never went abroad again. He lived largely as a recluse. His house and the extensive grounds became his laboratory.

Down House was bought for the public in the 1920s and the furniture and furnishings are largely intact, well cared for. The drawing room is big, encouraging a stroll; the dining room could comfortably seat twenty; the billiard room match-size. It is the home of a comfortable country gentleman with a study brimming with aids to his trade and an adjoining lavatory for relief of that persistent undiagnosed illness which some have seen as psychosomatic, others as the result of a bug picked up on the voyage, an illness which, Darwin said, sometimes disabled him from working altogether and on many occasions for merely half the day. Even so his writings and experiments were prodigious.

It was here that he wrote some fourteen thousand letters – the greatest number to close scientific friends – Charles Lyall, Joseph Hooker, Thomas Henry Huxley – but also those he searched out to help him on specific issues – pigeon fanciers (in abundance), kennel hands, fur trappers and residents of India, Jamaica, Canada, Australia, New Zealand, China, Borneo and the Hawaiian Islands. In other rooms he studied the infant grimaces and smiles of his children and visited zoos to compare them with the infant grimaces of the orang-utan – and found them precisely similar.

It is a house, rather like Chartwell, Churchill's house, also in Kent, structured entirely around the work and comfort of the patriarch.

It is arguable that the grounds and the garden tell you even more about him. This is where for decades, with the patience of the true scholar, Darwin bred his pigeons, grew seeds in the outhouses, observed bees busy among the flower beds; this is where the great man with the appearance, increasingly, of a Victorian illustration of an Old Testament prophet, counted blades of grass on his lawn. It was here in a laboratory attached to where the greenhouse now is, having tracked worms in the local fields for his great and final work on the essential contribution of the common earthworm to the well-being of the planet, that he examined minutely all the plant and animal life obtained in his garden with as much intensity and to as great an effect as the exotic loot bagged on the voyage of the *Beagle*.

There is a Thinking Path in the grounds of Down House. It skirts the edge of a copse and along the way is a bower; plain, but a bower none the less, presumably for resting and further thinking. Thinking while walking seems to be not uncommon to men of great achievement. Perhaps it is something to do with the pace of the stride matching the beat of the heart settling the state of the brain.

Many poets – Wordsworth is the outstanding example – composed as they walked, and Wordsworth too, at Rydal Mount, has the equivalent of a Thinking Path. In the study I sat at his desk and hoped for an inkling of an evolutionary thought or even a twitch of a visitation from the 'other side'; on the Thinking Path I thought I might catch his thinking. No luck.

It is important to note that, like others in this volume, Darwin did not arrive at his studies out of nowhere. His five years' fieldwork on the *Beagle* preceded the vast amount of reading he then set himself to do at Down House. In short, he was a naturalist well before he was a theorist.

Two major works that preceded and influenced Darwin's *Origin* were Lamarck's *Philosophie Zoologique* in 1809 and Robert Chambers's *Vestiges of the Natural History of Creation* in 1844. Though influential, bold and innovating, both had major flaws.

Lamarck's work was distorted by the time frame in which he thought evolution must have occurred. Broadly he agreed with the seventeenth-century vice-chancellor of Cambridge University who, after careful study of the scriptures, declared with all his authority that 'Men were created by the Trinity on October 23rd 4004 B.C. at nine o'clock in the morning'. That settled the matter for many, including Lamarck. Yet his doctrine of continual successful adaptation to an organism's needs was one of the ideas which impressed Darwin.

Robert Chambers proposed a scheme of evolution of all living creatures from one simple form – similar in outline though not in detail to Darwin's scheme. He based much of his evidence on fossils. Unfortunately he wrote that a new species might arise directly from a 'monstrous birth'. Critics pointed out that this could suggest that a pig gave birth to a woodpecker. Chambers was ridiculed despite being a best-seller in his day and read by Disraeli and Abraham Lincoln. Darwin wrote that Chambers displayed 'little accurate knowledge and a great want of scientific caution'. Yet he

A *page from Darwin's original manuscript for* On the Origin of Species.

was grateful to him for his 'excellent service in this country in calling attention to the subject, in reviving prejudice and in thus preparing the ground for the reception of analogous views'. Darwin, though, was warned by the reception given Chambers of the probability of public scorn and he took note of this.

Just as evolution had a history – which started back with the Ancient Greeks – so the idea of natural selection was not new. For instance, Darwin, in the Historical Sketch section of the *Origin* in which he refers to thirty predecessors, quotes a passage from a paper by Dr W. C. Wells written in 1818 in which, Darwin writes, 'he distinctly recognises the principle of natural selection but he applies it only to the race of man'. He goes on, 'Dr Wells observes, firstly, that all animals tend to vary in some degree and, secondly, that agriculturalists improve their domesticated animals by selection; and then he adds, but what is done in this latter case by art, seems to be done with equal efficacy though more slowly by nature in the formation of the varieties of mankind fitted for the country which they inhabit.'

There were many other theories. Where Darwin surpassed all was with the comprehensive nature of his theory and the unmatched evidence that supported it.

Yet for twenty years Darwin would not publish his main work. The idea of transmutation of species was held by radicals and liberals and not by the circle of conservatively inclined country gentlemen and their peers whose respect Darwin wanted.

He was forced to publish. He was sent an essay by Alfred Russell Wallace, from whom Darwin had requested the skins of some Malayan poultry. In the Malayan jungle, Wallace had independently arrived at virtually the same theory of evolution by natural selection that Darwin believed to be his own. Darwin was desperate. 'So all my originality whatever it may amount to will be smashed.'

His friends convinced Darwin that he ought to write an outline of his theory alongside that of Wallace. Darwin could live with the joint publication. 'A very gentlemanly reasonable solution,' he called it and from the beginning he was firm in giving Wallace his due.

But now he had to write it. Even though he described it as only 'an abstract of an essay', this is what became the great *Origin*. He worked not at his desk but in a big armchair with a board across his knee. 'I fear I shall never be able to make it good enough. It is a mere rag of a hypothesis with as many flaws and holes as sound parts. My question is whether the rag is worth anything.' By 1856, the 'essay', still incomplete, was 250,000 words long and now referred to by Darwin as 'my big book on species'.

It went to the Edinburgh publisher John Murray, who was not impressed. As an amateur geologist he thought the book's central argument was 'as absurd as though one should contemplate a fruitful union between a poker and a rabbit'. Murray sought a second opinion from the Reverend Whitwell Gavin, the editor of the distinguished *Quarterly Review*. He suggested that Darwin rewrite the book concentrating on the studies of pigeons. Many people were interested in pigeons, he said, and the book should sell well. Murray was rather taken with the idea but Darwin was not amused. Pressed by Darwin's influential friends and given generous terms, Murray finally and reluctantly agreed an initial print run of 500. But he had his way on the title.

Darwin had called it *An Abstract of an Essay on the Origin of Species and Varieties through Natural Selection.* Under Murray's influence it was transmuted to *On the Origin of Species by Means of Natural Selection, or the Preservation of Favoured Races in the Struggle for Life.*

I think Darwin's opening paragraphs say much that is important about the man and his work. After the generous Historical Sketch which appears in the New Impression of 1900, he sets out his Introduction under the heading 'Origin of Species'.

When on board H.M.S. 'Beagle' as naturalist, I was much struck with certain facts in the distribution of the organic beings inhabiting South America, and in the geological relations of the present to the past inhabitants of that continent. These facts, as will be seen in the latter chapters of this volume, seemed to throw some light on the origin of species – that mystery of mysteries as it has been called by one of our greatest philosophers. On my return home, it occurred to me, in 1837, that something might perhaps be made out on this question by patiently accumulating and reflecting on all sorts of facts which could possibly have any bearing on it. After five years' work I allowed myself to speculate on the subject and drew up some short notes; these I enlarged in 1844 into a sketch of the conclusions, which then seemed to me possible; from that period to the present day I have steadily pursued the same object. I hope that I may be excused for entering on these personal details, as I give them to show that I have not been hasty in coming to a decision.

My work is now (1859) nearly finished; but as it will take me many more years to complete it, and as my health is far from strong, I have been urged to publish this Abstract. I have more especially been induced to do this, by one who is now studying the natural history of the Malay Archipelago, and has arrived at almost exactly the same general conclusions that I have on the origin of species. In 1858 he sent me a memoir on the subject with a request that I would forward it to Sir Charles Lyall who sent it to the Linnaean Society and it is published in the third volume of the Journal of that Society. Sir C. Lyall and Dr Hooker, who both knew of my work, the latter having read my sketch of 1844 – honoured me by thinking it advisable to publish with Mr Wallace's memoir, some brief extracts from my manuscripts.

This Abstract, which I now publish, must necessarily be imperfect . . .

This was the book, 502 pages long, bound in green cloth and rather expensive at 14 shillings, which would change the world. It was an instant best-seller. The first print run (3,000 copies) was oversubscribed. A month after publication there was a long enthusiastic review in *The Times*. Darwin wrote to a friend at Harvard, to organise an American edition. It was translated into French and German almost immediately. By the time the sixth edition came out in 1872 (Darwin made changes and additions for each reprint), it was priced for the pocket of the skilled working man, the word 'evolution' was in the text for the first time and sales quadrupled. But as its popularity grew so the tide of opposition swelled.

William Whewell, past president of the Geological Society and Master of Trinity College, Cambridge, refused to allow the book into the college library. Darwin's old friend, the geologist Adam Sedgwick, wrote, 'Parts of it I admire greatly, parts I laughed at until my sides were sore; other parts I read with absolute sorrow because I think them utterly false and grievously mischievous.' Later in the *Spectator* he wrote that Darwin's argument would 'sink the human race into a lower grade of degradation than any into which it has fallen since its written records tell us of its history'. The *Christian Observer* dismissed the book, the *Rambler*, a Catholic journal, rebuked him and there was outrage in academia that it had reached a wide public and was even on sale to commuters at Waterloo station.

There was praise, too. The Reverend Charles Kingsley wrote, 'It awes me. If you be right I must give up much that I have believed.' Henry Watson, a botanist, wrote to him, 'Your leading idea will assuredly become recognised as an established truth in science, i.e. Natural Selection . . . You are the greatest revolutionist in natural history of this century, if not of all centuries.' Among intellectuals, men of the quality of Hooker, Huxley and Lyall publicly declared their support in important periodicals.

MONKEYANA.

One of the many satirical cartoons inspired by
On the Origin of Species.

Yet Darwin had every reason to fear he was being persecuted. Soon the *Origin* was popularly known as 'The Monkey Theory'. The *British Quarterly* carried a cartoon in which a monkey proposed marriage to a lovely young girl in a crinoline. There were pottery statuettes of a monkey contemplating a human skull. Harry Johnston posed as a 'real living Man Monkey' in Leicester Square. A New York agricultural firm advertised its gargling oil with an ape that sang 'If I am Darwin's grandpa/It follows don't you see/ That what is good for man and beast/Is doubly good for me'. Many churchmen forced their congregations to choose – Christ or Darwin; was man created by God or is he just a baboon? At a meeting in 1860, Bishop Samuel Wilberforce asked of T. H. Huxley, Darwin's friend (who became known as 'Darwin's Bulldog'), whether he claimed descent from an ape on his mother's or his father's side? Huxley replied that he would rather have an ape for a grandfather than a man who misused his gifts to obscure important scientific discussion by rhetoric and religious prejudice. Darwin wanted all the details of that exchange.

Wilberforce expressed a common misconception. But as Darwin observed to his friend, the geologist Sir Charles Lyall, 'our ancestor was an animal which breathed water, had a swim bladder, a great swimming tail, an imperfect skull, and undoubtedly was a hermaphrodite'. Ultimately, as he wrote in one of his notebooks, 'Animals may partake from our common origin in one ancestor . . . we may all be melted together.'

Yet Darwin was not wholly unprepared for what became an onslaught. He had noted the scorn meted out to Chambers after *Vestiges of Creation*, published in 1844. And when he had first told his thoughts on evolution to a friend, Darwin said that it was like 'confessing a murder'. It was not only the stiff canopy of Christianity overlying almost all cultivated Victorian Britain that inhibited him, it was his own residual beliefs. His fears, though real, and the reaction, often vitriolic, could not stop the spread of the book: the advent of relatively inexpensive printing, the rise of literacy in the second half of the nineteenth century and the increasing popularity of periodicals swept the book across the land. By the time of his death, Darwin had collected and classified references in more than a hundred journals and newspapers in Britain alone. His collection also includes 347 reviews, 1,571 general articles and 336 items kept separately because of their large size.

It was a great trial for Darwin that his findings and his subsequent theory explained that living beings were created not by divine diktat but by natural processes. Not only had he been on course for the Church, he was closely bound to the public views of his time. He was a man who sought to avoid any form of protest or disorder. Many commentators have suggested that his very long gestation period is proof of a deep reluctance to publish and be damned. He was aware of what the book's conclusions would do to those of faith. Even Darwin, however, cannot have been aware of how powerful and long lasting an effect the book would have.

In Darwin's nature, the many fail that the few might progress. In mid-nineteenth-century Britain and increasingly in the world ever since, this insight, especially with its absence of morality, its freedom from the shackles of an omnipotent God, even an omnipotent good, not only caught the mood of modern times, it helped make modern times. It inculcated in the minds of millions the idea that the best adapted would survive and breed at the expense of the rest, and in the garden and in the study of Down House this painstaking classifier of nature had proved it.

Parallels between the organic kingdom and the political and economic state of the world were plucked from the heart of the *Origin*. Karl Marx, who read it soon after publication, seized on it. 'Although developed in the crude English fashion,' he wrote, 'this is the book which in the field of natural history provides the basis for my views . . . Darwin's work is most important and suits my purpose in that it provides a basis in natural science for the historic class struggle.' Apart from the fact that Darwin's 'crude English fashion' has far outsoared in influence the decreasing impact and slowing intellectual dynamo of Karl Marx's Germanic fashion, apart from the wonderful patronising tone and the polite rebuff from Darwin when Marx offered to dedicate the English edition of *Das Kapital* to him, this is a perfect illustration of everyone seeing themselves in Darwin's mirror held up to nature.

Darwin's success was partly to do with the accessibility of his prose and the common currency of his proofs. All those connections with pigeon fanciers and sailors seem to have induced in him a respect for the ordinary, a delight even in what was regarded then as the humble (his lifelong observations of the earthworm fit in here) which coloured his arguments and made them effortlessly available. This style he has handed on to his great successors, men like Richard Dawkins and Steve Jones, whose own Darwin-inspired works reach tens of thousands of readers. Like many of the others in this volume, Darwin inspired a multitude of disciples and set in motion a great train of research and study which goes on to this day. Universities have grown rich in scholarship and numbers because of Darwin.

There have been consequences which Darwin could not have foreseen, I believe, most especially in the areas of politics and the social sciences. 'Natural selection', 'the survival of the fittest' and the publisher John Murray's unfortunate, in my view, insistence on the subtitle including the phrase 'the preservation of the favoured races in the struggle for life' – 'favoured races' being raw meat for the big cats in the jungle – allowed and allows the theory to be simplified and brandished as a scientific proof of many forms of authoritarianism.

All those in power could declare themselves 'the fittest' by which they would mean the strongest, the best adapted and therefore by a law more powerful because more provable than God's law, it was right that they ruled. It was used everywhere. W. G. Sumner, an American academic, said to Andrew Carnegie that 'millionaires are the product of natural selection' and there is little doubt that the 'greed is good' mantra of stock-exchange capitalism, openly expressed at the end of the twentieth century, perpetuates that belief system. At the other end of the spectrum there is a sense in which Marx saw Darwin as empowering the proletariat as the fittest in the new class order.

There was worse, though. Professor Borrow writes:

> Filtered through innumerable hack popularisations, it [Darwin's theory] formed a vital ingredient in the stew of racialism, nationalism and anti-semitism swallowed by the young Hitler in the public reading rooms of Munich and Vienna. Racial doctrines entered European thought before Darwin, as an offshoot of developments in anatomy and philology, and Darwin himself did not endorse the application of his theory in social contexts – Huxley [one of Darwin's chief disciples] indeed explicitly repudiated it – but inevitably it provided a kind of crucible into which the fears and hatreds of the age could be dipped and come out coated with an aura of scientific authority.

Social Darwinism, it was argued by Darwinists, was based on a misreading of Darwin. The theory of evolution is not a contest which leads to a super-species or race; rather it emphasises the common beginnings of all life and represents a celebration of the eventual diversity. In some ways Darwinism more properly underpins the new age of Gaia theory, emphasising the common heritage, the interconnections, the oneness of the planet, just as some early philosophers thought the Earth itself had a soul. In this scheme of things, racial differences are of minor importance.

Yet Darwin did open a Pandora's box and it has to be said that evidence from his own writing does not help matters. He was, as everyone is, of his own age, steeped in the culture of the times in which he lived. He accepted the Victorian view that there are 'savages' who have a 'low morality' and a 'weak power of self-command'. A. N. Wilson, in his book *The Victorians*, accuses certain passages of *The Descent of Man* of coming unnecessarily close to justifying homicide – as long as it is performed by the British. That is only one of the reasons why the *Origin* takes precedence over *The Descent of Man*.

Yet 'the survival of the fittest' will not go away. It is perhaps too good a phrase; additionally, it strikes too deeply. Darwin borrowed the phrase from the writer Herbert Spencer to replace his own 'natural selection', which could have been as much a mistake as yielding to John Murray's 'favoured races'. Yet Darwin's own words finally exonerate him.

'As many more individuals of each species are born than can possibly survive,' he wrote,

> and as, consequently, there is a frequently recurring struggle for existence, it follows that any being, if it vary however slightly in any manner profitable to itself, under the complex and sometimes varying conditions of life, will have a better chance of surviving and thus be *naturally selected*. From the strong principle of inheritance, any selected variety will tend to propagate its new and modified form.

In the margin of his copy of Chambers's *Vestiges*, he writes, 'Never use the words higher and lower' and in the *Origin* he writes that he believes in 'no law of necessary development'.

There is one other point here, to do with common experience. We know that we can, by selective breeding, produce faster horses, bigger and smaller dogs, more perfect pigeons, fatter cattle; and in plant life too we have sought for thousands of years to improve the quality and succeeded. Darwin seemed to validate that: or rather he

differing from the Progne purpurea of both Americas, only in
being rather duller coloured, smaller, and slenderer, is considered by Mr. Gould as specifically distinct. Fifthly, there are
three species of mocking-thrush—a form highly characteristic
of America. The remaining land-birds form a most singular
group of finches, related to each other in the structure of their
beaks, short tails, form of body, and plumage: there are thirteen
species, which Mr. Gould has divided into four sub-groups.
All these species are peculiar to this archipelago; and so is
the whole group, with the exception of one species of the sub-
group Cactornis, lately brought from Bow island, in the Low
Archipelago. Of Cactornis, the two species may be often seen
climbing about the flowers of the great cactus-trees; but all
the other species of this group of finches, mingled together in
flocks, feed on the dry and sterile ground of the lower districts.
The males of all, or certainly of the greater number, are jet
black; and the females (with perhaps one or two exceptions) are
brown. The most curious fact is the perfect gradation in the
size of the beaks in the different species of Geospiza, from one as

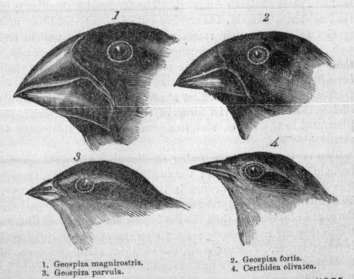

1. Geospiza magnirostris.   2. Geospiza fortis.
3. Geospiza parvula.   4. Certhidea olivacea.

large as that of a hawfinch to that of a chaffinch, and (if Mr.
Gould is right in including his sub-group, Certhidea, in the main

*Four species of Galapagos finch from Darwin's journal published
in 1890 relating the findings of the voyage of the* Beagle.

has been used and misused to validate that in the case of humans. Darwin gave extreme eugenicists intellectual respectability. The argument was simple: why should selective breeding not be applied to the human race? Of course it has been. In Sweden until well into the second half of the twentieth century, those thought unfit to bear children were sterilised, as had happened, most intensely and on a huge scale in Germany. But it was also applied to an extent in America and other countries. The idea of keeping a gene pool pure is one basis of the caste system in India, while the notion of strength through selective and controlled breeding dominates the specification of family in China.

In North America, Austria, New Zealand, Tasmania, in Central America and many parts of Africa, the indigenous populations were reduced chiefly through violence and disease and have largely disappeared. The grounds for this were bound up in the idea, pre-Darwin but retrospectively 'justified' by certain phrases offered in Darwin and his observations on animal life, that there were 'higher and lower' and the 'fittest', most often interpreted as the strongest and the best, were destined to triumph. I fear that this has not gone away and while Darwin is in no way responsible, and though his theories are counter to supremacism, it ought to be considered, I think, that the perverse consequences of a theory could also be counted as real consequences.

Darwin's head-on crash at the time was with Christianity. It is a collision which continues to this day with the Creationists, most dramatically in the USA, where many still refuse to admit the truth of Darwin's description of the origin and development of life. It was presented in Darwin's own time as a stand-up fight: were you for Christ or Darwin?

Despite the undermining of religion by a great number of thinkers before Darwin, there was still a wide acceptance of what could be called a natural theology. Natural seemed proof enough. In

'The Excursion', the most famous poem Wordsworth published in his lifetime, he had written (pre-Darwin):

> How exquisitely the individual Mind
> (And the progressive power perhaps no less
> Of the whole species) to the external World
> Is fitted: and how exquisitely too . . .
> The external World is fitted to the Mind.

God was out there: in the beauty and mystery of nature and in the capacity for spirituality He could be seen and felt in its mirror, the human mind.

Darwin took this argument. 'We behold the face of nature bright with gladness,' he wrote.

> We often see superabundance of food; we do not see or we forget, that birds which are idly singing around us mostly live on insects or seeds and are thus constantly destroying life; or we forget how largely these songsters, or their eggs, or their nestlings, are destroyed by birds and beasts of prey; we do not always bear in mind that though food may now be superabundant, it is not so at all seasons of each recurring year.

The *Origin* pointed out in reasonable terms that the universe had no need of God and that, for many people, was intolerable. Professor Borrow wrote of men suddenly finding themselves in a 'cold, passionless universe'. Nature had no meaning. Meaning was unnecessary. Morality was not rooted in any divine or favoured notion of mankind. To many Christians Darwin's world was unbearably empty of all they valued about life. Existentialism owes the foundation of its bleak, aimless, soulless philosophy to Darwinism. And Darwin's universe seemed to throw into question the very notion of rights. If they were not inspired by a higher authority, then what were they but temporary arguments, man-constructed to seal over imperfections for a few generations at most?

Copernicus had removed the Earth from the centre of the universe. Darwin removed God as the central force of life. It was the beginning of a continuing stripping away of the long-held conviction that the human species was special, supreme and chosen. Perhaps we exist merely to carry genes. Or are we transport vehicles for the conquering march of bacteria? And how do our claims to any sort of immortality compare with the billion-years-old creatures below the ocean floor and the cosmic dust from the Big Bang?

Crick and Watson's double-helix structure describing DNA, almost a century on from the *Origin*, showed that what Darwin had arrived at through meticulous observation and hard thinking was there in the genes, his theory, as it were validated. From there to the Human Genome Project, thought by Steve Jones to be over-hyped, although there are others, Matt Ridley for instance, who believe its completion 'will transform the production, prevention, treatment and understanding of disease'. He even adds, 'Above all there are genes that promise to solve old mysteries of determinism and free will.'

Since 1859, Darwin's theories have been tested and examined and become accepted as the foundation of all the biological sciences. And yet, even at the beginning of the twenty-first century, the theory of evolution is subject to attack by religions and by anti-evolution Creationists who put forward the theory of 'intelligent design'. America has been the focal point of this argument at least since 1925, when John Scopes was prosecuted for teaching evolution in Tennessee. Still today in the USA a poll shows that 64 per cent of people are in favour of teaching Creationism alongside evolution and 38 per cent believe that Creationism ought to replace evolution. President Bush declared, 'I think that part of education is to expose people to different schools of thought,' and agreed that 'intelligent design' should be taught as part of science, even though it will yield to no scientific tests. Professor Kenneth Miller, a biologist at Brown University, Rhode Island, said, 'Every single scientific society in the United States that has taken a position on this issue has taken a position against intelligent design and for evolutionary theory.' British scientists, led by Richard Dawkins, are horrified at the implication of the increasing influence of Creationism.

It shows, though, that the religious opposition to Darwin will not easily be overcome. It could be said that in some quarters Darwin's theories have fortified the belief of the Creationists.

God was always the big problem for Darwin and in the sixth edition of the *Origin*, printed in 1872, Darwin makes a rare reference to God in his conclusion.

I see no good reason why the views given in this volume should shock the religious feeling of anyone. It is satisfactory, as showing how transitory such impressions are, to remember that the greatest discovery ever made by man, namely the law of the attraction of gravity, was also attacked by Leibniz, 'as subversive of natural and inferentially of revealed religion'. A celebrated author and divine has written to me that 'he has gradually learnt to see that it is just as noble a conception of the Deity, to believe that He created a few original forms capable of self-development into other and needful forms, as to believe that He required a fresh act of creation to supply the voices caused by the action of His laws.

Darwin is confident of the future of his theory. 'I look with confidence to the future,' he writes, 'to young and rising naturalists, who will be able to view both sides of the question with impartiality. Whoever is led to believe that species are mutable will do good science by continually expressing his conviction; for thus only can the load of prejudice by which this subject is overwhelmed, be removed.'

The final, firm words in this careful, quiet but revolutionary book could be read as Darwin's credo: 'There is a grandeur in this view of life,' he writes, 'with its several powers, having been originally breathed by the Creator into a few forms or into one; and that, whilst this planet has gone cycling on according to the fixed law of gravity, from so simple a beginning endless forms most beautiful and most wonderful have been and are being evolved.'

TIMELINE
ON THE ORIGIN OF SPECIES

1859   Charles Darwin publishes *The Origin of Species* which goes into a second
        edition the following year

1860   T. H. Huxley and Bishop Samuel Wilberforce engage in their famous
        debate on Darwin's theory of evolution

1867   Volume I of Karl Marx's *Das Kapital* is published, drawing on
        Darwin's 'survival of the fittest' notions to explain aspects of
        Communist social theory

1869   DNA is discovered by Swiss biochemist, Johann Miescher

1872   The sixth impression of *The Origin of Species* adopts the term 'evolution'
        for the first time

1882   Walter Flemming observes chromosomes while studing the dividing
        cells of salamander larvae

1902   Walter Sutton determines that chromosomes carry the cell's unit of
        inheritance and that they occur in distinct pairs within a cell's nucleus

1910   Thomas Hunt Morgan's fruit-fly experiments reveal that some traits are
        sex linked and reside on a special pair of chromosomes

1925   Governor Austin Peay of Tennessee signs an Act prohibiting the
        teaching of evolution theory in all universities and public schools in
        Tennessee

        The 'Scopes Monkey Trial' begins in Dayton, Tennessee, in which John
        Scopes challenges this anti-evolution law

1930s   The marriage of genetics and Darwinian natural selection creates Neo-
        Darwinsim, or the New Synthesis

Nazi Germany uses Social Darwinism to justify the 'superiority' of the Aryan race during the Second World War

1944   Oswald Avery finds that a cell's genetic information is carried in DNA

1950   The encyclical Humani Generis, issued by Pope Pius XII, states that evolution was not necessarily in conflict with Christianity

1952   The first animal cloning occurs as Robert Briggs and Thomas J. King clone northern leopard frogs

1953   Francis Crick and James Watson describe the double-helix structure of DNA.

1968   The *Epperson* v. *Arkansas* case finds the Arkansas law prohibiting the teaching of evolution unconstitutional as it was not science-based

1969   The Harvard Medical team isolate the first gene

1973   Stanley Cohen and Herbert Boyer create the first recombinant DNA organism through 'gene splicing'

1976   Richard Dawkins publishes his controversial book *The Selfish Gene*

1978   The first child conceived through in vitro fertilisation, baby Louise, is born

1979   James Lovelock publishes *Gaia: A New Look at Life on Earth*, developing the theory that life on Earth not only made the atmosphere but also regulated it

1981   A law is passed stating that public schools within Arkansas must give balanced treatment to creation-science and evolution-science

1982   The *McClean* v. *Arkansas* case finds that the Arkansas law is unconstitutional

The first genetically engineered drug approved: a form of human insulin produced by bacteria

1984   Steen Willadsen clones a sheep from embryo cells

1987   The *Edwards* v. *Aguillard* trial decides that Louisiana's 'Creationism Act', which prohibited the teaching of evolution unless balanced by biblical Creationism, invalid

1990   The *Webster* v. *New Lenox* case rules that school boards should have the right to prohibit teaching Creationism

        The International Human Genome Project formally begins

1991   The gene responsible for breast cancer in women is identified

1993   The gene responsible for Huntington's disease is identified

        Human embryos are first cloned

1996   Dolly the sheep is the first organism to be cloned from adult cells

1998   University of Wisconsin scientists publish their discovery of human embryo stem cells

        Nineteen European nations sign a ban on human cloning

2000   The National Institute of Health issues final guidelines for funding stem cell research. George W. Bush opposes federal funding of such research. Former President Bill Clinton supports the guidlines

2003   The Human Genome Project announces the completion of a final draft of the human genome sequence

ON THE ABOLITION
OF THE SLAVE TRADE

1789

by

William Wilberforce in Parliament, immediately printed in several versions

5. " That the slave trade has been found, by experience, to be peculiarly injurious and destructive to the British seamen who have been employed therein; and that the mortality among them has been much greater than in his Majesty's ships, stationed on the coast of Africa, or than has been usual in British vessels employed in any other trade.

6. " That the mode of transporting the slaves from Africa to the West Indies necessarily exposes them to many and grievous sufferings, for which no regulation can provide an adequate remedy ; and that, in consequence thereof a large proportion of them has annually perished during the voyage.

7. " That a large proportion of the slaves so transported, has also perished in the harbours in the West Indies, previous to their being sold. That this loss is stated by the assembly of the island of Jamaica at about four and a half per cent. of the number imported ; and is, by medical persons of experience in that island, ascribed, in great measure, to diseases contracted during the voyage, and to the mode of treatment on board the ships, by which those diseases have been suppressed for a time, in order to render the slaves fit for immediate sale.

8. " That the loss of newly imported negroes, within the first three years of their importation, bears a large proportion to the whole number imported.

9. " That the natural increase of population among the slaves in the islands, appear to have been impeded principally by the following causes. 1st, The inequality of the number of the sexes in the importations from Africa. 2nd, The general dissoluteness of manners among the slaves, and the want of proper regulations for the encouragement of marriages, and of rearing children. 3d, Particular diseases which are prevalent among them, and which are in some instances attributed to too severe labour or rigorous treatment, and in others to insufficient or improper food. 4th, Those diseases which affect a large proportion of negro children in their infancy, and those to which the negroes newly imported from Africa have been found to be particularly liable.

10. " That the whole number of slaves in the island of Jamaica, in 1768, was about 167,000. That the number in 1774, was stated by governor Keith about 193,000. And, that the number in December 1787,

as stated by lieut. governor Clarke, was about 256,000. That by comparing these numbers with the numbers imported into and retained in the island, in the several years from 1768 to 1774 inclusive, as appearing from the accounts delivered to the committee of trade by Mr. Fuller ; and in the several years from 1775 inclusive, to 1787 also inclusive, as appearing by the accounts delivered in by the inspector general ; and allowing for a loss of about one twenty-second part by deaths on ship board after entry, as stated in the report of the assembly of the said island of Jamaica, it appears, That the annual excess of deaths above births in the island in the whole period of nineteen years, has been in the proportion of about seven eighths per cent., computing on the medium number of slaves in the island during that period. That in the first six years of the said nineteen, the excess of deaths was in the proportion of rather more than one on every hundred on the medium number. That in the last thirteen years of the said nineteen, the excess of deaths was in the proportion of about three-fifths on every hundred on the medium number; and that a number of slaves, amounting to 15,000, is stated by the report of the island of Jamaica to have perished, during the latter period, in consequence of repeated hurricanes, and of the want of foreign supplies of provisions.

11 ". That the whole number of slaves in the island of Barbadoes was, in the year 1764, according to the account given in to the committee of trade by Mr. Braithwaite 70,706. That in 1774, the number was, by the same account 74,874. In 1780, by ditto 68,270. In 1781, after the hurricane, according to the same account 63,248. In 1786, by ditto 62,115. That by comparing these numbers with the number imported into this island, according to the same account (not allowing for any re-exportation), the annual excess of deaths above births, in the ten years from 1764 to 1774, was in the proportion of about five on every hundred, computing on the medium number of slaves in the island during that period. That in the seven years from 1774 to 1780, both inclusive, the excess of deaths was in the proportion of about one and one-third on every hundred, on the medium number. That between the year 1780 and 1781, there appears to have been a decrease in the number of slaves of about 5000. That

The historian, G. M. Trevelyan, writing on the abolition of the British slave trade, was unequivocal. It was, he wrote, 'one of the turning circumstances in the history of the world'. Although it came about through a combination of events and voices over a century, no one then or since has doubted that there was one man who finally made it happen: William Wilberforce. The key moment in his campaign was a four-hour speech delivered in the House of Commons on 12 May 1789. The consequences of that speech are evident everywhere today. The force of its arguments still stirs the blood; the extension of the arguments were to include many other areas of emancipation and unleash a new power of mass public morality into the world. And in a world still polluted by slavery, the call to arms in terms defined by Wilberforce remains urgent.

The speech is considered one of the most notable ever delivered in the House of Commons. Perhaps the only other real contender would be a defining speech of Churchill when Britain 'stood alone' in 1940. There was no official record of speeches made to Parliament in Wilberforce's time (and Hansard, Parliament's own record of its business, did not then exist) but newspapers recorded their versions of speeches. The printed versions mattered essentially. Some of these were remarkably detailed, full and regarded as accurate. Naturally they could be skewed towards the agenda of a proprietor but his speech was printed immediately, in more than thirty different versions. The speech was reprinted verbatim in *Cobbett's Parliamentary History of England*, published in 1806. So by virtue of Cobbett it comes into the category 'book', and surely in our time when so many concoctions call themselves books it can be allowed this definition. The time-defying speeches of great politicians, from Demosthenes to Mandela, can, if printed between hard covers, be called, I think, their books. But on Cobbett I rest. And it is in print that it has had its greatest effect.

Wilberforce's speech set out a damning critique of the slave trade. His words evoked the appalling conditions of the slave vessels, the misery of the slaves, the role played by the trade in creating wars in Africa and the trade's damaging spiritual effect on the relationship between men.

It was received with passionate approval and then for eighteen years during which Wilberforce never gave in, his cause was subject to a series of setbacks, some accidental, others designed. Time and again these threatened to sink the attempt to turn Wilberforce's outcry into the law of the land.

Elizabeth I had said that the slave trade would 'call down the vengeance of heaven', and there was a strain in English life and thought which was opposed to the slave trade from Elizabeth up to contemporaries of Wilberforce. William Paley, for instance, rejected slavery in 1785 in his book *Principles of Moral and Political Philosophy*. Adam Smith, in *The Wealth of Nations*, condemned slavery for rather different reasons, as an inefficient system of production, as slaves had no prospect of owning property and were promised no incentive to work.

Between the utterance of Elizabeth I and the speech of Wilberforce, it has been estimated that more than 10 million West Africans were enslaved by European traders. Slavery had been in operation on the continent of Africa, run by Arab merchants and local African chiefs for centuries, and the Western European traders were at the end of a long line which began often several hundred miles from the coast. The Portuguese and the Spanish were the first Europeans to drive the slave trade. Britain, which came in later, soon became the biggest slave-trading nation. By the early eighteenth century, it is estimated that more than a quarter of all Londoners were involved in the slave trade; Bristol and Liverpool exploded in wealth and population as a result of the trade.

Yet in the same period, about twenty thousand black people settled in the UK as slave servants or free men. There was a consistent though probably not a prevailing view that while slavery was acceptable abroad, it did not sit comfortably with the basic notion of liberty and the free individual at home. This can be seen as hypocrisy. It could also have provided a platform for Wilberforce's great leap into the unthinkable.

The sums of money involved in the slave trade were staggeringly large. In present-day terms it generated the equivalent of the entire housing market or the IT industry. In one year alone £17 million came into Liverpool – a massive sum for those times. Fine houses were built in the slave-trading cities, fine churches erected, along with public buildings and monuments which still remain. It is one measure of the strength of the arguments, the tenacity and the political skills of Wilberforce that he managed to persuade those who benefited so royally to give up the source of their wealth. It is difficult to believe that one man, a man of no political office, could effect such a change for the better today. Even when we think of Mandela we see him in the wake of Wilberforce.

The slave trade worked as a triangular system. Ships from Bristol and other English ports would take goods to Africa where they would be sold, the money used to buy slaves, up to sixty thousand a year, who would be transported to America or the West Indies, the ships protected by the Royal Navy. The slaves would be sold and the money used to bring back luxury goods, among them sugar, coffee, rum and tobacco.

The road to Wilberforce was paved with outrage. In 1781, for instance, Luke Collingwood, captain of a ship called *Zong*, threw shackled but living slaves overboard as they were too weak to sell and he could use the excuse that this act served the safety of the ship and thus allowed him to claim insurance. When this became known there was uproar; pamphlets were issued and later in 1787 anti-slavery campaigners formed the Committee for the Abolition of the Slave Trade. Abolishing the trade seemed attainable. It could be said that what Wilberforce put forward was an idea whose time had come, and yet a champion was badly needed.

There is a view that in order truly to understand the ills of mankind you need to have suffered from them. Wilberforce spikes that. He was born into a wealthy merchant family in Hull. The wealth took him to Cambridge and landed him a seat in Parliament at the age of twenty-one. He was a close friend of the young William Pitt who was first the Chancellor of the Exchequer and then the youngest ever prime minister. Wilberforce was moved by his religion to do a great thing for humanity and there is a sense in which he looked around for a fit cause and found it in the abolition of slavery.

Nor does he appear to have had the commanding presence of the born leader. He had, by all accounts, a beautiful voice but, according to James Boswell, he looked like 'a shrimp'. At the time of his speech he was thirty years old, short, snubnosed and weak eyed.

This was the man who rose to his feet in the crowded House of Commons in May 1789. He began:

> When I consider the magnitude of the subject which I am to bring before the House — a subject in which the interests not just of this country, nor of Europe alone, but of the whole world and of posterity are involved . . . it is impossible for me not to feel both terrified and concerned at my own inadequacy to such a task . . . the end of which is the total abolition of the slave trade.

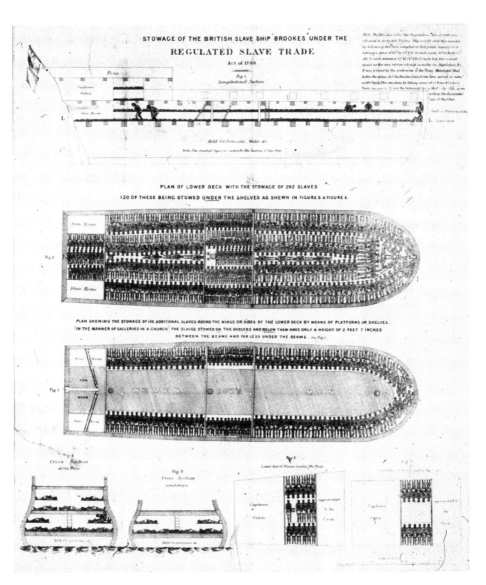

The slave ship Brookes *carried 292 slaves on the lower deck and 130 crammed round the edge.*

Four hours later he emerged as a man of heroic moral stature, a man whose words would move the world.

I find it fascinating that although this speech was to inspire and move multitudes, it was couched in the calm classical English of the new Enlightenment. The intention of this comparatively young man was to effect a seismic shift in opinion. He succeeded. His language, though, was not only measured and restrained, it deliberately set out to reassure its audience that it was not a mere pulling at the teats of the cow of guilt: it was with reason that he would prevail.

'It is not', he wrote, and said to the House of Commons, 'their passions' (written as 'paſſions')

> I shall appeal to – I ask only for their cool and impartial reason; and I wish not to take them by surprise but to deliberate point by point on every question. I mean not to accuse anyone, but to take the shame upon myself, in common, indeed, with the whole Parliament of Great Britain, for having furthered this horrid trade to be carried on under their authority. We are all guilty – we ought all to plead guilty and not to exculpate ourselves by throwing the guilt on others . . .

Wilberforce stuck to his guns throughout and appealed to reason as he saw it. Yet behind his Enlightenment, just as behind the powerful theories expressed in mathematical terms by one of the fathers of the Enlightenment, Isaac Newton, there was a profound belief in God. God and the good drove Wilberforce.

It is also, I think, worth noting that the 'we are all guilty' notion, expressed by Wilberforce to a group of legislators, that is to say people who could change the organisation of life, has now become a tired and tiresome slogan, meaningless most of the time. People in Britain today do not and, I think, should not be shackled with the idea that they bear guilt for the seventeenth- and eighteenth-century slave trade. Like many great phrases, it has been used for good and ill. Wilberforce was talking to a group of men (all men) who could and did change society. He did not, I believe, think that the labourers in rural Norfolk, the industrial wage slaves in the North, the liberal-minded intellectuals in the coffee houses of London were 'all' equally guilty. He was attacking those at the centre of power. He knew that in terms of a mood and economic revolution they were the men who mattered.

The *Star* reported that 'the gallery of the House of Commons on Tuesday was crowded with Liverpool merchants who hung their heads in sorrow.'

It is often said that the speech was a masterpiece of cunning, a tactical manoeuvre. William Hague, his latest biographer, inclines to that opinion. I do not think this was Wilberforce's intention. His Christianity was profound. He believed deeply in the Sermon on the Mount. He demanded the best from those he faced not because it was clever or Machiavellian to do so but because he was a follower of the New Testament. Thus one of the most remarkable features of what he wrote was his extraordinary empathy – for its time – with those in Africa.

What should we suppose must naturally be the consequence of our carrying on a slave trade with Africa? With a country vast in extent, not utterly barbarous, but civilised in a very small degree? Does anyone suppose a slave trade would help their civilisation? Is it not plain that she must suffer from it; that her civilisation must be checked; that her barbarous manners must be made more barbarous; and that the happiness of her millions of inhabitants must be prejudiced by her intercourse with Britain? Does not everyone see that a slave trade carried on around her coasts must carry violence and desolation to her very centre? . . . If her men are all converted into goods, and become commodities that can be bartered, it follows they must be subject to ravage just as goods are . . .

163

This focus on the damage to Africa came out of a belief, Christian-based, in the equality of mankind. In pursuing this, to great effect and admirably, Wilberforce did not take on the complicity of the Africans themselves, and this is part of his gift to posterity. The still-prevailing notion that the slave trade was all the fault of wicked white Europeans and most culpable of all, wicked white Englishmen (the other countries in the United Kingdom like to shuffle away from inclusion in this one) is just plain wrong. But we have to remember that this book of spoken words was narrowly directed. In his attempt to convince his peers in a wealthy, privileged and by contemporary standards unacceptably corrupt legislative House, he was forced to, or perhaps he believed that he had to, present the case in stark terms. One unfortunate consequence is that these stark terms have become a stigma on the English above all others ever since.

Wilberforce drew on, as Enlightenment intellectuals did, a range of arguments. He was, for instance, unafraid to talk about what he saw as the essential appetites, the core evil condition of mankind. After a rather individual view of African strife, he remonstrates with the House of Commons for what he considers to be the introduction of alien vices to the African continent. African kings, he declared, are pushed into bad ways under the influence of the slave trade.

'In Europe', he writes, 'it is the extension of commerce, the maintenance of national honour or some great public object that is ever the motive to war with every monarch; but in Africa it is the personal avarice and sensuality of their kings.' Today we stand amazed at the beautifully balanced sentences poised on such sketchy proofs which resonated with their intended audience as certain truths. Dauntless, he went on:

> these two vices of avarice and sensuality, the most powerful and
> predominant in natures thus corrupt, we tempt, we stimulate in all
> these African princes, and we depend upon these vices for the very

maintenance of the slave trade. Does the King of Barbessin want brandy? He has only to send his troop, in the night time, to burn and desolate a village; the captives will serve as commodities, that may be bartered by the British trader.

No matter that the King of Barbessin seems to get off, morally, scot-free compared with the British trader, the force of the moral dynamic in this world-changing speech is in full flow. 'Some', he adds, driving his point in deep, 'have admitted the slave trade to be the chief cause of wars in Africa.'

Then he turns his attention to totally verifiable facts and, it turned out, to revolutionary effect. He told it like it was. Most of those in the House of Commons did not know the facts; the country did not know the facts. They did, after 12 May 1789. Wilberforce had researched them.

'I must speak,' he said,

of the transit of the slaves to the West Indies. This, I confirm, in my own opinion, is the most wretched part of the whole subject. So much misery contained in so little room is more than the human imagination had ever before conceived. I will not accuse the Liverpool Merchants. I will allow them, nay, I will believe them, to be men of humanity and I will therefore believe . . . if it were not for the enormous magnitude and extent of the evil which distracts their attention from individual cases, and makes them think generally, and therefore less feelingly on the subject, they never would have persisted in the trade. I verily believe, therefore, if the wretchedness of any one of the many hundred negroes stowed in each ship could be brought before their view, and remain within the sight of the African market, that there is no one among them whose heart would bear it.

This has been considered by many commentators to be Wilberforce's master stroke. Not for him the easy accusing finger, the self-indulgent adjectives of opprobrium, the phrases making pariahs of the Liverpool merchants – here was an open appeal to noble hearts. It was stunningly effective. It has been copied ever since. But it came again, I think, in Wilberforce's case, not from tactics but from a creed. He believed in the essential goodness of humanity, fed by Christianity and by the new creed of Natural Innocence in the works of Rousseau and others. He was also carried forward by the Enlightenment mission to obliterate ancient superstitions of guilt-saturated mankind and replace them with all the possibilities of reasoned optimism. Possibly more than anything else in this great speech, it was Wilberforce's direct address to the Liverpool merchants in the gallery of the House of Commons which most emphatically influenced the abolition cause.

Then he came back to the facts. 'Let anyone imagine to himself six or seven hundred of these wretches chained two and two surrounded by every object that is nauseous and disgusting, diseased and struggling under every kind of wretchedness.'

He turned his guns on a Mr Norris, 'one of the Liverpool delegates', who, Wilberforce said, had described the slaves 'in a manner which I am sure will convince the House how interest can draw a film over the eyes, so thick that total blindness could do no more'.

'Their apartments', he said, quoting Mr Norris,

are fitted up as much for their advantage as circumstances will admit. The right ankle of one, indeed, is connected with the left ankle of another by a small iron fetter, and if they are turbulent by another on their wrists. They have several meals a day – some of their own country's provisions with the best sauces of African cooking and, by the way of variety, another meal of pulse etc. according to European taste. After breakfast they have water to wash themselves while their apartments are perfumed with frankincense and lime juice. Before dinner they are amused after the manner of their country. The song and dance are permitted . . . the men play and sing while the women and girls make fanciful ornaments with beads with which they are plentifully provided.

'What will the House think,' said Wilberforce, 'when, by the concurring testimony of other witnesses the true history is laid open? . . . The pulses which Mr Norris talks of are horse beans and the scantiness of both water and provision was suggested by the very legislature of Jamaica . . . to be a subject that called for the interference of parliament.'

'Mr Norris,' he continued,

talks of frankincense and lime juice: when the surgeons tell you the slaves are stored so close that there is not room to tread among them . . . in the evidence of Sir George Young . . . 'the stench was intolerable' . . . the song and dance are permitted, says Mr Norris . . . the truth is, that for the sake of exercise, these miserable wretches, loaded with chains, oppressed with disease and wretchedness, are forced to dance by the terror of the lash and sometimes by the actual use of it . . . and it may be observed also, with respect to food, that an instrument is sometimes carried out in order to force them to eat, which is some sort of proof how much they enjoy themselves in that instance also.

Wilberforce was relentless. 'As to their singing, what shall we say when we are told that their songs are songs of lamentation upon their departure which, while they sing, are always in tears, insomuch that one captain . . . threatened one of the women with a flogging because the mournfulness of her song was too painful for his feelings.'

Finally he turned to statistics. 'Death', he said, 'is a sure ground of evidence, and the proportion of deaths will not only confirm but, if possible, will even aggravate our suspicion of their misery in the transit.'

LADIES' DEPARTMENT.

'Am I not a Woman and a Sister?'

White Lady, happy, proud and free,
Lend awhile thine ear to me ;
Let the Negro Mother's wail
Turn thy pale cheek still more pale.
Can the Negro Mother joy
Over this her captive boy,
Which in bondage and in tears,
For a life of wo she rears ?
Though she bears a Mother's name,
A Mother's rights she may not claim ;
For the white man's will can part,
Her darling from her bursting heart.

A poem published in the American anti-slavery newspaper The Liberator *in 1849.*

He had the figures to hand. Twelve and a half per cent of the cargo perished in the Middle Passage. Reports from Jamaica said that 4.5 per cent died onshore before the sale. Thirty-three per cent die 'in the seasoning and this in a country exactly like their own . . . the diseases . . . which they contract on shipboard, the astringent washes which are to hide their wounds and the mischievous tricks used to make them up for sale are a principal cause of this mortality . . .' He quotes from the Jamaica report: 'upon the whole . . . here is a mortality of about 50 per cent, and this among negroes who are not bought unless quite healthy at first and unless (as the phrase is with cattle) they are sound in wind and limb.'

He then turns the argument closer to home.

Let us then make such amends as we can for the mischiefs we have done to the unhappy continent; let us recollect what Europe itself was no longer ago than three or four centuries. What if I should be able to show this House that in a civilised part of Europe in the time of Henry VII there were people who actually sold their own children? What if I should tell them that England itself was that country? What if I should point out to them that the very place where this inhuman traffic was carried on was the city of Bristol? . . . Let us put an end at once to this inhuman traffic – let us stop this effusion of human blood.

The true way to virtue is by withdrawing from temptation. Let us then withdraw from these wretched Africans the temptation to fraud, violence, cruelty and injustice, which the slave trade furnishes. Wherever the sun shines, let us go around the world with him, diffusing our benevolence . . . Total abolition is the only cure for it.

The speech was such a triumph that it was thought the matter had been carried there and then. The *Star* reported: 'the African occupation of bolts and chains is no more.'

It was to take another eighteen years before a Bill was passed. During this time Wilberforce was constantly vilified, sometimes by the greatest in the land. Lord Nelson said, 'I was bred in the good old school and taught to appreciate the value of our West Indian possessions and neither in the field nor in the senate shall their just rights be infringed, while I have an arm to fight in their defence or a tongue to launch my voice against the damnable Wilberforce and his hypocritical allies.'

Wilberforce suffered politically and personally. There were vitriolic attacks in some newspapers. He faced death threats and was physically assaulted. He had to travel with an armed body-guard.

By the time Wilberforce's proposals came before Parliament for legislation, the anti-abolition forces had gathered strength. The manufacturers of Birmingham, for instance, who faced ruin, were among the foremost of his opponents. Supporters of the trade said that Britain's wealth depended on the slave trade and that if Britain stopped it several European countries would take advantage.

But the greatest initial obstacle to Wilberforce was the French Revolution in 1789. This inspired a slave rebellion in St Domingue in 1790. The liberated slaves' barbarous treatment and butchery of their former masters set off alarm bells in all the state legislatures of Europe. More than that, though, the French Revolution, which was to lead to a long war of survival against France, simply crowded out the attention and the time needed to see through this humanitarian initiative. Parliamentary business was completely disrupted.

Then the delaying tactics kicked in.

It was not until 1791 that the Bill came before Parliament, when, because of anti-abolitionist propaganda and the slave rebellion, it was defeated by a majority of seventy-five. Anna Laetitia, a poet who was a supporter of Wilberforce, wrote verses which began:

The slave rebellion on the island of St Domingue (Haiti)
in 1790 was inspired by the French Revolution.

> Cease Wilberforce, to urge thy generous cause,
> Thy country knows the sin and stands the shame . . .

But Wilberforce did not cease. More petitions were collected, more meetings, more pamphlets and a boycott of sugar were organised.

In 1792 Wilberforce once again brought the Bill into the Commons and this time the MP Henry Dundas introduced the fatal word 'gradual'. With this word the Bill was passed by 230 votes to 85. Gradual abolition became the law with a final date of 1796 set.

More delaying tactics meant that although Wilberforce introduced the Bill every year throughout the 1790s, little progress was made. There were powerful speakers against him, not only Lord Nelson. And they too took what they saw as a principled stand. One MP said he 'declined to gratify his humanity at the expense of the interests of his country and . . . thought that we should not enquire too closely into the unpleasant circumstances with which [the slave trade] was perhaps attended'. Even William Pitt, prime minister and friend of Wilberforce, could not push it through in these years.

But just as the French Revolution had triggered the baulking of the Bill, so the new Emperor of France, Napoleon, rather unexpectedly came to its rescue. He had a great hostility to emancipation and once that was widely known the British fear and hatred of their enemy allowed the abolitionists to recruit new vigorous members. From 1804 they regrouped for what proved to be, after annual debates, their final and great success in 1807. In that last debate, the Solicitor General, Sir Samuel Romilly, concluded a long speech with a moving tribute to Wilberforce in which he contrasted the happiness of Wilberforce in his bed with the tortured sleeplessness of Napoleon Bonaparte. Wilberforce wept. The House rose and cheered him. The Bill was passed. On 25 March 1807 it received the Royal Assent.

There was still much to be done, and for the rest of his life Wilberforce did as much as he could. He became a magnet for emancipators of all kinds and campaigned for an end to the institution of slavery.

Wilberforce's health declined in late middle age. He had some financial difficulties. In 1825 he resigned from the House of Commons to live just outside London. His last public appearance was at a meeting of the Anti-Slavery Society in 1830. On 26 July 1833 slavery was abolished – the planters were richly compensated. Wilberforce said, 'thank God that I have lived to witness a day in which England is willing to give twenty millions sterling for the Abolition of Slavery.' Three days later, on 29 July, he died and was buried in Westminster Abbey.

He had changed the views of a nation and an empire. He had great and important allies, from William Pitt to Thomas Clarkson to Josiah Wedgwood, whose brooches depicting a slave and a slave owner with the inscription 'Am I not a man and a brother?' became articles of fashion in Britain and America. The abolition was not Wilberforce's single-handed achievement, but it was his single-mindedness that saw it launched and, despite heavy opposition, saw it through.

The slave trade, abolished in Britain in 1807, set off a domino effect. In 1808 it was abolished in the United States and in 1838 throughout the British colonies. In 1865 slavery itself was abolished in the United States, in 1886 in Cuba and in 1888 in Brazil.

It can be argued convincingly, I think, that Wilberforce's legacy was evident not only in the slave trade. It changed the world even more fundamentally. It was the foundation of the worldwide human rights movement. His anti-slavery movement has been called 'the first genuine mass movement this country had seen'. The inspiration for suffragettes, for instance, and the movements for majority and minority rights of all denominations can be traced back to Wilberforce.

An illustration from Uncle Tom's Cabin, *first published in 1852.*

He remained and remains, though, most powerful as an influence in the movement to have Africans and by extension all other non-Caucasians recognised as wholly equal to all others. Wilberforce personified the Christian arm of the Enlightenment at its best and it is not too much to claim that he set the world on a different and a finer course.

His name and what he achieved has become a touchstone. Wilberforce University, the oldest private university in the USA dedicated 150 years ago to the education of Afro-Americans, is a place where his praises are sung daily. The black students, 95 per cent of whom are there on scholarships and from poor backgrounds, speak of him with enormous pride and affection, as they made evident when we filmed there for the TV series. And back in his home town of Hull there is the Wilberforce Institute for the Study of Slavery and Emancipation (patron Archbishop Tutu, from a country in which Wilberforce is also venerated). At the Institute, Professor David Richardson not only maps out the extension to Wilberforce's emancipating Bill but is swift to point out that the struggle over slavery is not finished. It is estimated that in Brazil up to 25,000 slave labourers are clearing Amazonian rainforests; in Mauritania up to 1 million people are held as 'inherited property'; in the Sudan militias take women and children in slave raids; in Europe and America boys and women are forced to be sex slaves.

Perhaps nowhere has his influence been more strongly felt than in America. There is a direct line from Wilberforce to Martin Luther King. At one point on that line is *Uncle Tom's Cabin* by Harriet Beecher Stowe, a book which had the most enormous influence on the American public's opinion of slaves. In it there is a passage where a Southern slave owner discusses the practice of separating female slaves from their babies and says it is better not to as it tends to affect their productivity. Harriet Beecher Stowe then writes, ironically, 'the trader leaned back in his chair and folded his arms with an air of virtuous decision, apparently considering himself a second Wilberforce'.

His first words on 12 May 1789 were:

> When I consider the magnitude of the subject which I am to bring before the House – a subject in which the interests not just of this country, nor of Europe alone, but of the whole world and of posterity are involved; when I think, at the same time, on the weakness of the advocate who has undertaken this great cause . . . it is impossible for me not to feel both terrified and concerned at my own inadequacy to such a task . . . the end of which is the total abolition of the slave trade.

The words which followed and flowed instantly into print can make a strong claim to have changed the world. Wilberforce both led and catalysed a mass morality which, despite many setbacks and failings, still marches on, and he did that by means of words first written, then spoken and immediately afterwards printed, and reprinted and repeated ever since. It is the access to posterity guaranteed by print that has given them their potency over the centuries.

Outside the splendid house in which he was born and lived in Hull there is a statue of Wilberforce. The inscription reads:

> England owes to him the Reformation of Manners
> The World owes to him the Abolition of the Slave Trade.

TIMELINE
ON THE ABOLITION OF THE SLAVE TRADE

1789 William Wilberforce delivers his four-hour speech on the end of slavery in the House of Commons

1790 Slave rebellion occurs in St Domingue (Haiti)

1791 Wilberforce's proposed Bill is defeated

1792 Following the second and successful petition campaign by the Society for the Abolition of the Slave Trade, 'Gradual' abolition becomes the law in Britain

1794 In France, Abbé Grégoire and the Convention abolish slavery but it is re-established by Napoleon in 1802

1803 Haitian slaves gain their independence and Haiti becomes the first black republic

1806 A verbatim record of Wilberforce's speech is published in *Cobbett's Parliamentary History of England*

1807 Britain passes the Abolition of the Slave Trade Act which outlaws the British Atlantic slave trade

1808 The United States passes legislation banning the slave trade

1811 Slavery is abolished in Spain and the Spanish colonies, except Cuba

1813 Slave trading is banned by Sweden

1814 Slave trading is banned by the Netherlands

1817 Slave trading is abolished by France although it is not made effective until 1826

1819 Portugal abolishes the slave trade north of the equator

1823 The Anti-Slavery Society is formed, campaigning for better conditions for slaves in the West Indies and for the gradual abolition of slavery

1828– British Parliament is presented with over five thousand petitions
30   calling for the immediate abolition of slavery

1829 Mexico abolishes slavery

1831 Seventy slaves kill sixty whites in two days during the Nat Turner slave rebellion

1833 The Abolition of Slavery Act is passed, bringing into effect the gradual abolition of slavery in all British colonies

Wilberforce dies and is buried in Westminster Abbey

1834 All slaves in the British Empire are emancipated but still indentured to their former owners

1838 The slavery apprenticeship system is finally abolished throughout the British colonies

1839 The British and Foreign Anti-Slavery Society is formed to campaign for the global abolition of slavery

Rebellion aboard the slave ship, *Amistad*, takes place and the rebelling slaves are eventually allowed by an American court to return to Africa

1841 Slaves successfully commandeer the slave ship *Creole*

1851 Slave trading is abolished by Brazil

Uncle Tom's Cabin appears in serial form in an abolitionist weekly

1856 Wilberforce University is founded in Ohio, USA, for young African-American students

1858 Slavery is abolished in Portuguese colonies although all slaves are subject to a twenty-year apprenticeship

1861 Slavery is abolished in the Dutch colonies of the Caribbean

1865 Slavery is abolished in the United States following the Civil War

1886 Slavery is abolished in Cuba

1888 Slavery is abolished in Brazil

1926 The Slavery Convention, an initiative of the League of Nations, becomes a turning point in banning global slavery

1948 Article 4 of the Universal Declaration of Human Rights is adopted by the UN General Assembly, explicitly banning slavery

1956 The United Nations Supplementary Convention on the Abolition of Slavery is convened to outlaw and ban slavery worldwide

1966 The UN General Assembly adopts the International Covenant on Civil and Political Rights which includes an Article banning slavery

2000 The Second World War Reparations and Repatriation Truth Commission includes a Petition for $777 trillion against the US, Canada and European Union members for 'unlawful removal and destruction of Petitioners' mineral and human resources from the African continent' between 1503 up to the end of the colonialism era in the late 1950s and 1960s

2007 The Wilberforce Institute for the Study of Slavery and Emancipation plans to open with its patron, Archbishop Tutu, coinciding with the bicentenary of the abolition of slavery

A VINDICATION OF
THE RIGHTS OF WOMAN

1792

by

Mary Wollstonecraft

A

VINDICATION

OF THE

RIGHTS OF WOMAN:

WITH

STRICTURES

ON

POLITICAL AND MORAL SUBJECTS.

By MARY WOLLSTONECRAFT.

LONDON:

PRINTED FOR J. JOHNSON, Nº 72, ST. PAUL'S CHURCH YARD.

1792.

'From the tyranny of men', Wollstonecraft wrote, 'I firmly believe the greater number of female follies proceed.' And she had 'a profound conviction that the neglected education of my fellow creatures is the grand source of the misery I deplore'.

In *A Vindication of the Rights of Woman*, published in 1792, which can fairly be called the first great feminist thesis, in which, among much else, she argued that the intellect will always govern, Wollstonecraft sought to 'persuade women to endeavour to acquire strength, both of mind and body, and to convince them that the soft phrases, susceptibility of heart, delicacy of sentiment, and refinement of taste, are almost synonymous with epithets of weakness.'

She was a passionate disciple of the Age of reason. Reason, once inculcated, would rule the world and usher in the egalitarian society. Her argument joins together Reason and Christianity. 'But the nature of reason must be the same in all if it be an emanation of divinity, the tie that connects the creature with the creator.'

Education was key and women must share in it. 'The present mode of education does not tend to enlarge the heart any more than the understanding.' And education was to be for women as much as for men. She wanted to set women free. 'Women are everywhere in this deplorable state for, in order to preserve their innocence, as ignorance is courteously termed, truth is hidden from them, and they are made to assume an artificial character before their faculties have acquired any strength. Taught from their infancy that beauty is a woman's sceptre, the mind shapes itself to the body, and roaming around its gilt cage, only seeks to adore its prison.'

In this polemic she wrote about love, passion, sex, property, marriage and the ambiguities of women who might believe that to be free they must be like men. Her views are still part of current debate on one of the great issues of the modern age, the place of women in society, debates which now penetrate aspects of life from the strictures of dress in Islamist fundamentalist countries to equal pay and 'girl power'. Her life – represented as reprehensible and a most dangerous example for generations – for a long time diverted from discipleship many of those at whom the book was aimed. But increasingly, especially in the last half-century, her life has been seized on as a symbol, a challenge which would disturb and eventually uproot a male domination which had held sway for millennia. It was a book that bided its time and when that time came it struck to the heart of a struggle still fiercely engaged in. It would be fair, I think, to see Mary Wollstonecraft not only as an iconic figure but as a founding philosopher, practitioner and activist for views on women which now contend for recognition in every intellectual and political marketplace around the globe.

Mary Wollstonecraft was born in April 1759 in Primrose Street, Spitalfields. Now part of the teeming sprawl of London, Spitalfields was then, as the name indicates, in the country, farming country. Her mother was an Irish Protestant. Her father inherited the then tremendous sum of £10,000 and used his new riches to set himself up as a gentleman, in his case a gentleman farmer. But the idea of the 'gentleman', long corrupted from Chaucer's notion of the knight-in-arms as a 'gentil man', was paramount. Trade was shown the back door. Extravagance came in the front. Incompetence was more of a governing factor than style. Ruin followed.

'All you need is a ball and and some kids and they all start speaking the global language of football'.

Charles Darwin: 'From so simple a beginning endless forms most beautiful and most wonderful have been and are being evolved'.

Crick and Watson's work on DNA in the 1950s validated Darwin's theories on the crucial importance of genes.

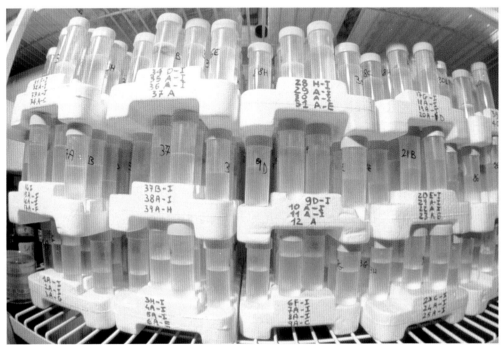

Test tubes containing the entire human genome in a laboratory refrigerator: taken as a whole, these tubes contain all the DNA found in a human cell.

William Wilberforce: 'When I consider the magnitude of the subject . . . it is impossible for me not to feel terrified and concerned at my own inadequacy to such a task'.

This 1963 civil rights demonstration, the March on Washington, embodied the process Wilberforce began with the abolition of slavery.

Civil rights leader Marin Luther King and activist Rosa Parks are commemorated by the naming of these streets in Detroit.

Mary Wollstonecraft: 'It is time to effect a revolution in female matters'.

1924: Suffragettes picket the Houses of Parliament in London.

1954: Equal Pay for Women demonstrators.

1971: a women's liberation march for equal pay and expanded rights and opportunities for women.

The six children – three boys, three girls, Mary the second child and eldest daughter – shifted around England and Wales in progressively smaller farms with her father growing more violent – Mary, we are told, frequently threw herself in front of her mother to prevent her father attacking her in one of his violent rages. She also describes nights sleeping in her mother's doorway when she feared her father might break in and wreak more violence on his wife – a wife who has been described by Miriam Brody, a professor at Ithaca College, New York, who has written extensively on Mary Wollstonecraft, as 'too willingly his victim'.

Mary's education was inadequate and intermittent. Embroidery and needlework were thought the most essential skills for middle-class girls and for all her father's spiral into poverty, Mary was and remained a middle-class girl, and it was to middle-class girls similarly afflicted by a derisory education that she addressed her exhortations. But from the beginning Mary sought out ways to nourish her mind. At Beverley in Yorkshire, for instance, she attended the public science lectures of John Arden, befriended his daughter, Jane, and was taught by Arden both geography by means of his globe and the elementary methods to be used in making philosophical points.

Later she met Frances (Fanny) Blood who was four years older than she was. They were passionate friends until Fanny's early death in Lisbon in 1786, of a complication in pregnancy. Mary had got herself to Portugal, kept vigil with prayer by her bedside, closed Fanny's eyes and cut a lock of hair to make a ring. She described her as 'a friend whom I love better than the entire world', and was always prepared to defend their friendship, on grounds of reason, as a perfectly fitting alternative to marriage.

During her early years she prised herself from her parents and looked for financial independence. She began in contemporary novel fashion as a companion to an elderly widow at Bath in 1778. Such posts continued. By 1783 she had hauled up her education to the

'Taught from their infancy that beauty is a woman's sceptre,
the mind shapes itself to the body' – Mary Wollstonecraft.

level of her determination and she established, as anyone in those days could, a school at Newington Green in London. It collapsed soon after Fanny's death, leaving Mary in debt. It was suggested to her by a friend that she follow the course set by hundreds of impoverished young men and a good number of women of the day and write for profit. There was a commercial market in books splendidly and quite recently exploited by Dr Johnson, a market run by booksellers (more like today's publishers) who saw a growing appetite for print and sought to feed and further grow it. In 1787 Mary wrote *Thoughts on the Education of Daughters*. It was published with little impact. But she was on her way.

One post as a companion was before her and it may well have played a crucial role in her larger education. She became a governess with the Kingsborough family – landed gentry in Ireland. She wrote to her sister: 'you cannot conceive the dissipated lives the women of quality lead. Five hours do many, I assure you, spend in dressing . . .' Her victim mother, her opulent propertied superior and employer, her faithful and equal female friend: her life was being fed on seeding experiences, her mind developed by wide reading.

It is important to remember that Mary was a Christian, a regular churchgoer, and her 'congregation' was important to her. As was her connection with London life and letters. She wrote to Joseph Johnson, the London bookseller who had published her *Thoughts* and he said he would publish her first novel, *Mary, A Fiction*. She moved back to London and engaged with a group of liberal intellectuals. They were fired by the idea of equality emerging from America. This was greeted with acclaim by English radicals, who saw the pursuit of liberty as part of their proper and essential inheritance. Mary aimed to become what was no longer rare, a woman professional writer. Her rarity consisted in part in her open criticism of femininity. She began, like the great exemplar, Dr Johnson himself, as a lowly hack, translating, writing reviews, doing all she was offered by her own Johnson, the editor of the *Analytical Review*. She got the best part of her education in hack work.

It may be useful here to chronicle the rest of her brief years. In 1792, at the home of Tom Paine in Paris, she met a charming American rogue, Gilbert Imlay. Though she did not fall in love with him for some months (she was romantically attached to Henry Fuseli) Imlay was to become a seismic force in her life. In August 1793 she was pregnant, out of wedlock. In September Imlay apparently registered her as his wife at the American embassy in Paris. Wollstonecraft's contemporaries said this was not a marriage but an acceptance of his protection. The child out of wedlock was to become an issue which badly wounded her reputation. In 1794 their daughter was born: Mary christened her Fanny. Imlay went back to London and pressed her to return from Paris since she was regarded as an important figure in the revolutionary activity there. Finally, most reluctantly, she complied and arrived to discover him in the throes of an affair with an actress. That year, 1795, she made two suicide attempts.

She set to work to support herself and her daughter, fortified not only by *Vindication* (1792) but by an account of the early years of the French Revolution. She moved in increasingly dangerous radical circles. One of the Dissenters she encountered was William Godwin, a friend of Tom Paine, an agitator for reform. They were two independently minded people with increasingly revolutionary ideas in a country closing its ears to everything that seemed to smack of France and turning its guns on what was seen as the deeply disturbing French state. By 1796, Mary was pregnant by Godwin and they decided to marry, with reservations. This marriage seemed to confirm that the alliance with Imlay had been no marriage. Both Mary and Godwin were, in principle, against the institution of marriage and both rejected conventional gender roles. Initially the couple worked and socialised separately. Yet they decided to tie the knot. Of their marriage, Mary wrote to Godwin:

WARD & LOCK'S

HANDBOOK

TO THE

MARRIED WOMEN'S PROPERTY ACT

1882.

ITS IMPORTANT CONSEQUENCES—

What it Does,

AND

What does Not Do.

London: WARD, LOCK & CO., Salisbury Square, E.C.
New York: 10, Bond Street.

This guide was published to explain the workings of the 1882 Act of Parliament.

'A husband is a convenient part of the furniture of a house . . . I wish you, from my soul, to be riveted in my heart: but I do not desire to have you always at my elbow.'

Godwin's literary experience helped her, even though she was upset by some of his criticisms of her headlong writing style. So much so that she even agreed to take lessons in grammar from her philosopher-husband.

It was a short partnership. Mary died in September 1797 of complications following childbirth, ten days after the birth of her daughter, Mary, who was to marry the poet Shelley and write *Frankenstein*. She is buried in St Pancras churchyard. In 1798 her husband published *Memoirs of the Author of A Vindication of the Rights of Woman*, a truthful account which, though lovingly intended, with its honest revelations of her life gave fuel to her enemies, scared off many of her natural supporters and drew a cloud over her work for generations to come.

In 1789, Dr Richard Price, a Unitarian minister, preached a sermon entitled 'On the Love of Country'. He congratulated the French National Assembly for the new possibilities of religious and civil freedom offered by the revolution. Its 'Declaration of the Rights of Man and of the Citizen', following on from the American Declaration of Independence in 1776, had made it possible, Price claimed, to be a citizen of the world. In this sermon, Price developed his idea of 'perfectibility' – that the world could be improved through human effort. It was a sermon which trumpeted a welcome to radical change.

Edmund Burke's response to the revolution and so to Dr Price's sermon could not have been more antagonistic. He saw the French revolutionaries' attack on and overthrow of authority as a sure way to disorder and chaos. In his *Reflections on the French Revolution*, which became a classic of conservative thinking, he argued that traditional authority could not be sacrificed for ideas of liberty, that the rights of man could not replace the rights of the monarch.

Thomas Paine, the English pamphleteer and philosopher whose political activism impressed America, France and England, wrote *The Rights of Man* in rebuttal of Burke. A great debate was begun.

Mary Wollstonecraft, though an Anglican, was an admirer of Dr Price and would attend his church to hear his sermons, often then a central force in political opinion-forming. She dashed off *A Vindication of the Rights of Men*, in which she argued passionately for the God-given rights of civil and religious liberty. It is intriguing that at precisely this time William Wilberforce was similarly driven by Christian, godly ideals. She attacked the French aristocracy as decadent but more tellingly, given what she was to write next, she censored Burke severely for his selective sympathy with regard to women. 'Your tears are reserved,' she wrote in *A Vindication of the Rights of Men*,

> very naturally, considering your character . . . for the downfall of queens, whose rank alters the nature of feeling, and throws a graceful veil over vices that degrade humanity; whilst the distress of many industrious mothers, whose helpmates have been torn from them, and the hungry cry of helpless babes, were vulgar sorrows that could not move our commiseration, though they might extort an alms.

Emboldened by the publication of this book, she turned to the book she will be remembered for, a book whose way had been prepared by the words of Price and Burke, of Paine and, in the background, Rousseau, as well as being sharpened on the grindstone of her own life. It is, in effect, both an extension of her previous book and a summary of thoughts and convictions which had been gathering force since those youthful lessons in philosophical argument from Mr Arden.

Wollstonecraft's book was multi-faceted. She has been called the 'mother of feminism' because her work is primarily concerned with the individual woman and her rights. She also insisted that women be judged not by men's standards but according to the realisation of their own nature. Her views on sexuality and gender, though not largely developed, still have a resonance in an area of strenuous current debate. Her views on rights and on duty in the family have led to her being claimed by communitarians. In her argument that men must change she is a precursor of political feminism, while in her demand that property be equalised she brings socialism to bear on the whole issue of a good life of true fellowship. Her book is still relevant in so many respects. Her accusation against women that they collude with their designation as mere sexual beings still resonates. In a recent survey of British girls aged between nine and sixteen, the career choice of the largest proportion (34 per cent) was glamour model or lap dancer.

Wollstonecraft is not addressing the great majority of the rural poor or the emerging working classes in the new industrialised towns. For one thing, only a small percentage of those women would have had access to books; for another, Wollstonecraft thought they had a clear function in their society, a job to do, a place fulfilled by work even though it could also be described as drudgery. Similarly she did not concern herself with artistic women, who were too well established already to need her guidance. It was the surplus of young middle-class females at whom she aimed many of her arguments. She wanted to let them into the man's world but she had no strategy for restructuring existing institutions. It was imperative though that women be given the opportunity, even if they failed. 'Further,' she writes, 'should experience prove that they [women] cannot attain the same degree of strength of mind, perseverance, and fortitude, let their virtues be the same in kind, though they may vainly struggle for the same degree; and the superiority of man will be equally clear, if not clearer; and truth, as it is a simple principle, which admits of no modification, would be common to both.'

There is a realisation here which allows for differences, some would say inequalities, between men and women, an argument now re-emerging shorn, through experience, of its previous only prejudiced acceptance. Difference can be accepted without a hierarchy being imposed.

Her argument that human beings have natural rights and that the denial of these rights 'daily insult[s] common sense' was part of the general rational argument and in this, as in other ways, she stood shoulder to shoulder with Paine and others, scorning the 'indolent puppet of a court' and all 'the dregs of ambition'.

In the book she indicates that she is pushing the argument beyond emancipation through education. 'As such politics diffuse liberty,' she writes, 'mankind, including women, will become more wise and virtuous.' There is an echo of the Ancients, Aristotle especially, in the raising of virtue as the mark of true civic liberty. This includes all of society and not just women, but only in a wholly liberated society can the virtue of men and women both be realised. She pushes it farther and puts it bluntly: 'If the progress of society depends on virtue in the citizens,' she writes, 'and if the present constitution of civil society is an almost insuperable obstacle, then the implication here appears very clear: the present state of civil society must be changed, if we are to progress.'

In short, root-and-branch revolution. This position is confirmed by Wollstonecraft's attitude to property. 'But 'til hereditary possessions are spread abroad,' she writes, 'how can we expect men to be proud of virtue? And 'til they are, women will govern them by the most direct means, neglecting their dull domestic duties to catch the pleasure that sits lightly on the wing of time.' From the relationship between men and women and the subjugation of women to the pleasure and purposes of men to the reassessment of the institutional and ancestral structures of society is a seamless flow in her arguments. She challenges the very basis of existing society, beginning with the sexual relationship. Yet her views on sexuality are capable of several different interpretations, some of which could be at odds with each other.

Rousseau, from whom she drew much, is wholly rejected here in his view that, to preserve the family, a woman must practise deceptions, flirtations, teasings. So how should men and women cohabit purposefully? How, in effect, can passion, which she acknowledged to be and experienced as being so powerful and so wretched, be educated?

Her response is that passion should be removed from any sensible equation since it does not last and in the fullest measure of life, plays only a small part. 'Friendship or indifference inevitably succeeds love,' she writes. 'When the husband ceases to be a lover,' she declares, 'and the time will inevitably come, her desire for pleasing will then grow languid, or become a spring of bitterness: and love, perhaps the most evanescent of all passions, gives place to jealousy and vanity.' It is friendship and fellowship that matter most. 'The woman who strengthens her body and exercises her mind will, by managing her family and practising various virtues, become the friend, and not the humble dependent on her husband.' Again and again in the book she rails against the condition of women which forces them merely to please men. 'Confined . . . in cages like the feathered race, they have nothing to do but to plume themselves and stalk with mock majesty from perch to perch . . . Why must the female mind be tainted by coquettish arts . . . ?' She also writes, 'gentleness, docility and spaniel-like affection are consistently recommended as the cardinal virtues of the sex . . . she was created as the toy of man.'

Reason should govern everything including sex. This has raised problems. There are those commentators who have said that on this point Mary Wollstonecraft is very near Marx's proposition that we eliminate the family as the basic unit of society.

And yet, as a Christian and a mother, she protests the value of the family – but on terms wholly untraditional. The woman's domain is still the home, but the home is integrated into the rest of life and not a separate pen, not a protected nursery for the raising of girls allowed to play only with dolls and taught only that beauty and guile can capture the attention of the ruling man. She sees this as uncoupling man from his proper responsibility and by allowing him irresponsibility, releasing the very force in him which will unseat the wife. 'I venture to assert', she writes, 'that all the causes of female weakness, as well as depravity which I have already enlarged on, branch out of one final cause – want of chastity in men.'

She offers her solution:

Would men but generously snap our chains, and be content with rational fellowship instead of slavish obedience, they would find us more observant daughters, more affectionate sisters, more faithful wives, more reasonable mothers – in a word, better citizens. We should then love them with true affection, because we should learn to respect ourselves; and the peace of mind of a worthy man would not be interrupted by the idle vanity of his wife . . .

True freedom, she maintains, comes from equality, especially in education. And this will be the beginning of a new chain of existence. 'Children will never be properly educated 'til friendship subsists between parents. Virtue flies from a house divided against itself and a whole legion of devils take up their residence there.' Which, it is possible to assume, takes her back to her own violent beginnings.

Vindication was written in six weeks and published with various errors in 1792. A second edition published in the same year is that on which readers now rely. It is 452 pages long and described by a librarian at the Women's Library in Whitechapel as 'a standard size hardback unremarkable in its appearance'.

Contemporary reaction was mostly hostile. Though read with

sympathy by some women, Wollstonecraft began no visibly effective woman's movement at the time. There was some public
support. Thomas Cooper, a radical Manchester cotton manufacturer
who later moved to South Carolina, said, 'Let the defenders of male
despotism answer (if they can) the Rights of Woman'. But her
arguments were scarcely addressed at all. Horace Walpole called her
'a hyena in petticoats'. A magazine was to print:

> For Mary verily would wear the breeches
> God help poor silly men from such usurping b . . . s.

Her association with Paine and his French connections worked
badly against her as France became the feared, monstrous and
deadly enemy against whom no propaganda was too black. Her
reputation was virulently assailed. At her death, one commentator
in the *Historical Magazine* predicted that her works would be read
'with disgust by every female who has any pretension to delicacy,
with detestation by everyone attached to the interests of religion
and morality, and with indignation by anyone who might feel any
regard for the unhappy woman whose frailties should have been
buried in oblivion'.

As mentioned earlier, Mary's husband, William Godwin,
published a memoir after her death. In it he spoke of her troubled
love affairs, her suicide attempts, her financial difficulties . . . in
all she grew as a monster to much of the public, monstered
further and later by her daughter's indecent liaison with Shelley.
She was one of the 'Unsexed Females' lambasted by Richard
Polwhele, and the dust raised by the beating of her character
threatened wholly to conceal the light of her radical, bold and
transforming ideas.

Even as recently as 1947, two Freudian psychoanalysts, Ferdi-
nand Lundby and Maryana F. Farnham, wrote:

The Seneca Falls Women's Rights meeting in 1848 was attacked by an angry mob.

Mary Wollstonecraft hated men. She had every personal reason probably known to psychiatry for hating them. Hers was hatred of creatures she greatly admired and feared, creatures that seemed to her capable of doing everything while women to her seemed capable of doing nothing whatever, in their own nature being perfectly weak in comparison with the strong, lordly male . . . Mary Wollstonecraft was an extreme neurotic of a complex type . . . out of her illness came the ideology of Feminism.

It was still the life, not the work, which claimed public attention. And yet in the second half of the twentieth century, it was the life which ironically increased respect for her, drew readers through her persistent life struggles to her writing, and inspired those who saw the truth and power in her analysis.

Yet she had not been entirely lost from view in the interim. Despite the kindly intended manner of her husband's devastating portrait of what was perceived as a depraved and uncontrolled woman, despite the hysteria provoked by anyone and anything, especially ideas, emanating from France, despite the big swing of the pendulum towards public primness and the female domestic goddess in the long and big-breeding age of Victoria, she had her disciples, those who carried the flame.

It is significant that her first disciples preferred to stay in the shadows. Mary Hays published *Appeal to the Men of Great Britain in Behalf of Women* in 1798, but she did so anonymously. Mary Robinson published *A Letter to the Women of England on the Injustice of Mental Subordination, with Anecdotes* in 1799, but under a pseudonym.

Scandal continued to spoil Mary's reputation well into the nineteenth century. The suicide of her first daughter, Fanny Imlay, and Mary Shelley's elopement with the married Percy Shelley, who abandoned a pregnant wife, only added fuel. It was very important to seem to be at one with the philosophy one expressed: a gap between the private person and the public view – whether of a hero, a statesman, a man of God or a great thinker – was often fatal to the regard in which one was held. Especially a woman. Nobility had to be all of a piece, as had idealism. Mary's philosophy of the place of women, seen as idealistic, was contaminated in the eyes of those who were against her by what were viewed as her irredeemable female failings, which undermined her ideas.

She is rarely cited by nineteenth-century feminists although she was well known to them and fed their work, an unacknowledged legislator. Barbara Taylor, who wrote Wollstonecraft's entry in the *Oxford Dictionary of National Biography*, has shown that the tracts and newspapers of the Owenite Society regularly reprinted parts of *The Rights of Woman* from the 1820s until 1845, together with admiring comments. Robert Owen, like Shelley and of course Godwin – all three radical, intellectual, influential – was a great admirer of Mary Wollstonecraft and would keep her work alive.

They were more open and direct in America. Mary Wollstone-craft's work was quoted in letters between Elizabeth Cady Stanton and Lucretia Mott, who were the guiding minds behind the Seneca Falls Declaration in New York in 1848 – the first feminist meeting and declaration of aims. It became known as the Declaration of Sentiments because of its deliberate imitation of the structure and language of the Declaration of Independence. Tyrannical men replaced the tyrannical British. The Seneca Falls meeting attracted 240 sympathisers and it is proof of a direct link with, even an inspiration from, the *Vindication* of 1792.

Dr Price had preached his sermon in a Unitarian church and the Unitarians were always loyal to Mary Wollstonecraft. Harriet Martineau refers to her in her autobiography and speaks of the high admiration for her in Victorian circles. Brilliant Unitarian intellectuals – Anna Barbauld, Helen Maria Williams and Mary Hays – kept alive her fame, and this group above all others made sure that her message was carried forward. The Langham Place Group in the 1850s, including Octavia Hill, Barbara Leigh-Smith

PROGRAMME
April 27th, 1909

MARY WOLLSTONECRAFT.
Born April 27th, 1759.

WOMEN'S
TRADES AND
PROFESSIONS

PROCESSION to ALBERT HALL
GREAT MEETING
in favour of
WOMEN'S SUFFRAGE

Mary Wollstonecraft's picture used on the programme for a suffrage meeting.

and Bessie Rayner Parkes, emerged as a new wave of feminists. All were from Unitarian families; all had access to Wollstonecraft's works. Yet among those and other feminists her life was constantly a problem. One of the methods they used to advance the feminist cause was to show that they were totally reasonable, sensible, reliable, prepared to be sound citizens, unthreatening though demanding: Mary's reputation as a scandalous bohemian woman was one with which they dared not be associated, much as they may have drawn from her work.

George Eliot was one of the few who publicly supported Wollstonecraft. She saw her as a victim of social prejudice, as she herself was on account of her relationship with a married man.

Her 'scandalous' life cast a long shadow. In 1857, in recognition of this, and in a bold attempt to clear her name, Mary Shelley's daughter-in-law, Lady Shelley, republished Wollstonecraft's *Letters to Imlay* and *William Godwin: his friends and contemporaries* with a memoir stressing that Mary had never lost her deep Anglican faith. This had an effect. Other books began to appear, biography and criticism and after more than half a century of relegation to the wings, the woman and her ideas began to reclaim their rightful position, centre stage, in a drama unfolding with what proved to be irresistible momentum.

J. S. Mill wrote *The Subjection of Women*; George Bernard Shaw wrote *The Intelligent Woman's Guide to Socialism and Capitalism*. The fuse lit by Wollstonecraft in 1792 began to reach the powder kegs of opinion.

The suffragists put sexual freedom on the agenda towards the end of the Victorian age, and Mary's ideas in that combustible area were in contention, the arguments in *Vindication* seen as still central to the debate. In 1860 Josephine Butler wrote about women and declared that all women have rights, most controversially, and in the bold tradition of Wollstonecraft, 'even' prostitutes – a scandalous claim to make at that time. Millicent Fawcett was another suffragist and it is evidence of the growth of a self-conscious acknowledgement of the debt to Wollstonecraft that it was the Fawcett Society which marked the bicentenary of Mary's birth in 1959 and in doing so brought her finally and firmly into the mainstream of respectability as well as intellectual debate.

As if that bicentenary event were a signal, there followed a rush of brilliant feminist authors who were pleased to pay respects to Wollstonecraft and whose ideas built on hers. To name a few who stand for many: Gloria Steinem, Erica Jong, Kate Millett, Betty Freidan and Marilyn French in the USA, Sheila Rowbottom, Germaine Greer and Juliet Mitchell in the UK. A book such as Germaine Greer's *The Female Eunuch* carried and still carries the seeds of *Vindication* around the world. The argument stemming from her argument goes on in innumerable poems, novels, plays, learned papers and magazines.

In Iran the relaxation of the strict Islamic code of dressing for women was hailed as a step forward for democracy; this relaxation is now being reined in and the protests are a focus for progressive politics. As Wollstonecraft pointed out, the woman is the key which can unlock the private and so alter the public life. In Iraq, in Afghanistan, in many parts of the Muslim world, a similar situation obtains. It is around the rights of women that some of the closest battles are being fought and on which countries and societies are being judged. In the USA and the UK in my adult lifetime the determination of women to obtain their rights has been a central strand in the new weave of the country. Equal pay has been and still is a testing ground. The divorce rate in itself questions marriage in a way which may prove that one of Wollstonecraft's more contentious notions (which she herself alas found it difficult to follow), that passion ought to play no more than an initiating and temporary role in marriage, is working its way through even though there are commentators who see this as harmful to future generations. She is still part of the current debate.

I want to end with another woman writer, Virginia Woolf, who has also been an inspiration to many women, many feminists and many writers of both genders. In her essay on Mary Wollstonecraft she writes: 'She is alive and active, she argues and experiments, we hear her voice and trace her influence, even now among the living.'

TIMELINE
A VINDICATION OF THE RIGHTS OF WOMAN

1792   First edition of *A Vindication of the Rights of Woman* published

1797   Mary Wollstonecraft dies

1798   Mary Hays, one of Wollstonecraft's 'disciples', publishes *Appeal to the Men of Great Britain in Behalf of Women* anonymously

1799   Mary Robinson, another of Wollstonecraft's disciples, publishes *A Letter to the Women of England on the Injustice of Mental Subordination with Anecdotes*

1848   Seneca Falls Declaration, New York, pioneered by Elizabeth Cady Stanton and Lucretia Mott, attracts 240 sympathisers

1852   Lucretia Mott writes *Discourse on Woman*, arguing that the inferiority of women can be attributed to their inferior educational opportunities

1866   The American Equal Rights Association is formed by Elizabeth Cady Stanton and Susan B. Anthony, dedicated to the goal of universal suffrage

1869   Girton College becomes the first residential college at Cambridge University for women. They are not considered full members of the university, however, and not admitted to degrees

1879   Lady Margaret Hall and Somerville, Oxford, become the first female colleges of Oxford University

1895   Elizabeth Cady Stanton publishes *The Woman's Bible*

1890   The National Woman Suffrage Association (NWSA) and the more conservative American Woman Suffrage Association (AWSA) combine to form the National American Woman Suffrage Association (NAWSA) under the leadership of Elizabeth Cady Stanton

1897   Millicent Fawcett founds the National Union of Women's Suffrage Societies (NUWSS), beginning the British struggle for female suffrage in earnest

1903   Emmeline Pankhurst founds the Women's Social and Political Union (WSPU), better known as the Suffragette movement, willing to use violence to make gains

1908   Suffrage campaigners chain themselves to the railings outside the prime minister's front door

1909   Marion Wallace Dunlop is the first suffrage campaigner to go on hunger strike

1910   Black Friday. Suffragette campaigners are beaten and trampled by policemen demonstrating outside the Houses of Parliament

1912   Suffragettes attack shops in Oxford Street and the Strand and throw stones at 10 Downing Street

1913   Suffragette Emily Wilding Davison throws herself under the king's horse at the Derby

1918   Representation of the People Act allows women with property over the age of thirty to vote; passed by an overwhelming majority in the House of Commons

1919   Nineteenth Amendment to the US Constitution is ratified, granting women the right to vote

        Sex Disqualification Removal Act makes it illegal to exclude women from jobs because of their sex

        Nancy Astor becomes the first female MP in England, winning Plymouth Sutton in a by-election

1920   Women are finally recognised as full members of Oxford University

1921   Women granted full title degree in Cambridge University

1923   The Equal Rights Amendment to the Constitution is first introduced into Congress

1928   Equal Franchise Act finally establishes equal voting rights for men and women in Great Britain

1929   Margaret Bondfield becomes the first woman to gain a place in the British cabinet

1959   The feminist Fawcett Society place a wreath on Wollstonecraft's grave in St Pancras churchyard, to commemorate the bicentenary of her birth

1960s   Second-wave feminists emerge, concerned with the issue of economic equality

President John F. Kennedy appoints a permanent Citizens' Advisory Council on the Status of Women

1963   Betty Friedan publishes *The Feminine Mystique*, detailing the frustrating lives of countless American women expected to find fulfilment through the achievements of husbands and children

Congress passes the Equal Pay for Equal Work Act

1970   Germaine Greer publishes *The Female Eunuch*

1979   Margaret Thatcher becomes prime minister

1981   Sandra Day O'Connor becomes the first woman appointed to the US Supreme Court

EXPERIMENTAL RESEARCHES
IN ELECTRICITY
(3 VOLUMES)

1839, 1844, 1855

by

Michael Faraday

*Royal Institution
from its faithful Servant
the Author*

EXPERIMENTAL RESEARCHES

IN

ELECTRICITY.

BY

MICHAEL FARADAY, D.C.L. F.R.S.

FULLERIAN PROFESSOR OF CHEMISTRY IN THE ROYAL INSTITUTION.

CORRESPONDING MEMBER, ETC., OF THE ROYAL AND IMPERIAL ACADEMIES OF
SCIENCE OF PARIS, PETERSBURGH, FLORENCE, COPENHAGEN, BERLIN,
GOTTINGEN, MODENA, STOCKHOLM, PALERMO, ETC., ETC.

———————

Reprinted from the PHILOSOPHICAL TRANSACTIONS of 1831—1838.

———————

LONDON:

RICHARD AND JOHN EDWARD TAYLOR,

PRINTERS AND PUBLISHERS TO THE UNIVERSITY OF LONDON,

RED LION COURT, FLEET STREET.

1839.

If you stroll west from Piccadilly Circus, which once marked the key point of reference for distances to all the countries which were part of the British Empire, you will reach Albemarle Street, elegant, rich in the finest goods and crowned, at its northern end, by the most magnificent building in the street, the classically columned Royal Institution of Great Britain. In the basement is a hidden museum, probably in its time the most fertile experimental laboratory not only in London and the British Empire but in the world. The work done in that modest and modestly equipped space by Michael Faraday in the first half of the nineteenth century changed the way we all live. His dedication to science was extraordinary. He spent his entire adult working life in that building.

It was there, some years ago, when I was making a series of radio programmes about scientists, that Professor Sir John Meurig Thomas, a previous director of the Royal Institution, showed me Faraday's lines of force using iron filings and a magnet used by Faraday himself, which is preserved behind glass, save for occasional demonstrations. That experiment, carried out by Faraday and later developed mathematically by James Clerk Maxwell, has become one of the main underpinnings of theoretical physics and has yielded information about galactic magnetic fields.

Meurig Thomas, a great enthusiast for Faraday, there in that subterranean laboratory, reeled off just a few of the aspects of the modern world which came from persistent and brilliant experiments, thousands of them, made and scrupulously recorded by a young man who left his parents' home to earn a living as an errand boy at the age of thirteen. 'He liquefied about twenty gases,' said Professor Thomas.

> Refrigeration becomes possible because of that. It did not have an immediate impact in that direction but his laws of electrolysis changed the nature of industry and manufacture. But his biggest impact theoretically was the notion of the field . . . He argued that you have to think of a field of a body exerting its magnetic or electrical or gravitational influence right throughout to the end of space . . . That is what has given rise to electronics – the fax machine, telephone, television, the wireless, the radio, the gramophone, they all go back to Faraday's understanding that you can have this force in the ether which you can tap and harness and pull out. So it is a magical thing. They all go back, step by step, to Faraday.'

And all and more of the proofs which led to these wonders are described in his book: *Experimental Researches in Electricity*. From countless patient experiments, Faraday uncovered sources of energy from which we benefit every hour of the day; and in the three volumes he published are the proofs, written plainly for all. He was a lifelong opponent of obfuscation and incomprehensible jargon.

Faraday's first step was taken south of London in an area now known as the Elephant and Castle. His parents had recently arrived from Yorkshire; his father was a blacksmith and they were Sandemanians, a small, strict sect of biblical literalists who also believed that their community should devote time and resources on a daily basis to care for one another. Faraday joined that sect and found his wife within it. His family were poor and at one time he was forced to subsist on a single loaf of bread a week. For this and much other information about Faraday's life, I am indebted to the biographies by Iwan Rhys Morus and James Hamilton.

After a year spent as an errand boy he had what proved to be a crucial stroke of luck and became an apprentice to a bookbinder. Here he taught himself, not unlike Jude the Obscure. He read the books he bound there – especially the physical and chemical works of the time which most engaged his interest. In the small furnace in the basement of the business he began to conduct his first experiments in the evenings. He started keeping notebooks, observations on the nature of life, chemistry, art . . .

It is notable how many who have made significant, even crucial, contributions to our country and to the world began young and without benefit of university education. Shakespeare left school at sixteen and sidestepped the university experience so prized by many of his contemporaries. Nelson, not only a hero in war but a brilliant strategist, joined the navy when he was twelve, as did so many who went on to form the most formidable navy the world has seen. For a twelve-year-old to join the navy would be thought a scandal today, just as Faraday's employers would be sent to court for allowing the young boy to do experiments in a furnace. Yet that early training may have made him. The experimental standards he set and the heights to which he rose through their pursuit inspired generations of young people to conduct their own juvenile experiments and, like Faraday, acquire the taste, the practice, when young. Not any more. Health and safety regulations applied with little concern for thought have driven the exciting parts of chemistry and physics out of the laboratories and out of the curriculum, and many of the best pupils have switched to other subjects as a result. Faraday and Nelson are just two examples of what seems to be a common thread – look at Newton, at Darwin, at Mary Wollstonecraft – that the best way to travel far, farther than before, is to start in early adolescence.

FOUR LECTURES

being part of a Course on

The Elements of

CHEMICAL PHILOSOPHY

Delivered   by

SIR H . DAVY

LL.D. Sec R S. FRSE. MRIA. MRI. &c &c.

AT THE

Royal Institution

And taken off from Notes

BY

M . FARADAY

1812

The frontispiece for Davy's lectures at the Royal Institution.

So when the young Faraday, then twenty-one, was given tickets by a satisfied customer for four lectures to be given at the Royal Institution by Sir Humphry Davy, he was fully prepared. But not for the impact of the man and his words.

John Meurig Thomas observed, speaking at the Royal Institution:

> Davy was a poet, a friend of Coleridge and many others. Davy was also a brilliant experimentalist. Faraday saw the experiments he gave, dazzling even now: we respect them here and it still brings the house down. They were tremendous theatre, magic, conjuring it seemed. [Faraday] sat up in the gallery above the clock and listened, mesmerised, to this man giving one lecture after the other. He wrote up those lectures, bound them and sent them to Davy. That, in effect, was it.

Faraday's ability to follow the experiments closely enough to take notes (in itself no mean feat at a live lecture) of sufficient accuracy to impress a man called 'the greatest experimentalist in Europe' is a tribute to his considerable talent and to the success of his self-education. The careful and elegant binding of the notes and their presentation to the great man were undoubtedly a sincere and unworldly tribute. The consequence of that gift changed not only his world but ours too.

On Christmas Eve in 1812, a grand carriage drew up outside Faraday's lodgings and out stepped not the great man but a bearer of the great man's note. Would Mr Faraday appear at the Royal Institution? He was taken on as Sir Humphry Davy's assistant at the Royal Institution laboratory, wage 25 shillings a week. It was the end of a fairy tale.

Davy in effect became his personal tutor. He was one of Europe's greatest experimental natural philosophers. The word 'scientist' was lying in wait on the not-too-distant horizon but even when it arrived, Faraday disdained it. He wanted to be, he was, a natural philosopher, like Newton, like Davy. Faraday saw the importance of being like Davy in several ways and spent money on elocution lessons from the eminent Mr Benjamin Smart. He also studied Davy's techniques of lecturing to the fashionable and important audience which treated the Royal Institution as its private theatre of natural philosophy. He was determined that when his time came he would let down neither himself nor them, and nor did he. He would never be the romantic man of culture nor the metropolitan darling of the salons: Davy was too hard an act to follow there, even had Faraday wanted to. But he would surpass his mentor as an experimental natural philosopher and in doing so cause friction and jealousy as the son challenged and surpassed the father.

Davy hired Faraday as what Meurig Thomas calls 'a bottle washer'. But 'within six months he was doing some of the most intricate chemical experiments that you can imagine, preparing capriciously explosive materials . . .'. Davy had just got married and wanted to take his wife and his laboratory on a grand European tour. The Napoleonic Wars appeared to present an obstacle but Davy wrote to the emperor who knew the reputation of this great man of natural philosophy and granted him a dispensation. Faraday was invited to accompany them.

It was a blessing for Faraday, though not unqualified. The trip lasted eighteen months, and they went to France, Italy, Belgium and Switzerland. They met many scientists whose generosity was put to the benefit of the education of the brilliant young apprentice. In Paris, with Faraday's help, Davy, his laboratory always at hand, discovered iodine from burnt seaweed.

But unfortunately there was Lady Davy, who treated Faraday not only as an inferior but even as a servant. He wrote to his friend Benjamin Abbot from Rome in 1815:

I should have but little to complain of were I travelling with Sir Humphry alone or were Lady Davy like him, but her temper makes it oftentimes go wrong with me, with herself and with Sir Humphry . . . She is haughty and proud to an excessive degree and delights in making her inferiors feel her power. At present I laugh at her whims which now seldom extend to me but at times a greater degree of ill humour than ordinary involves me in affray which on occasion creates a coolness between us all for two or three days.

When they returned to London, Faraday was made 'Assistant and Superintendent of the Apparatus of the Laboratory and Mineral Collection'. He assisted lecturers and he himself lectured, but most of all he assisted Davy in his experiments and also pursued his own experiments, sometimes at the prompting of Davy and sometimes not, which, when Faraday's skills and reputation grew, caused increasing difficulties between the two men.

For instance, Iwan Morus relates that

In the 1820s . . . things got into quite a mess . . . Faraday was doing his work on chlorine. Davy was the one who initially told Faraday 'Michael, go and do this'. Then, when Faraday wrote up the experiments to be sent to the Philosophical Transactions for the Royal Society, Davy insisted that Faraday put a footnote . . . 'Sir Humphry Davy instructed me to carry out these experiments'.

After his work on chlorine, Faraday turned his attention to electricity. He was the first to show (and write down in his notes and then in his books) that a magnetic field could produce a current. That is why most science dictionaries credit him with the invention of a primitive electric motor. It made Faraday's name but caused his relationship with Davy to sour even further. John Meurig Thomas explains:

Davy was a vain man. He was a passionate man. He loved the applause of the multitudes far more than Faraday. What happened was that in 1821 – this was the turning point – Faraday heard another great scientist talking to Davy about the experiment that had been done in Copenhagen by Oersted, a Danish medical scientist who had spotted that if you passed a current through a wire then a needle of a compass would twitch. This was a significant observation. What did this mean? What should he do with it? Faraday went away and worked out how to create an electric motor from that idea. He sent the paper off, it was published and it brought him international fame. Davy was very annoyed because he thought the idea had come really from him, and more especially from Woollaston . . . Davy, then President of the Royal Society, started imputing in public that Faraday had stolen the idea . . . vanity and jealousy . . . he saw this man who was going to be better than him. Very hard to take. It must be the same these days.

It is worth remembering that Faraday was a strictly religious man and unyielding in his faith and equally in any conviction he had that he thought was right. He is also reported to have had a 'fiery' temper. This story of patronage followed by rivalry is worth the length of telling, I think, because it throws so much light on the turns of fortune in Faraday's career. Meurig Thomas insists that

> Faraday loved him [Davy] right to the end. When Faraday was touching seventy, he wrote an account of his experiments, and he writes a footnote on the first ever paper he published. He said 'this is a very precious paper for me. I published it as a result of work given to me by Sir Humphry Davy at a time when my fear far exceeded my confidence and when both exceeded my knowledge.'

The fact was that by the mid-1820s, Faraday had no need of Davy's guidance.

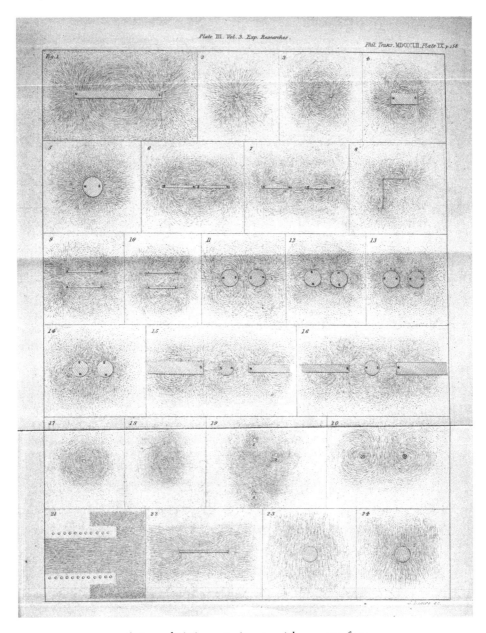

A *page depicting experiments with magnets from*
Faraday's Experimental Researches in Electricity.

His three experimental research volumes grew out of forty years of meticulous note-keeping. Reports of all his investigations were numbered up to 16,041, in March 1860. Periodically he would write up his experiments in order to publish them in the learned magazines of the Royal Institution, but he wanted his work to reach a wider audience (this was always an ambition, only partially satisfied by his packed-house lectures) and so he gathered together the forty-five linked papers which lay down the fundamental laws which guide the natural power of electricity and published them in his book *Experimental Researches in Electricity* in three volumes (1839, 1844 and 1855). In the book he uses the same method of numbering paragraphs – 3,242 in all. The volumes reflect Faraday's omnivorous curiosity about all aspects of nature from the refraction of light to the chemistry of a candle flame. His diagrams illuminate his words perfectly. But it was electricity and magnetism which fascinated him most of all.

The publishers were Taylor and Francis, a publishing house which still exists and publishes numerous journals and new books each year.

He avoided jargon and mathematics, and made the books far less daunting than was the usual case. They are, given their subject matter, very accessible – at the opposite end of the spectrum to the work of Newton. In fact Faraday was challenging the dominant Newtonian mathematical paradigm. He proposed an alternative vision, according to Iwan Rhys Morus, in which carefully designed and skilfully executed experiments allowed natural laws to be revealed directly and unambiguously with a minimum of theoretical presuppositions. Instead of proposing theories in mathematical formulae, he used his experiments as demonstrations, and it was through these that he transformed the science of electricity. His demonstration, also written out in the books, that electrical current could be produced by a moving magnet was an insight that lay at the heart of the nineteenth-century electrical power industry.

James Hamilton writes:

In the 21st century, Michael Faraday's discoveries and improvements have been given facts and facilities. Electricity comes out of the plug in the wall . . . we wear spectacles with precision-made lenses, stir tea with electroplated spoons, we fly in aeroplanes free of harm from lightning strikes, we sail in ships warned off rocks by effective lighthouses; and we swim in pools tinctured by liquid chlorine . . . If Faraday had not made the scientific discoveries he did [it can be argued that] someone else or a chain of other people would quite rapidly have done so. Life would have been recognisably similar but for one particular. Faraday never patented anything . . . Faraday saw his role as reading 'the book of nature . . . written by the finger of God' . . . which he gave as general knowledge to humanity . . . the world's electrical industry is founded on the laws Faraday discovered and tabulated and, like the Declaration of Human Rights, they have been added to but never superseded.

Faraday stopped his research work in 1855 because of problems with his mental health. He had endured a nervous breakdown connected, perhaps, to his temporary expulsion from the Sandemanian community for what seems a rather unimportant and uncharacteristic failure of obedience to their strict laws. His mental powers declined but he continued as a lecturer until 1861. A series of six children's lectures published in 1860 as *The Chemical History of a Candle* has become a classic of scientific literature. His mental health grew worse. He was given refuge and a residence in Hampton Court by Queen Victoria, who, together with her husband Prince Albert, was a great admirer of his work. He died in 1867 and is buried not alongside Newton in Westminster Abbey but in Highgate Cemetery.

It was electricity that fascinated him most of all. When Faraday began his career, electricity, like magnetism, was thought of as a magical force, utterly mysterious. Electricity, it was thought, might prove a cure-all for disease and electric 'parties' became the vogue. In these often rather erotic sessions every part of the body was made to tingle and by tingling apparently become more healthy.

In 1803 Giovanni Aldini created a sensation in London when he demonstrated that a high voltage passed through a freshly executed criminal caused the body to convulse. It was thought that electricity was on the verge of resurrecting the dead. Frankenstein's monster was conceived there in the old operating theatre at St Thomas's. Static electricity had been observed for some time but although the sparks could be spectacular it provoked little extended interest. Faraday referred to it as 'ordinary electricity'. In paragraph ten in his book he writes: 'By ordinary electricity I understand that which can be obtained from . . . the atmosphere, or cleavage of crystal or a multitude of other operations, its distinctive character being that of great intensity.'

In 1813, Alessandro Volta, who invented the battery, had personally given one to Faraday. It is now in the Faraday Museum. Faraday was intrigued by the properties of voltaic electricity. He set himself the task of settling the controversy over whether apparently different types of electricity were in fact one fundamental force. He laid out the problem in his usual methodical way, seeking to establish whether lightning and static electricity are identical to electricity generated by eels, crystals and batteries. He starts by enumerating the various memorable effects of electricity. This is how he set it out: 'The effects of electricity in motion or electrified currents may be considered as 1st evolution of heat; 2nd magnetism; 3rd chemical decomposition; 4th physiological phenomena; 5th spark. It will be my object to compare electricities from different sources, and especially common and voltaic electricities, by their power of producing these effects.'

Aug 29th 1831.

1. Effects on the production of Electricity from Magnetism &c

2. Have had an iron ring made (soft iron), iron round and inches thick & ring 6 inches in external diameter. Wound many coils of copper wire round one half the coils being separated by twine & calico — there were 3 lengths of wire each about 24 feet long and they could be connected as one length or used as separate lengths. By trial with a trough each was insulated from the other. Will call this side of the ring **A**. On the other side but separated by an interval was wound wire in two pieces together amounting to about 60 feet in length the direction being as with the former coils — this side call **B**.

3. Charged a battery of 10 pr plates 4 inches square. Made the coil on B side one coil and connected its extremities by a copper wire passing to a distance and just over a magnetic needle (3 feet from iron ring) then connected the ends of one of the pieces on A side with battery — immediately a sensible effect on needle. It oscillated & settled at last in original position. On breaking connection of A side with Battery again a disturbance of the needle.

Made all the wires on A side one coil and sent current from battery through the whole. Effect on needle much stronger than before.

The effect on the needle then but a very small part of that which the wire communicating directly with the battery could produce.

A page from Faraday's diary recording his discovery of electromagnetic induction, 1831.

He then draws an elegant table which summarises his results. It shows that electricity from a battery makes sparks, whereas electricity from an eel cannot. But, crucially, animal electricity causes the deflection of a magnetic needle just like the electricity from a battery or a static electricity machine. He notes that all three have 'a physiological effect'. They give you a shock! 'The general conclusion which must, I think, be drawn from this collection of facts is that electricity, whatever may be its source, is identical in its nature. The phenomenon in the five kinds of species quoted differ not in their character, but only in degree.'

What most of all made Faraday's book world-changing was that he established the interdependence between electricity and magnetism. In 1821 he discovered that an electric current could create magnetic forces, and this is the principle behind his first, and the world's first, electric motor. Ten years later, still persistent in daily experiments in the basement of the Royal Institution, he discovered that the reverse is also true. Magnetism can create electricity.

The apparatus he used is still there. He wound 220 feet of copper wire around a tube of stiff waxed paper and attached both ends to a galvanometer to detect any electricity. His book takes up the story:

> Then a cylindrical bar magnet $\frac{3}{4}$ inch in diameter and $8\frac{1}{2}$ inches in length had one end just inserted into the end of the helix cylinder – then it was quickly thrust in the whole length and the galvanometer needle moved – then pulled out again and the needle moved but in the opposite direction. This effect was repeated every time the magnet was put in or out and therefore a wave of electricity was so produced from mere approximation of a magnet and not from its formation in situ.

Within days he had developed the theory of electromagnetism. Electricity, which had been thought of as a form of theatrical entertainment or a health cure or the property of atheists, materialists and revolutionaries disturbingly connected with the French, became, through Faraday's experiments, transformed into a force which would one day light up cities and power great ships. He came to his conclusions after ten days' application.

Soon after this, the first electrical generator was made, and exactly the same principle is still used in every power station in the world today, whether it is fuelled by coal, gas or plutonium. Enormous quantities of coils of wire are set in motion between massive magnets, generating millions of volts. Beneath the elegance of Albemarle Street, like a sorcerer working under the skin of the earth, Faraday brought to an end the age of steam and the age of electricity was born. Within fifty years of what now seem Neanderthal experiments under the privileged and wealthy canopy of Mayfair, London, entrepreneurs such as Marconi, Edison, Ferranti and Swan had electrically driven cookers, cleaners, heaters and light bulbs in the shops. (Faraday took no interest in the commercial exploitation of his work: knowledge was meant to show humanity the fuller light of God's greatness.)

Like Darwin (whose work was published just a few years before Faraday's death), Faraday could explain his ideas in language and diagrams. He did not need, he was not accomplished in, mathematics. Yet mathematical equations in science are thought to be the truest conductors, and it is a fortunate coincidence that James Clerk Maxwell, thought to be – by Einstein among others – the most brilliant theoretical physicist of all time, was born in 1831 and twenty-four years later distilled Faraday's results into what Meurig Thomas calls 'four Everlasting Equations. It has been said that when mankind dies away and even when Shakespeare's poetry is forgotten, those Maxwell Equations will stay forever. They are some of the greatest equations that you can have.' It was through these equations that Faraday, through Maxwell, reached Einstein and quantum physics.

Clerk Maxwell's equations were submitted for his Cambridge

thesis on Faraday's writings on lines of force. 'With that work', says Meurig Thomas, 'we understand that the nature of electromagnetic radiation – all the light that you can have from gamma rays, from X-rays, right through the infrared to radio waves – they are all the same. They have a unity and they will be understood by the principles initially perceived very vaguely by Faraday and fully understood by Maxwell.'

Faraday's reaction to Maxwell's paper speaks for many aspects of the man: his rootedness to the importance of experiments, his natural inclination to reach out to the wider public, his manners. This letter is dated 13 November 1857:

My dear Sir,

There is one thing I would be glad to ask you. When a mathematician engaged in investigating physical actions and results has arrived at his own conclusions, may they not be supported in common language, as fully, clearly and definitely as in mathematical formulae? If so, would it not be a great boon to such as we to express them so – translating them out of their hieroglyphics that we might work upon them by experiment? I think it must be so because I have always found that you could convey to me a perfectly clear idea of your conclusions, which, though they may give me no full understanding of the steps of your process, give me the results neither above nor below the truth and so clear in character that I can think and work from them.

If this be possible would it not be a good thing if mathematicians, writing on these subjects, were to give us their results in this popular useful working state as well as in that which is their own and proper to them?

Ever, my dear Sir, most truly yours

Faraday made landmark discoveries in applied science that made possible the dynamo or generator, and led eventually to dozens of domestic appliances, to lights, computers, ECT machines. He discovered the magnetic field which has been used to elucidate molecular structure and yield information about galactic magnetic activity as well as, via Clerk Maxwell, undertaking work leading to radio and telegraph and, farther down the line, the electric car and the extraordinary Maglev train in Germany, propelled by a travelling magnetic field. He also discovered the Law of Electrolysis and coined the words 'anode', 'cathode', 'ion' and 'electrolyte', all of which would be revealed to the public in his lectures and in his books. Faraday, in 1825, also spent time synthesising chlorocarbons and discovering benzene, which led to an understanding of all the aromatics.

Aromatics are so called because of their distinctive smell: they are substances derived from crude oil and, in small quantities, from coal. The chief aromatics apart from benzene are toluene and the xylenes. These are used as the starting materials for a wide range of consumer products. Transport, for example, relies on components made from aromatic-based products. In a car the body, bumpers, lighting, dashboard, seats, upholstery, fuel systems and under-bonnet components are all derived from aromatics.

Cumene and phenol – both derived from benzene – are key ingredients of aspirin and penicillin. CDs and DVDs are reliant on aromatics, as are plastic, acrylic and nylon for clothes.

It would be foolish to pretend that Faraday foresaw all this. It would be wrong to suggest that the line of cause and effect is simple. But it is direct, and a cause of wonder that out of fifty years of continuous experiments in that dark, cramped laboratory came so much that makes up what is modern about the modern world. The three volumes of his experiments are still the bible for experimenters, and the proof that what is often thought of as the humdrum work in research, the carthorse option, the unintellectual can, and has, yielded results of profound significance.

Faraday became enthused and entranced with the mission of

Faraday lecturing on magnetism at the Royal Institution.

sharing his knowledge. As has been noted, he took elocution lessons and developed a high and dramatic style of lecturing. A contemporary, Juliet Pollock, wrote:

> It was an irresistible eloquence which compelled attention. There was a gleaming in his eyes which no painter could copy, which no poet could describe. His enthusiasm seemed to carry him to the point of ecstasy when he expiated on the beauty of nature, and when he lifted the veil from his deep mysteries. His light lithe body seemed to quiver with its eager life. His audience took fire with him, and every face was flushed.

It was always a full house. Charles Dickens came occasionally, Charles Darwin regularly. Prince Albert, *le tout Londres*, or the thinking stratum of *tout Londres*, had to have visited the Royal Institution for a Friday-night lecture.

They could be melodramatic. John Meurig Thomas describes one experiment Faraday carried out in the lecture theatre:

> He built a cage, a cube, twelve feet by twelve feet by twelve feet, of wood. He covered it with metal, metal foil, metal wire. He stepped inside with delicate electrical instruments and then he had his assistants charge up the cage to something like a hundred thousand volts. All the people around were watching sparks flying everywhere, and he was inside not feeling a tremor. He predicted that. What a hell of a thing to do! You could be killed if you did not know your science well enough, and he came out and that was that. This was one side of his showmanship.

His determination to popularise science could be said to mark yet another achievement – we now have Richard Dawkins, Charles Simonyi Professor of the Public Understanding of Science at Oxford, and scores of scientists and journalists following the route pioneered by Faraday.

This was fully recognised in his day, as this 1830 letter attests:

Dear Sir,

It has occurred to me that it would be extremely beneficial to a large class of the public to have some account of your late lectures on the breakfast table, and of those you addressed last year to children. I should be exceedingly glad to have some papers in reference to them published in my new enterprise 'Household Words'. May I ask you whether it would be agreeable to you and if so whether you would favour me with the loan of your notes of these lectures for perusal.

With great respect and esteem I am, dear Sir, your faithful servant
Charles Dickens

He kept the notes for his own books. And of his drama in the lecture theatre, the most famous example of them all is the lecture he gave in 1849 on the chemical history of the candle.

Now I must take you to a very interesting part of our subject – the relation between the combustion of a candle and that living kind of combustion that goes on within us. In every one of us there is a living process of combustion going on very similar to that of the candle, and I must try to make that plain to you. For it is not merely true in a poetical sense – the relation of man to a taper, and if you will follow, I think I can make that clear . . .

You will be astonished when I tell you what the curious play of carbon amounts to. A candle will burn some four, five, six or seven hours. What then must be the daily amount of carbon going up into the air in the way of carbonic acid! What a quantity must go from each of us in respiration! What a wonderful change of carbon must take place under these circumstances of combustion or respiration! A man in twenty-four hours converts as much as seven ounces of carbon into carbonic acid; a milch cow will convert seventy ounces and a horse seventy-nine ounces, solely by the act of respiration. That is, the horse in twenty-four hours, burns seventy-nine ounces of charcoal or carbon in his organs of respiration to supply his natural warmth in that time.

There is so much more to say about Faraday, as about all the others in this book, but there are thankfully many larger studies available, some of which are mentioned in the Acknowledgements. We have his own books. And as in Faraday's lifelong interest in the natural world, which led him out into the countryside to spot birds, name plants and flowers, there is always awe at the grandeur of it all. This, I think, is linked with his religion, a demanding religion in terms not only of its faith but of its works, attending the elderly every week, playing a full social part in that enclosed community.

It seems to me that, not unlike Newton, for Faraday his science and his idea of God were not only ballast but perhaps even co-dependent inspirations, essential inspiration for his work as an experimenter.

In 1845, in his laboratory, he came across some glass that he had made by a special chemical means. When a polarised ray of light was passed through it and a magnetic field applied to it, its polarisation was tilted. Magneto-optics began on that day. Writing up the experiment Faraday says: 'I have long held an opinion almost to conviction in common I believe, with other lovers of the natural worlds, that all the forces of all base matter have one common cause.'

TIMELINE
EXPERIMENTAL RESEARCHES IN ELECTRICITY

1839–55   Taylor and Francis publish Faraday's *Experimental Researches in Electricity* in three volumes

1839   The first fuel cell appears

1841   Joule's law of electrical heating is published

1845   Gustav Robert Kirchhoff publishes 'circuit rules' for calculating electrical quantities in loop and junction configurations

1851   Heinrich Ruhmkorff invents doubly wound induction coil which leads to the development of AC transformers

1864   James Clerk Maxwell describes electromagnetic field in four classic equations, which also allow calculation of the speed of light

1869   William Crookes and Johann Wilhelm Hittof independently discover 'cathode rays'

1871   Gramme introduces the first commercially significant electric motor

1876   Invention of the telephone by Alexander Graham Bell and, independently, by Elisha Gray

1878   Edison Electric Light Co. (US) and American Electric and Illuminating (Canada) are founded

1879   The first commercial power station opens in San Francisco, using Charles Brush generator and arc lights

The first commercial arc lighting system is installed in Cleveland, Ohio

Thomas Edison demonstrates his incandescent lamp

Experimental Researches in Electricity

1881   The first electric public railway opens in Germany

1882   The world's first central electricity generating system, Edison's Pearl Street Station, opens in New York

1883   The second electric public railway, built by Magnus Volk, opens in Brighton

       The transformer is invented

1884   Charles Parsons builds a steam turbine; this technology would become widespread in power generation

1888   Nikola Tesla designs the alternating current (AC) power generator, which revolutionises industry and commerce

       Turbine-driven electric power generators begin to appear

       Heinrich Hertz discovers and measures radio waves, predicted by Faraday and Maxwell

1892   The General Electric Company is formed by the merger of Thomson-Houston and Edison General Electric

1895   Marconi pioneers the wireless telegram

1896   The 'Zeeman effect' is first observed

1897   A radio message is sent by Marconi over a twenty-mile distance from the Isle of Wight to Poole, Dorset, England

1903   Ductile tungsten used in light bulbs is invented by William Coolidge

       The first successful gas turbine appears in France

       The world's first all-turbine station opens in Chicago

       Shawinigan Water & Power (Canada) installs the world's largest generator and the world's largest and highest voltage line

1906   In the United States, James Murray Spangler invents the electric vauum cleaner

1907 Lee De Forest invents the electric amplifier

1908 The first electric washing machine is invented by Alva J. Fisher

1913 The first domestic refrigerator appears

1915 The first electrical clothes driers appear

1919 The first commercial quench-hardened steel magnets are made available

Mass production of electric washing machines and refrigerators begins

1926 The UK National Grid is introduced following the Electricity Supply Act

1927 The first electric refrigerator to see widespread use is produced by General Electric

1937 The hand-held vacuum cleaner is introduced

1947 The transistor is invented

1956 The development of fibre optics is concluded after two years' work

1965 9 November: Great Northeast blackout

1977 13–14 July: New York City blackout

1985 Citizens Power, first power marketer, goes into business

1999 Electricity is marketed on the internet

2003 14–15 August: power blackout in northeastern and southern Canada

PATENT SPECIFICATION FOR ARKWRIGHT'S SPINNING MACHINE

——

1769

by

Richard Arkwright

A.D. 1769 . . . . N° 931.

SPECIFICATION

OF

RICHARD ARKWRIGHT.

SPINNING MACHINE.

LONDON:

PRINTED BY GEORGE E. EYRE AND WILLIAM SPOTTISWOODE,
PRINTERS TO THE QUEEN'S MOST EXCELLENT MAJESTY:

PUBLISHED AT THE GREAT SEAL PATENT OFFICE,
25, SOUTHAMPTON BUILDINGS, HOLBORN.

Price 6d.   1856.

This may seem, at first glance, a curious addition to the list of twelve. The patent is three pages long – but length need not define a book; Seneca wrote 'books' one page long and a poem can be a poem whether it is fourteen or 140 lines long. There are books on law from Cicero onwards which could not incongruously be labelled legal pleas and yet they are books.

This patent is the plea of a manufacturer to 'His Most Excellent Majesty King George III'. 'Manufacturer' might be a clue to the apprehension I sense about this inclusion. The subtext of this book is the devotion of writers to the idea itself, to that which is outside price and concerned only with value. A 'manufacturer' in the United Kingdom has for more than a century now been considered below the salt. Yet until quite recently these small islands could fairly claim to be the Workshop of the World. Once, with less than 2 per cent of the world's population our manufacturers claimed 35 per cent of the world's trade.

Once, to be a manufacturer was to be a new man, a man of science and the future, a challenger to the landed aristocracy, the first great social force outside the concentric circles of titled and would-be titled praetorian guards which had spun around the monarchy since 1066, indeed since Alfred's reign, as the planets spun around the Sun. The Industrial Revolution changed all that. And Richard Arkwright's patent could be claimed as a principal catalyst of an English revolution which, arguably, has had and continues to have a greater impact on the world than the American, the French, the Russian or even the Chinese. We live in a factory-powered world and the first cotton factory powered anywhere on the planet was in Cromford in Derbyshire, built by the cunning, tenacity, flair and financial skills of Richard Arkwright. If this book is to make some attempt to take in a breadth of life, then manufacturing, money, labour, the grit of life cannot be omitted, and Richard Arkwright best exemplifies these.

I would have loved to write, as I thought I would, 'a patent is an inventor's book'. But Arkwright was not an inventor. He was not of the class of James Hargreaves with his Spinning Jenny (1767), or James Watt with his steam engine (1769) or Samuel Crompton with his spinning mule loom (1779). No fine inventor's hand and mind took him into that galaxy of creativity, which in the unlikely setting of remote northern Britain gave birth not so much to a Renaissance as a new making of the means and methods of engaging with the production of goods for a material life that has expanded ever since. Even in our clerical world, the word 'inventor' has a glamour, a swagger, respect. Entrepreneur is not so shiny. But entrepreneur is what Arkwright was. And without Arkwright the entrepreneur and others who followed in his slipstream the works of the inventors might have remained as nothing much more than curiosities, strictly local improvements, commercially null. Entrepreneur Arkwright is: world-changing the patent was.

Arkwright's patent revolutionised the powerful cotton manufacturing industry – an industry key to the Industrial Revolution. It established a factory system which dominates world industry and has remained fundamentally unchanged since Arkwright's day. Its success stimulated scores of ancillary manufacturers, helping form an industrial cluster which had a snowball effect – a process still at work today. The Industrial Revolution, in which he was so influential, accelerated and integrated a vast social

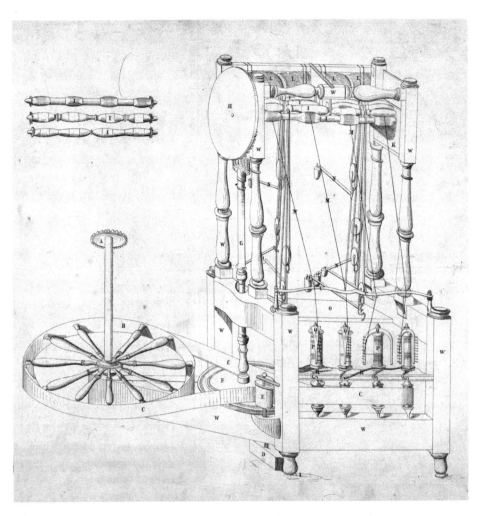

Arkwright's 1769 patent drawing for a spinning machine.

transformation which has gone global. It energised the mass movement from the country to the town and the lift-off of the capitalist
economy. In the overgrown, hidden, tangled little gullies of Derbyshire can still be seen the remains of the mills that harnessed the
water to the factories that made the cotton at a speed and volume of
production which at that time beggared belief. While in the great
mill standing at Cromford, magnificiently restored can be seen the
might and power of industry, all the more startling for being lodged
in a wild North Pennine landscape. The original power remains to
this day. The modern world had been born, and it made Arkwright
the richest businessman the world had hitherto known.

Of the several books consulted for this chapter, the two I found
outstanding were *The Lunar Men* by Jenny Uglow and *Richard
Arkwright and Cotton Spinning* by Richard Hills, and to both I am
indebted for some of what follows.

Arkwright's background was not unlike that of many of the men
who invented, fashioned and drove the Industrial Revolution – it
runs parallel to the early experience of Faraday, save that he had even
less education than Faraday and did not share in Faraday's luck in
respect of book learning when he set to work. The youngest of
thirteen children, born in Preston in 1732, Arkwright was taught to
read and write by his cousin Ellen as his parents could not afford to
send him to school. His father was a tailor and managed to find his
son an apprenticeship in the barber's trade when he was thirteen. A
few years later, Arkwright started up his own wig-making business
and travelled widely collecting hair. He married twice, honed his
entrepreneurial skills in the hair trade and on his travels in the North
and the Midlands came into contact with the excitement surround-
ing attempts to invent new machines aimed at making even more
profitable the well-established textile industry.

He met John Kay, a clockmaker from Warrington, who was
attempting to invent a new spinning machine in collaboration with
Thomas Highs of Leigh. The two of them had run out of money.

This was common among the largely untutored inventors in the pre-industrialised North at the time, and Arkwright saw and began to take advantage of – some said exploit – an opportunity. Slyly, he employed John Kay, Highs's colleague, and paid him to build moulds of Highs's invention. He sought out other local craftsmen and together they produced a model of the spinning frame which he used to attract potential investors. It seems very unlikely that Arkwright had much intellectual input. It is equally unlikely that the operation would have got under way without him. He made it his own and owning it was paramount. Yet there would be those who might employ the term 'visionary' about him.

The machine involved three sets of parallel rollers that turned at different speeds. While these rollers produced yarn of the correct thickness, a set of spindles twisted the fibres firmly together. The machine was able to produce a thread that was far stronger than that made by James Hargreaves's Spinning Jenny, patented in 1770.

Cotton was king of the early Industrial Revolution. Arab merchants had brought it to Europe around AD 800. Columbus found cotton growing in the Bahamas, and when this was introduced into Florida and Virginia by seventeenth-century colonists it set off a substantial trade in cloth for fabrics and furnishings. On the other side of the world, the East India Company had developed a profitable trade in Indian calico cloth which at the end of the seventeenth century was threatening the famous and long-established English woollen industry. By 1750 Manchester was already a world centre of the cotton industry and around that booming city satellites like Bolton, Leigh and Bury also fed well off the trade.

But it was highly skilled work. The quality depended on the feel of the fibres moving through the fingers and also on putting in an equal number of turns on each twist. The race was on to speed up the process. As Arkwright pounded the land seeking hair for his wigs – there are desperate and poignant stories of girls sacrificing their sole treasure for a few pence to provide the crowning glories for women who lived in another England – he picked up on the excitement and the gossip, the gossip of intelligent men. There is no suggestion that Arkwright was anything but an exceptional autodidact of practical learning. He saw commercial possibilities.

This revolution was driven by inventors, Northern men mostly, little schooled in book learning, eager and hungry for knowledge of mechanics, fascinated by the ceaseless ripple effect of Newton, believing that the world could be changed through science and that they in their modest way were in Newton's slipstream, making things that made change. The mechanisation of the spinning of cotton was where most of these men put their energy.

There was, as an early instance, John Wyatt, the eldest of eight brothers. He has been described as a mechanical and mathematical genius. From the 1730s, he worked on machines which would achieve what became the inventors' holy grail – replacing manual labour and cottage drudgery. There was a humanitarian impulse here as well as the excited desire to do it and of course a commercial goal. Wyatt was a disaster at commerce, as so many British inventors have been and continue to be, which is why on occasion the contribution of a forceful entrepreneur is vital. Wyatt invented a machine to cut files and sold it to a gunsmith who went bankrupt. He designed the first suspension bridge for which airy fancy there were no buyers. He invented ball bearings, drew up plans for piped water supplies and had no impact at all.

A meeting with another inventor, Lewis Paul, led towards the crock of gold, for out of this came Wyatt's development of the first machine for spinning cotton yarn using rollers revolving at different speeds: this was patented in 1738. Inspired by Wyatt, Paul invented the carding machine and he and Wyatt set up a mill in Birmingham and another in Northampton which employed fifty people. This has some claim to be the first textile factory, but it failed. Twenty-five years later, Arkwright's factory, served by a better machine employing 5,000 people and organised with Arkwright's unique flair, established the lasting foundation for the first leap of the revolution.

James Hargreaves has to have a place in this chapter. He was both a carpenter and a weaver, again a man of no formal education, never taught to read or write. His Spinning Jenny (named after Jenny, his wife) was a hand-powered multiple spinning machine that was the first machine in the long history of cotton to improve upon the spinning wheel. This decreased the number of skilled workers required and in 1768 a group of spinners broke into Hargreaves's house and destroyed his increasingly elaborate machines, fearing they would take away their work. But Hargreaves's machine had a drawback: it produced thread that was too coarse to be used for warp work, that is, threads extending lengthways up the loom; it could only be used for weft work, the crossing yarn.

By now the search for The Machine was intensifying. In 1761, the Society for the Encouragement of Arts, Commerce and Manufactures offered a prize of £50 for the invention of a successful spinning machine. Arkwright began to move in. Significantly it is not entirely clear how he developed his machine. He continued to employ John Kay to help him and some hold that Kay merely copied Highs's machine and, with Arkwright, took the credit.

The patent application for this 'new Piece of Machinery' (number 931) was submitted to the king by Richard Arkwright on 15 July 1769. The most relevant passages are:

> Whereas I, the said Richard Arkwright, did by my petition humbly represent to His Present most Excellent Majesty King George the Third, that I had by great study, and long application invented A new Piece of Machinery never before found out, practiced, or used, for the making of weft or yarn from cotton, flax, and wool, which would be of great utility to a great many manufacturers in this His Kingdom of England, by employing a great number of poor people in working the said machinery . . .

The second relevant passage reads:

I, the said Richard Arkwright, my executors, administrators and assigns should and lawfully might have and enjoy the whole profit, benefit, commodity, and advantage from time to time coming, growing, accruing, and arising by reason of the said invention for and during the term of years therein mentioned, to have, hold, exercise and enjoy the said license, powers, privileges and advantages therein before granted or mentioned to be granted unto me . . .

This is the abstract autobiography of an entrepreneur. From the start Arkwright saw that he could employ unskilled and therefore cheap labour. From the first he seems to have been aware of the vast commercial potential and made certain of his own interest. His was not the first system to use water power (water-powered silk mills in Derby dated back to the seventeenth century), but the reach of Arkwright was immeasurably greater, even though he was faced with strong contemporary competition. Crompton's mule spinning, introduced in 1779, grew so rapidly that by the early nineteenth century there were 4.4 million mule spindles in use compared with Arkwright's 310,000 water-frame spindles.

Nor was it a flash of lightning which out of nowhere and on its own illuminated the way forward. There had been a low level of mechanised industry before Arkwright and it took time for the revolution to take hold. By the end of the eighteenth century, thought of as the heyday of the Industrial Revolution, non-factory workers still outnumbered factory workers in the national labour force. Not all industrialists were keen on mechanisation and it was only after the mid-nineteenth century that mechanised industry became the giant hand blocking out the sun across the British Isles. As yet it was an uneven process, unevenly distributed.

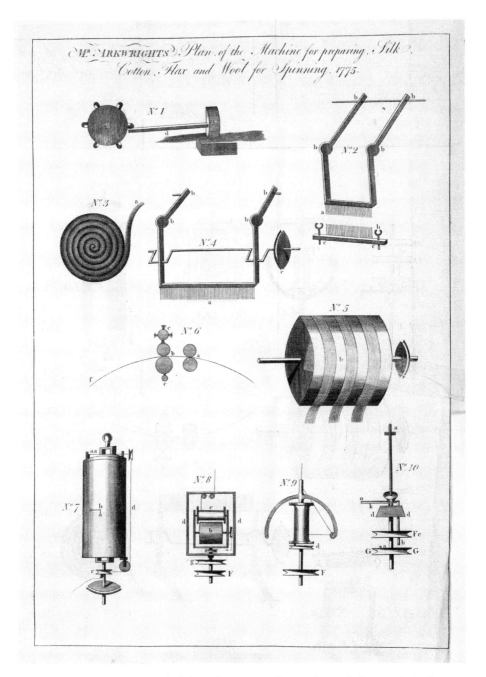

This engraving was included in the account of a trial in which several rivals attempted to repeal Arkwright's patent for his machine to prepare yarn for spinning.

Yet Arkwright's combination of powered machines and a continuous process retains its role as the trigger point in the Industrial Revolution especially, and vitally, because Arkwright's factory system introduced rigour and efficiency to the method of production that were a qualitative as well as a quantitative change and swiftly spread abroad. The machines grew stronger, the factory system bigger; mass production arrived and his influence is everywhere.

It is useful, I think, in respect of clarifying the extent to which Arkwright had a crucial role, to uncover the track which he took to the patent for the water frame.

The pursuit of the perfect machine became as much an obsession with Arkwright as with the inventors he met, borrowed from, used and employed. That his motives were different was the essence. But the inventors needed his entrepreneurial genius and his bulldog determination.

At the end of the 1760s, Arkwright sought out Ichabod Wright, a Nottingham banker, to seek funds to expand his business. The size of his operation was important. It had to satisfy Arkwright's financial ambitions. And it had to be built to last. Most previous attempts had failed for lack of finance or lack of financial control. Wright introduced Arkwright to Jedediah Strutt and Samuel Need, who were impressed with the water frame and came in with him. At last what would be the hub of the revolution was to get proper funding.

From the beginning the ancillary consequences were substantial. After Arkwright set up the first big factory next to the River Derwent in Cromford in Derbyshire, yarn was to be produced so much more cheaply by the water-frame machine that despite a total lack of the natural resource – cotton – on which the industry was based, English merchants captured a very large proportion of the world market for cotton cloth. Where they went other British manufacturers followed. The growth of trade meant many more mills; it meant more waterwheels, and later steam engines to drive them; it led to the development of machine tool industries, and the new factory buildings created a further demand for timber, iron, bricks, leather . . .

Early on in his pursuit, Arkwright could have made machines and sold them locally as Hargreaves had done. But he had his eye on the much bigger picture and for that he needed considerable investment. His patent was a way to protect his profit and to attract investors. If a patent were granted, the holder had a sole right to it for fourteen years. He could develop the machines himself or license them out.

Before he thought he was fully ready to launch his patent application – not a simple process, nor inexpensive, nor guaranteed of success – he made an agreement with two more people who were to become 'Joint Adventurers and Partners' in his venture. John Smalley was a publican and paint merchant from Preston and David Thornley a merchant from Liverpool.

These two men agreed to 'advance in equal Proportions all such sums of money as might be necessary in applying for a Patent as aforesaid and for improving, Enlarging, Using and Working the machine already Invented and others to be constructed for the same, or like purposes, and all incident Charges and Expenses that might attend the same.'

The patent was granted on 3 July 1769.

It was a time of machine wrecking and Arkwright moved away from the North-West, the fiery towns of Lancashire where weavers locked in the traditions of centuries feared for their livelihood and expressed themselves violently. He moved first to Nottingham and then into the romantic, beautiful and, to the dreamer's eye, idyllic landscape of Derbyshire. In 1775 he applied for and got a second patent, this time for a carding engine for his machine, adding in the improvements he had made to the water frame and of course, in the process, extending his monopoly.

Now he set about making money and in the course of that the modern factory system was born. It came to be thought of by

utilitarians as the bringer of great benefits to mankind; by huma-
nitarians as the principal cause of the exploitation and oppression of
the individual; and by those who cared for the soul as the enemy of
everything most precious.

Arkwright needed workers. The following appeared in the *Derby
Mercury*: 'Wanted at Cromford, Forging and Filing Smiths, Joiners
and Carpenters, Frame-Knitters and Weavers with large families.
Likewise children of all ages may have constant employment. Boys
and young men may have trades taught them, which will enable
them to maintain a family in a short time.'

In 1781, Samuel Need died and Arkwright and Strutt decided to
dissolve their partnership. Strutt was worried about Arkwright's
imperial ambitions to build factories in Manchester, Winkworth,
Matlock Bath and Bakewell. He feared for his investment. Arkwright went it alone and made a fortune. He had read the market
brilliantly.

Arkwright's employees worked from six in the morning until
seven at night, six days a week. He would not employ children
under the age of six which was considered, by some, to be almost
enlightened. Two-thirds of his workforce were children and he was
reluctant to employ anyone over the age of forty.

The mill was built like a fortress and Arkwright introduced a
primitive but effective method of surveillance which has been copied
and refined ever since. His house – Rock House – was part of the mill,
as was common with the early generation of self-made industrialists.
Into an otherwise blank wall which overlooked the mill he built a
window which became known as 'the Cromford window'. It provided
an uninterrupted view of the yard and the main mill buildings, giving
workers the feeling they were being watched the whole time, even
when they knew Arkwright was away. He kept a cannon loaded with
grapeshot just inside the mill as a warning to any mob which might
attack his machinery as they had the Spinning Jennys of Hargreaves.
The *Derby Mercury* reported in 1779:

There is some fear of the mob coming to destroy the works at Cromford, but they are well prepared to receive them should they come here. All the gentlemen in this neighbourhood being determined to defend the works, which have been of such utility to this country, 5,000 or 6,000 men can be at any time assembled in less than an hour by signals agreed upon, who are determined to defend to the very last extremity the works by which many hundreds of their wives and children get a decent and comfortable livelihood.

This loyalty was despite savage discipline. In 1779 the *Derby Mercury* informed its readers: 'John Jeffries, a gunsmith of Cromford, has been committed to the House of Correction at Derby for one month, and to be kept to hard labour. John Jeffries was charged by Mr Arkwright, Cotton Merchant, with having absented himself from his master's business without leave (being hired a servant).'

Our reaction to this today, as to the employment of children aged six, is outrage. It is salutary to read the *Derby Mercury* on the loyalty of the workforce. This is, of course, not to condone that sort of Anglo-Saxon industrial child slavery for a moment. But the facts seem to indicate that here, as in many of the areas in which he operated to bring the new system to fruition, Arkwright's experience and ambition rendered him in tune with his times.

Arkwright, in my view, introduced, above all, mass-produced, low-cost, universally desirable goods and laid the foundation for the mass consumer market. The labour force in the Arkwright mills was overwhelmingly unskilled women and children. The spinning mules, by contrast, were operated by skilled men whose wages were much higher. As long as the two systems were seen to have a reasonable approximation in quality, other entrepreneurs and the public placed their money on Arkwright. And thousands of mills have been built, often with baroque, fantastical extravagance on the template of Arkwright, and his factory method has been refined ever since, in the USA, in India, throughout Europe, in Russia and now in China.

Women and children attending to textile machinery in 1835.

Arkwright's genius was not only to embody his times and to read them, but to have the nerve to seize on what he thought most effectively pushed forward the crucial ideas of the day. When he built new factories in Staffordshire and Scotland, he used steam power developed by James Watt and Matthew Boulton and in doing so he championed the cause of steam. Envious competitors sent in spies and tempted away employees with bribes which some took despite the draconian penalties exacted on anyone caught breaching the patent in any way. Other mills were built in which Arkwright's roller drawing system was used illegally and clandestinely. He tried to prevent this through the legal monopoly of his patent.

He was willing to sell licences, for a short term, to allow people to copy his machines. They were sold in units of a thousand spindles. Gardom and Pares, for instance, who built a mill at Calver on the Derwent in 1780, paid a flat fee of £2,000 for using Arkwright's first patent, £5,000 for using his second, and a royalty of £1,000 per annum. These were very big sums at the time. Collinson and Watson started a mill in Preston. Arkwright sold licences to many entrepreneurs in the Midlands and elsewhere and he charged excessively. This encouraged chancers to build mills without his permission. In 1781, Gardom and Pares – and probably others – stopped paying royalties, partly because they felt they had paid more than enough and partly because others were simply not paying. Arkwright moved to protect what he correctly saw as his legal rights. He chose his opponent carefully and took to court Colonel Mordaunt, who had a very small mill. In June 1781 he lost the case and his second patent became void. This was probably his first misreading of the century he was drawing into wealth beyond the dreams of even his own ambitions.

His first patent still ran to 1783 and he petitioned Parliament to extend it to 1789. His petition was rejected and from 1783 anyone who had the capital and the plan could build a cotton mill. There was a cotton rush; within two years £150,000 had been spent on new mills. This patent was declared void in 1785 largely as a result of testimony by John Kay which cast doubts on Arkwright's intellectual contribution to the invention. Nevertheless, in 1786 George III awarded him a knighthood.

Yet it was from this time that his reputation began to plummet. It was the faults in his nature which laid him low among his business contemporaries. He was detested and scorned. Thomas Carlyle wrote of him: 'He is a plain, almost gross, bag-cheeked, pot-bellied man, with an air of painful reflection, yet almost copious free digestion.' The barber's apprentice was a very long way below the salt. Snobbery kicked in and kicked out manufacturing as the high-born and highly educated have done, largely, ever since. Matthew Boulton, the inventor and a contemporary, wrote of him: 'Tyranny and an improper exercise of power will not do in this country . . . if he [Arkwright] had been a more civilised being and had understood mankind better, he would now have enjoyed his patent.' But it has to be argued that it was perhaps the 'improper exercise of power' itself which made Arkwright such a catalyst and such a success. This drew Boulton and scores of inventors; Gardom and Pares and hundreds of businesses; and men, women and children, into enterprises, fortunes and wages they could not have enjoyed without him. And the country grew very rich.

It is worth underlining, though, how powerful this appreciation of his achievement was at the time. The Americans, having recently secured independence from the British Crown, none the less kept in close touch with their former rulers especially in matters which would enrich their new country. They were fully aware of Ark-wright's great advances and tried in several ways to steal the secret from the despised former mother country. Their opportunity came in 1789 when a young man, Samuel Slater, arrived in New York after finishing a six-year apprenticeship with one of Arkwright's partners, Jedediah Strutt.

THE GRAPHIC

AN ILLUSTRATED WEEKLY NEWSPAPER

No. 527.—Vol. XXI.
Reg'd at General Post Office as a Newspaper]

SATURDAY, JANUARY 3, 1880

ENLARGED TO
TWO SHEETS [

PRICE SIXPENCE
Or by Post Sixpence Halfpenny

NOTES AT THE PATENT MUSEUM, SOUTH KENSINGTON

*Arkwright's spinning machine (bottom left)
was widely held to be one of the wonders of the age.*

Britain had early appreciated the commercial importance of trade secrets and in 1774 passed a series of laws which outlawed the emigration of engineers. Slater, who had read of the bounties being offered in New York, disguised himself as a farm worker and crossed the Atlantic. He linked up with Moses Brown, a Rhode Island factory owner. Slater built the first water-powered textile mill in America from memory. The mill, called 'Almy and Brown', still stands in Pawtucket, Rhode Island. Slater's wealth soon grew to 1 million dollars and at his death he owned all or part of thirteen textile mills. His impact on American manufacturing was enormous. In 1790 America was producing about 2 million pounds of cotton a year; by 1835 it was 80 million. There is also a preserved mill in Düsseldorf, and UNESCO recently inaugurated a large section of the Derwent Valley in Derbyshire as a World Heritage site.

When Arkwright died, at Rock House, he left, according to the *Gentleman's Magazine*, 'Manufactories the increase of which is greater than that of most German Principalities . . . His real and personal property is estimated at little short of half a million' (more than £200 million in today's terms).

In 1835, Edward Bernes wrote, 'To Arkwright and Watt, England is far more indebted for her triumphs than to Nelson and Wellington. Without the means supplied by her flourishing manufactures and trade, the country would not have borne up under a conflict so prolonged and exhausting.'

A person could now be rich without inheriting land. Many industrialists wanted both and bought their way into the aristocracy, with land, houses and titles. The Industrial Revolution completely changed the context and nature of manufacturing and the experience of work in the lives of the majority. Increasingly it was concentrated in cities, increasingly it was concentrated in factories, increasingly it opened up the capital, the opportunities and the material possibilities of life to millions whose ancestors had lived a life quite near that of the state of nature described by Thomas Hobbes – 'solitary, poor, nasty, brutish and short'.

Despite the much-described drawbacks and iniquities of the factory system, huge numbers enjoy benefits and facilities only a century ago undreamt of. It has boosted science and technology yet by its success denuded villages and made some thinkers fear that an essential and umbilical link with nature has been severed by these 'dark satanic mills'. The sweatshops of northern Britain have been relocated to the East and so has the character of the workforce. Almost 250 million children are still engaged in child labour. That too is part of the inheritance. So is the wealth that builds universities and hospitals for the many in Europe, North America, Australia and an increasing number of other countries.

It is odd to think that much of the power for this came from cotton, such a gentle thing. But it became, as Arkwright foresaw, a huge and, you might say, seeding industry. In 2003, the global textile sector was worth $958.6 billion. Today it is China that leads the trade, followed by the USA and India. In India, cotton accounts for a fifth of all industrial production and a third of total exports.

And so much else is now made from cotton: automobile tyre cord, plastic reinforcing; fibre from the stalk is used for pressed paper and cardboard. Cottonseed oil, now a separate industry, is used in a refined state in cooking oil, cosmetics, soap, candles . . .

These products came from factories organised in a way directly descended from Arkwright's prototype in Derbyshire. His patent is not a flower of English prose but, like many other examples in this book, it proves the force of the written word and its ability to spin its web around the globe and transform it.

TIMELINE
PATENT SPECIFICATION FOR
ARKWRIGHT'S SPINNING MACHINE

1769   Arkwright's specification for the patent of his spinning machine is published and his water-powered frame automates the weft

1770   Hargreaves's Spinning Jenny is patented

1775   Watt produces the first efficient steam engine

Arkwright applies for and gains a second patent, for a carding engine for his machine

Arkwright and his partners finally persuade the government to remove the crippling import tariff on raw cotton, which had been imposed earlier in order to protect the woollen industry

1777   The Grand Trunk Canal establishes a cross-England route connecting the Mersey to the Trent and the industrial Midlands to the ports of Bristol, Liverpool and Hull

1779   The first steam-powered mills appear

Crompton's spinning mule loom combines Hargreaves' and Arkwright's machines, fully automating the weaving process

Arkwright's mill in Chorley, Lancashire, is destroyed by a mob of labourers as a protest against his machinery which reduced the need for manual labour

1781   Arkwright sets out his ambitions to build factories in Manchester, Winkworth, Matlock Bath and Bakewell, all of which become a great success

Arkwright prosecutes nine different companies for breach of his patents

1785 Cartwright patents the power loom. It is improved upon by William Horrocks in 1813

Arkwright's patents are cancelled as it is proved in court that the intellectual property for many of the inventions lay not with him but with a selection of his partners, friends and rivals

There is a rush among manufacturers to use Arkwright's technology and it is estimated that within two years £150,000 was spent on new mills

1786 Arkwright installs a Watt engine in the Albion cotton mill, Blackfriars Bridge, London

Arkwright is knighted by George III

1787 Cartwright builds a power loom

Cotton goods production had increased tenfold since 1770

1789 The Thames–Severn Canal links the Thames to the Bristol Channel

Samuel Slater takes Arkwright's textile machinery design to the US

Cartwright patents a wool-combing machine

1790 Arkwright builds the first steam-powered textile factory in Nottingham, England

1792 Arkwright dies in Rock House, Derbyshire

1793 Eli Whitney develops his cotton gin, a device to clean raw cotton

Thomas Telford builds his two great iron aqueducts, over the Dee and the Ceirog valleys

1800 There are roughly 4.4 million mule spindles in use

Thanks to the Industrial Revolution, London is the only city in the world to hold in excess of 1 million people

1801 Richard Trevithick demonstrates a steam road locomotive, the first to carry passengers

1804   Joseph Marie Jacquard invents the Jacquard loom which made it possible to weave complex designs by using a sequence of punched cards to control the warp and weft threads

1811   The Luddites begin to meet in secret to plan the destruction of power spinning machinery

1813   The Luddite riots: labourers attack factories and break up the machines they fear will replace them

William Horrocks invents the variable speed batton for an improved power loom

1830   The Liverpool and Manchester Railway begins first regular commercial rail service

1835   Thanks to their new methods of spinning, America is now producing 80 million pounds of cotton a day

1850s   British manufacturing goods dominate world trade

1851   Only 9 per cent of the British population is now employed in agriculture

1856   William Perkin invents the first synthetic dye

2001   UNESCO designates a 24-km stretch of the Derwent Valley, between Matlock and Derby, as a heritage site

2003   The global textiles sector reaches a value of $958.6 billion

THE KING JAMES BIBLE

1611

by

William Tyndale and Fifty-four Scholars Appointed by the King

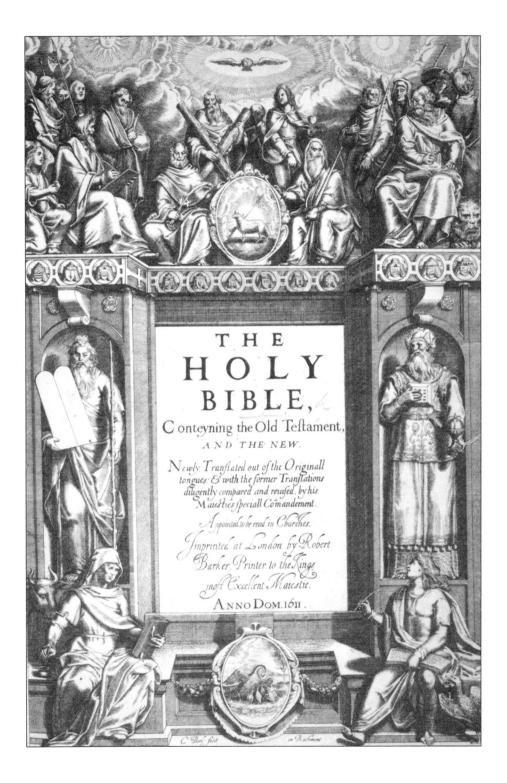

THE
HOLY
BIBLE,

Conteyning the Old Testament,

AND THE NEW.

Newly Translated out of the Originall
tongues: & with the former Translations
diligently compared and reuised, by his
Maiesties speciall Comandement.

Appointed to be read in Churches.

Imprinted at London by Robert
Barker, Printer to the Kings
most Excellent Maiestie.

ANNO DOM. 1611.

The Gideon Society website reports that annually 'the Gideon International is placing and distributing more than 63,000,000 (sixty-three million) Scriptures worldwide. To God be the Glory! This averages more than one million copies of the Word of God placed every seven days.'

This is the King James version of the Bible, which is both the standard scriptural text throughout the English-speaking world and, for centuries, the best-selling book in the English-speaking world. It was put together about four hundred years ago in Oxford, Cambridge and London by more than fifty scholars over a number of years and still remains the English Word of God. Revisions have not touched the hem of its majestic garment. There are those who believe that the English Churches, especially the Church of England for which this work was originally commissioned, will only find the way back to the true path and to the hearts of a mass congregation when the King James Bible is reclaimed, when this version is put back in the centre of its worship.

This bible had a spiritual effect on those who attended church and heard it and on those whose prize possession it was in their home, where for centuries it was read aloud. It has informed the English language more powerfully even than Shakespeare. It enabled the political debates in the seventeenth-century civil wars in Britain and its stories and sentences were used from then on in the debates about rights and justice and democracy, especially in the United States of America. Not least is its presence felt in key speeches by Martin Luther King, for instance, and President John F. Kennedy. It can be seen as an influence on writers from John Milton to John Steinbeck, on Negro spirituals and gospel songs and popular musical lyrics. It has for centuries been both a sacred text and a fund of tales, parables, wonders and wise sayings, and it is still today accepted by many as the very Word of God.

It is worth dwelling for a moment on the name of the book. It is King James's Bible. It is the gift of the monarch. It is the property of the king. It has royal authority going before it. It declares that God and King James are as one and that the authority of the kings and queens of this country is sanctified by God Almighty Himself through this Word. (Some also say it was the final proof that God was English.) It has underpinned English speaking colonisation.

After the death of Queen Elizabeth I, King James VI of Scotland travelled south to claim his new throne. He was well fit to become, as he would, the patron of this bible. He had studied other bibles – in several languages – throughout his childhood and written religious sonnets. Benson Bobrick described him as 'a true bibliophile'. He came from a Scotland in a ferment of Presbyterianism, a country in which the Puritans distrusted any evidence of Anglican imagery that borrowed (as much still did, even more than sixty years after the Reformation) from Rome. The Puritans were also against the bishops and distrustful of links between kingship and the Church.

James seems to have had a passion for unity. On his twenty-first birthday, already James VI of Scotland, this physically rather unprepossessing young man – he had over-prominent eyes and, it was said, 'waddled like a duck' owing to a bout of rickets in childhood – summoned the great men of Scotland to walk through the streets of Edinburgh hand in hand. We are told that the

The title page of the 1568 'Bishops' Bible'.

warlords submitted to this royal request and that their novel unity did indeed see out the whole day.

England, centralised under the Tudors, must have seemed a haven, but as he set out on his royal progress south James was beset by English Puritans. Clearly coordinated petitions reached him from all parts of the country. One of them, the Millenary Petition, had been signed by a thousand ministers. It attacked the bishops and called for further reformation of the Church. Reformation fever had not abated: they wrote against 'the superstitious ceremonies and tirannie of Prelates'. The bishops mounted their own counter-attack on the new king, who decided to hold a conference. Delayed because of a plague, it was convened in Hampton Court in January 1604. Apart from anything else it would give the king the opportunity to demonstrate his brilliance in theological debate.

At first it seemed that the king listed towards the arguments of the Puritans. One commentator, Lancelot Andrewes, wrote, 'the King did wonderfully play the Puritan that day'. But the gravitational pull of a centralised monarchy intertwined with a centralised Church with one man head of both was far too strong. 'No Bishop, no King,' was James's terse conclusion. He had nobbled the arguments of the Puritans by the ingenious device of laying on them the burden of proof. It was up to them, he said, to prove that there were writings in the Bible which openly condemned such matters as the bishops' administration of confirmation, the use of the cross in baptism, the ring in the wedding ceremony, kneeling for communion or the very existence of the bishops themselves. They could not.

John Reynolds, one of the leading Puritans, suggested during this debate, perhaps to salvage something for the losing side or perhaps sensing that he had found a cunning opportunity to further the Puritan cause in the long run, 'May it please Your Majesty that the bible be new translated'. James, flattered, approved, with strict conditions. The work got under way almost immediately.

There were several bibles at large, but of the flock two were most used. One, translated by the bishops in 1568 and henceforth known as the Bishops' Bible, was Elizabeth's own. The frontispiece showed Elizabeth and her ministers presiding over a Church dominated by bishops. The Puritans saw it as an instrument of the royalist-episcopal forces of neo-Papism and preferred the version of English Calvinists translated in Geneva in the 1550s, called, inevitably, the Geneva Bible. The great feature of this translation was the huge number of notes. These could be openly anti-royalist. The word 'tyrant', for instance, not used once in the King James version, appears over four hundred times in the Geneva version.

The Bishops' Bible was already a royal work. Despite its clunking prose (instead of 'cast thy bread upon the waters', the bishops wrote, 'lay thy bread upon wet faces') and its low reputation, James insisted that it be the bedrock of the new translation. In the end less than 8 per cent of the King James version was derived from the bishops, evidence not only of a lack of enthusiasm among the new translators but, more importantly, of a stealthily executed lack of loyalty which proved that the Bible was seen as a melding pot, rife with deliberate ambiguities to allow numerous interpretations.

King James laid down other rules. These were kept. He decreed that 'no marginal notes should be allowed – having found them which are annexed to the Geneva translation . . . some notes very partial, untrue, seditious and savouring too much of dangerous and traitorous comments'. This is a clear recognition of the political power of the Bible: James was on to it. In the royal draft document of 'Rules to be obeyed', there were fourteen rules of King James, including the process of delivering of authority; first to those chosen to lead the translation teams from the conservative universities of Oxford and Cambridge, then to the bishops, the Privy Council and finally the king himself. Moreover, this translation would be the only one that could be read in churches, this and 'no other'.

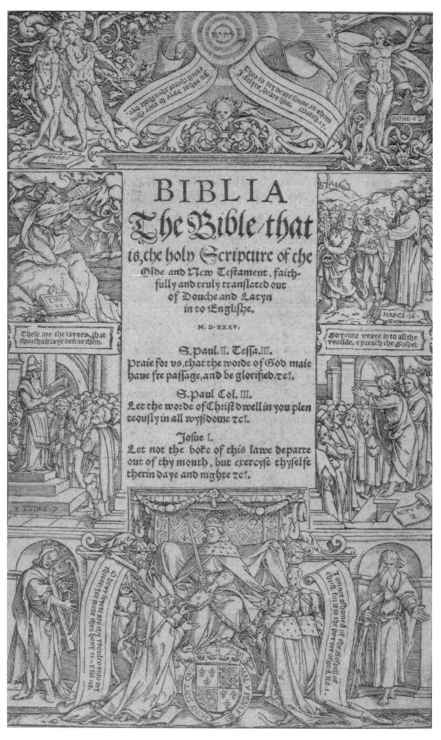

The title page of the 1535 Coverdale Bible.

Translation was regarded as a high and serious art. Miles Smith, in his preface to the King James version, wrote: 'Translation it is that openeth the window, to let in the light; that breaketh the shell, that we may eat the kernel; that pulleth aside the curtain, that we may look into the most Holy place; that removeth the cover of the well, that we may come by the water; even as Jacob rolled away the stone from the mouth of the well.'

There were six groups of translators, each one called a 'company'. It was an age of companies – the actors' companies are well remembered now but at that turn of the century, when the small island off the mainland of Europe turned its eyes, its trade, its intelligences and its guns on the globe itself, the word ran regally through the land – the Muscovy Company; the Levant Company; the Guinea Company for West Africa; and the East India Company, given royal approval in 1600.

Each of the six translating companies (numerologists have pointed out that six is the number of the Trinity multiplied by the number of the testaments) had eight members, which made forty-eight translators, each company led by a director. Forty-eight is the number of the Apostles multiplied by the four evangelists. They were a formidable translating force.

The First Westminster Group, for example, to which was assigned Genesis through to the Second Book of Kings, was led by Lancelot Andrewes, the Dean of Westminster. He learned fifteen languages including Latin, Greek, Hebrew, Syriac and Chaldee. According to Benson Bobrick, from whose work much of this information is taken, T. S. Eliot much admired his gifts of language, saying he had a way of 'taking a word and deriving a word from it'. John Reynolds, who had suggested the project in the first place, whose Puritan-leaning views were known, was in the First Oxford Company. They tackled Isaiah to Malachi. The Second Oxford Company took on the Gospels, Acts and Revelation. And so it went. They laboured for six years.

It is worth mentioning here, I think, the two greatest precursors in the long battle to see the Bible translated into English. Both of them were scholars of Oxford, once thought of as a docile medieval preparatory school for future tools of the establishment of the day. Not the case with these two men, John Wycliffe and William Tyndale. Both were devoted to the idea of a bible printed in the common language of the land. Both gave their lives to this task. Both were persecuted and hounded by a Roman Catholic England which wanted no voice heard but its own official and closely guarded Latin.

Under cover of sympathetic protectors and helped by equally zealous and bold young men from Oxford, especially Nicholas Hereford, a fine translator, Wycliffe produced and published the first bible in English. It was a best-seller but the Church moved against him with a show trial in 1382 in Blackfriars in London. Wycliffe was accused of heresy. His bible was banned, his followers condemned. Wycliffe became ill, paralysed by a stroke, and died in 1384.

In 1521, four years after Luther's revolutionary pamphlet was nailed on the church door at Wittenberg, as the Reformation began to burn through Europe, William Tyndale started to preach in public and set out on a journey which would, in my opinion, lead to an enrichment of the English language greater than that made by any other man. He was forced into exile in the Low Countries; he saw his translation of the Bible reach England despite the search-and-destroy mission of the king's navy and the burning of his books on the steps of St Paul's Cathedral by the Bishop of London. Henry VIII set his spies and assassins on him and in 1536, some years after Henry had turned Protestant and was crying out for English translations of the Bible, the assassins caught up with Tyndale and strangled him. But his bible lives on. It is the body of the King James version, the greatest quarry of our language.

'We never sought to make a new translation,' wrote Smith in his preface, 'nor yet a bad one to make a good one, but to make a good one better; or out of many good ones, one principal good one.'

Arguments still gather around the question – whose bible is it?

Both Adam Nicolson, in his book *Power and Glory: Jacobean England and the Making of the King James Bible* and Benson Bobrick, in his *The Making of the English Bible*, are in no doubt that the King James version is taken from many bibles, Tyndale's most of all, though enriched and rephrased by the fifty or so scholars in crucial often small ways which transform the originals and allow the King James version to stand certain on its own. There had been several bibles produced since Tyndale's version: the Coverdale Bible in 1535, largely poached from Tyndale; the Matthew Bible in 1537, an amalgam of Tyndale and Coverdale; and the Great Bible of 1539, again much taken from Tyndale. This had an introduction by Cranmer and became the official bible.

All these went into the King James version, printed by Robert Barker, 'Printer to the King's Most Excellent Majestie', in 1611. One passage illustrates dramatically how these several versions could be, as it were, stitched together. It is from Paul's Epistle to the Corinthians.

> You are also helping [Bishops' Bible] together [Geneva, 1557] by [Bishops' Bible] prayer for us, that [Tyndale] for the [Geneva, 1560] gift [Great Bible] bestowed upon us [Geneva, 1557] by the means of many [Tyndale] by [Geneva, 1557] many on our behalf [Tyndale].

This, in my view, though totally accurate does not give a proper picture of what was going on. Nailing my colours to Tyndale, I would contend (and few oppose this on a word count) that at least 80 per cent and probably more comes from William Tyndale.

The argument then moves on. Though this is admitted, some-times rather grudgingly, the point made by Nicolson and Bobrick –

both of whom know far more than I do — is that it is the modifications made by the King James scholars which are critically important. They call as their chief witness T. S. Eliot, who spoke of the King James version's 'auditory imagination . . . a feeling for syllable and rhythm, penetrating far below the conscious levels of thought and feeling, invigorating every word'.

Tyndale is, in effect, dismissed as the journeyman, almost the journalist, the bluffer, the scaffolder lacking the richness of scholarship and the muscle for rhythm displayed by James's scholars.

Examples are produced to prove this case and it is worth examining a few of them.

This is Tyndale's opening to Genesis, and perhaps it is important to stress that Tyndale wrote a bible to be read aloud, to be preached from, and this vital basic thrust, I suggest, was appropriated wholesale by the King James scholars (I have updated the spelling throughout):

> In the beginning God created heaven and earth. The earth was void and empty, and darkness was upon the deep and the spirit of God moved upon the water.

According to Adam Nicolson, the Geneva Bible took Tyndale's opening and made it 'more fluent':

> In the beginning God created the heaven and the earth. And the earth was without form and void, and darkness was upon the deep, and the Spirit of God moved upon the waters.

For 'more fluent' I would substitute 'less dramatic, less telling'. The definite article softens it — Tyndale's 'heaven and earth' is bolder than 'the heaven and the earth'. I would make a similar judgement in favour of Tyndale's 'the earth was void and empty', far bleaker and more harsh than 'and the earth was without form, and void'. I have read both aloud and see no gain in fluency, much loss in tension.

The King James version, worked on by the awe-inspiring Lancelot Andrewes, provokes ecstasy in Nicolson, Bobrick and T. S. Eliot. It reads:

> In the beginning God created the heaven, and the earth. And the earth was without form, and void, and darkness was upon the face of the deep. And the Spirit of God moved upon the face of the waters.

Thirty-nine words compared to Tyndale's twenty-nine. Again Tyndale's 'void and empty' strikes me as finer than 'without form and void', more sure of itself, clearer. Nicolson makes much of the comma after 'Heaven' and the colon after 'deep', by which he says Andrewes adds an 'aural fluency . . . a pace of deliberate and magisterial slowness'. First I would question whether the art of punctuation in the time and condition of Tyndale's publication was as advanced as it became. More importantly, I would suggest that any practised public reader will find in Tyndale's version the 'aural fluency' and the 'deliberate and magisterial slowness' for himself or herself. I think it is impossible to be in any sense final in a comparative judgement here. But Tyndale must take the palm for his originality and the choice of what are the key words – 'void', 'darkness', 'the face of the deep'. In my view, 'the face of the waters' in the King James version might possibly be regarded as unnecessary repetition and Tyndale's 'upon the water' more ominous.

The same polishing but diminishing of Tyndale's work can be seen in the shortest phrases. Take one line: 'Jesus Christ, the same yesterday, and today, and for ever'.

The King James version takes Tyndale's words but amends them to: 'Jesus Christ the same, yesterday, and today, and for ever'.

'The martyrdome of Master William Tindall in Flanders.'

The revising of Andrew Downes, who did this, was to do with sound, not with sense. 'If the words are arranged in this way, the statement will be more majestic.' As well as revealing the desire to please His Majesty, the statement reveals an attitude a little apart from that concentrated intention to be true to God's Word which drove Tyndale. And once again I beg to differ with the judgement. I think that Tyndale, by introducing the words 'the same' immediately after 'Jesus Christ', sets the agenda for the sentence in such a way as to open up its wonder. By comparison the Downes version seems a mite tricksy.

Here is a final example from the New Testament, from the Last Supper. Tyndale reads:

> And he took bread, and gave thanks, and brake it, and gave it unto them, saying: 'This is my body which is given for you, this do in remembrance of me.' Likewise, also, when they had supped, he took the cup, saying: 'This is the cup, the new testament, in my blood, which shall for you be shed.'

Adam Nicolson comments: 'The 1611 translators took that over, as so much else from Tyndale, very nearly wholesale, altering only the very last phrase, changing "which shall for you be shed" to the more accurate, pregnant and memorable "which is shed for you", a change, as ever, which is minuscule but formative.'

Once again I disagree. When Tyndale says 'which shall for you be shed' he is saying so much more than 'which is shed for you'. He is being more accurate, predicting his bloody crucifixion. As importantly, by saying 'for you be shed' he makes us think of an individual, a disciple, a follower, oneself, a particular person in receipt of this great gift. 'Shed for you' lets the word 'you' escape into ambiguity: is it singular or plural? While to end the sentence with 'you' is once again much softer and less Word-of-God-like than 'shed'.

This is not to deny that there was some finer tuning, some enrichment, some added resonance. Yet at its heart, this is still the bible of Tyndale. We listen in wonder at the most profound sermon ever given and it is to these words, Tyndale's original words, that we listen:

Blessed are the poor in spirit: for theirs is the kingdom of heaven.

Blessed are they that mourn: for they shall be comforted.

Blessed are the meek: for they shall inherit the earth.

Blessed are they which do hunger and thirst after righteousness: for they shall be filled.

Blessed are the merciful: for they shall obtain mercy.

Blessed are the pure in heart: for they shall see God.

Blessed are the peacemakers: for they shall be called the children of God . . .

That is true majesty, I think, and it is, as well, the pulse which will beat through much of the most ambitious English language, poetry and prose and song for centuries to follow.

Nor did the Bible's gift to the language stop there. Tyndale introduced hundreds of new words and phrases into a vocabulary we still use today. 'Let there be light'; 'the powers that be'; 'my brother's keeper'; 'filthy lucre'; 'fight the good fight'; 'flowing with milk and honey'; 'the apple of his eye'; 'a man after his own heart'; 'the spirit is willing but the flesh is weak'; 'signs of the times'; 'ye of little faith'; 'eat, drink and be merry'; 'broken-hearted'; 'clear-eyed' and more, many more. We talk Tyndale daily.

What the King James version has is an atmosphere of instant antiquity which the scholars must have knowingly engineered. It was printed in Gothic type in folio format (16 by 10 inches). It was laid out in double columns with ornamental capitals at the beginning of every chapter. In the beginning this rather backfired. It was thought too old-fashioned. The Puritans were to stick to their

Geneva version for some time. Over the years, however, that sense of antiquity began to work in its favour. It did indeed acquire the aura of God's Word in English. The idea of the English and God having a unique compact, an idea most likely borrowed from the Old Testament and the experience of the Jews, had arrived on the scene in England as early as the seventh century. Here it was sealed and, it was thought, sanctified. George Bernard Shaw had his say. 'To this day,' he wrote, 'the common Britisher or citizen of the United States of North America, accepts and worships it as the single book by a single author, the book being the Book of Books and the author being God.'

It is a book that has had a strong formative effect on other books by great writers such as John Milton, John Bunyan, Walt Whitman, Daniel Defoe, William Wordsworth, D. H. Lawrence, Gerard Manley Hopkins and T. S. Eliot. And for generations, when church attendance was nigh compulsory and most schools began their day with a church service including readings from the Bible, millions of young people were fed poetic prose so fine it lasted a lifetime and provided an unmatchable set of keys to the word-world. In the old colonies and the old commonwealth, the Bible and this version of the Bible became the staple of serious talk, of moralising, of wise saws and ancient instances, of vocabulary and tutelary stories. For many it was their skin of language.

It made its way everywhere, in the hymns in the Anglican Church, in the hymns of the Methodist and other nonconformist churches, and some of the hymn writers, such as John Wesley, fully capable of memorable lines, set to memorable melodies, carried words from the Bible across hills and fields the earth over. The laments of the early Afro-Americans and their liberationist spirituals used the words and deeds in the Bible all the time, and these flowed into soul music, into the blues, even into pop music. The Bible was a goldmine for the nuggets which inspire fine lyrics.

Makers of many speeches have reached for the sonorities of Tyndale and the Elizabethan scholars. After Martin Luther King said, 'I have a dream that one day every valley shall be exalted, every hill and mountain shall be made low', he quoted directly from Isaiah, chapter 40, verses 4–5 in the King James version: 'the rough places will be made plain and the crooked places will be made straight, and the glory of the Lord shall be revealed, and all flesh shall see it together'. In his inaugural address, John F. Kennedy also quoted from Isaiah, chapter 58, verse 6: 'Let both sides unite to heed, in all corners of the earth, the command of Isaiah – to "undo the heavy burdens, and to let the oppressed go free."' A quotation from Romans, chapter 12, verse 12 appears in another resounding passage: 'Now the trumpet summons us again – not as a call to bear arms, though arms we need – not as a call to battle, though embattled we are – but as a call to bear the burden of a long twilight struggle, year in and year out, "rejoicing in hope, patient in tribulation", a struggle against the common enemies of man: tyranny, poverty, disease and war itself.'

Today, in Northern Ireland, the Reverend Ian Paisley, a pastor of the Free Presbyterian congregation, defends the King James version with vigour, although King James himself may have wondered at the turn of history which led to one of those he once thought of as being dissident appearing so hot in defence of 'his' bible.

'Then there arose a glorious company of translators,' Paisley writes,

> who set to work to give the world the Bible in their mother tongue . . . I hail this book this day. It remains amid the passing and injuries of time a holy temple, unprofaned by the foot of the enemy. It remains an invincible building of God amidst the crumbling ruins of the century. God has preserved his book and will preserve it.

'Explorer David Livingstone reads the Bible to his men' — an engraving from 1874.

Although the Pilgrim Fathers took the Geneva Bible to America, the set-apart, embattled Puritan character of the settlers quite soon loosened its hold as they became the establishment. They were a people of the book and as their settlements grew in size and strength, so they enforced the teachings of the Bible with, as it were, a 'state' authority and support which King James would have recognised and even envied. As Adam Nicolson points out, in seventeenth-century Massachusetts, heresy, witchcraft, profanity, idolatry and breaking the Sabbath were all civil offences to be dealt with by the civil courts. It needed a bible to match its new condition: the Geneva separatist version had served its purpose. America turned to and embraced and embraces still the King James version.

The consequences of that are hard to overestimate. It was a factor in enforcing the primacy of English as the language of the new continent-nation. It was a factor in giving its citizens a deep loyalty to the Word of God which persists to this day to the extent that every day in the White House begins with a prayer and the current president of the United States unblushingly reveals that God talks directly to him and uses his Christian name. The grip that Protestantism has on the United States is strong, and fundamentally influential in its political practices. The majesty of the language, so transparently established in America's great public spoken moments, such as Lincoln's Gettysburg Address, informs and is embraced by the leading democratic nation on the planet. Through this bible the Protestant voice in English became the ruling tongue of two successive world empires. It also said to the world that Christianity was the leading faith, the Christian God the one true God and Christ the true and only Redeemer. This bible has had more impact on the ideology of the last four centuries than any other creed, manifesto or dogma.

The publication of the Bible in English and its reach, through the churches, to so many people whose ancestors had been hitherto ignorant of its content enabled there to be common debate and discussion. This undoubtedly helped lay the ground for democracy.

Now that this Bible of many books, of tumultuous, extraordinary, awesome events, Delphic sayings and fierce strictures, was on the street, argument was licensed. You could make criticism of tyranny through a debate on one of the Kings; you could plan revolution through a discussion of the true meaning of the Sermon on the Mount; you could out-prophesy the prophets and talk of vengeance, justice, a promised land, another Eden, a City of God to be attained on earth – through impeccably correct religious references to the Bible. The Bible could set you free.

In the English Civil War, a furnace of ideological conflict, Charles I was convinced that unrestricted access to the Bible, conjured up and enforced by his father, had nourished the discontent of the people. Throughout the Civil War, one extreme group after another sought and found the justification for its radical social views and political actions in the sacred pages of the King James version.

Yet after the Civil War, this began to change, and change quite rapidly. The King James version was now seen as a bedrock of monarchy and of Englishness. And so it remained for more than three hundred years until, in a misguided fit of mere modernising, it was 'revised', that is to say adulterated, diminished, stripped of everything that had made it last and made it count.

It was a small step from the English Civil War to the American civil rights movement: in both, the Bible was key as an inspiration against brutal and tyrannical authority. Yet in America, as in England three hundred years previously, once the blood was let, the King James version reverted to its natural home, which is at the centre of a Christian state. It was a position planned for it by the theologically brilliant Scot who rode south from Edinburgh to claim the throne left him by Elizabeth I. He was determined to see the authority of the crown fortressed by the Word of God. The greater consequence was the production and publication of a book of continuing universal influence.

TIMELINE
THE KING JAMES BIBLE

1611   The King James Bible is published

In Jamestown, Virginia, attendance of daily morning and evening prayers is made mandatory under 'Dales Laws'

1624   Virginia becomes a royal colony, required to conform to the Church of England

1636   King Charles I decides to impose the Anglican Prayer Book on Scotland

1642   The English Civil War begins

*c.*1660   Birth of Daniel Defoe whose great list of publications drew significantly on the King James Bible

1667   John Milton publishes *Paradise Lost*, his work is greatly influenced by the King James Bible

1678   John Bunyan publishes the first part of *The Pilgrim's Progress*, arguably one of the most widely known Christian allegories ever written

1691   Freedom of worship is guaranteed in New England and New York for all Protestants

1699   Thomas Bray founds the Society for Promoting Christian Knowledge (SPCK)

1701   Thomas Bray founds the Society for the Propagation of the Gospel, which sponsors over three hundred missionaries in the colonies over the next century

1776   The Declaration of Independence by American colonies. Two-thirds of the signatories are nominal members of the Church of England

1794   The Missionary Society, later named the London Missionary Society, is founded, aiming to spread Christian knowledge to the 'unenlightened' nations

1807   Following the abolition of the slave trade, Anglican missionaries convert large numbers in Sierra Leone and much of West Africa. One of these missionaries was Samuel Ajayi Crowther, a liberated slave educated by the Anglican Church Missionary Society and ordained first as a priest and then as the first black bishop in Africa

1814   The Anglican Mission is established at the Bay of Islands, New Zealand

1821   Sierra Leone, Gambia and the Gold Coast are combined to form British West Africa

1834   The Anglican British Church Missionary Society and the American Foreign Mission Society send missionaries to China

1850   Scottish missionary David Livingstone's exploration of Africa paves the way for missionaries, European adventurers and traders

1863   Abraham Lincoln draws on the King James Bible in his Gettysburg Address

1875   Bugandan King Mutesa allows Christian missionaries to enter his realm

1878   Livingstonia Central Africa Mission Company from Scotland begins work to develop a river route into Central Africa to enable trade

1899   The Gideon Society is formed in Janesville, Wisconsin

1901   The American Standard Version of the Bible is published

1906   The English Hymnal is published

1908   The Gideon Soceity votes to place bibles in all hotel rooms and within twenty years the association has distributed one million bibles

1921   Canadian School of Missions begins to train Anglicans, among others, for overseas missions

1928   New US Prayer Book is published

1940   Winston Churchill draws on the King James Bible in his 'Finest Hour' speech inaugurating the Battle of Britain

1947   Church of South India is formed as a result of the union of Anglican, Presbyterian, Methodist, and Congregational churches

1952   Revised Standard Version of the Bible is published and proves enormously popular

1961   John F. Kennedy's inaugural address quotes extensively from the King James Bible

1963   Martin Luther King delivers his 'I have a dream' speech containing a number of King James references

1970   The Church of North India is formed, uniting Anglicans, Presbyterians, Methodists and Congregationalists

1977   Ronald Reagan makes a radio broadcast devoted to the superiority of the King James Bible

1983   Ian Paisley publishes 'The Authority of the Scriptures vs. the Confusion of the Translations' on the unique and special nature of the King James Bible

1986   New English Hymnal is published

2000   The Book of Common Prayer now exists in 170 languages

AN INQUIRY INTO THE NATURE AND CAUSES OF THE WEALTH OF NATIONS

1776

by

Adam Smith

A N

I N Q U I R Y

INTO THE

Nature and Caufes

OF THE

WEALTH of NATIONS.

By ADAM SMITH, LL. D. and F. R. S.
Formerly Profeffor of Moral Philofophy in the Univerfity of GLASGOW.

IN TWO VOLUMES.

VOL. I.

LONDON:

PRINTED FOR W. STRAHAN; AND T. CADELL, IN THE STRAND,
MDCCLXXVI.

Adam Smith's book, commonly known as *The Wealth of Nations*, was published in the same year as the American Declaration of Independence It has been argued that the global effect of Smith's work has exceeded that of the American constitutionalists. And if the wealth of a nation or a people is the foundation of all else, then from Hong Kong and Shanghai to Peru, from the oil and gas fields of Russia to the United States itself, from Estonia to Australia, it can be claimed that the principles and economic dynamics at work in all these places come from a book by a scholar of Scotland published before the French Revolution, before the Industrial Revolution and eighty-four years before *Das Kapital* by Karl Marx.

Alan Greenspan, the American economic guru, writing of Adam Smith with regard to his contemporaries, says, 'one hears a good deal of Franz Joseph Haydn in the string quartets of Wolfgang Amadeus Mozart; yet to my ear, at least, Mozart rose to a plateau beyond anything Haydn and his contemporaries were able to reach. So, too, in his sphere, did Smith.' Compared with some claims made for his work (the bible of capitalism; the founding text in modern economics) Greenspan's is a comparatively modest tribute, but it does show how highly regarded Smith still is by current leaders and thinkers, a verdict expanded by the admiration and influence expressed for it by the leading political duo of the 1980s, Margaret Thatcher and Ronald Reagan, whose economic policies reintroduced Smith's idea to great and often devastating effect. On the negative side, anti-capitalist enemies and doubters of the word of Adam Smith believe that *The Wealth of Nations* unleashed unbridled rapacity, licensed greed and ignored inequality and suffering.

For some time, Adam Smith's reputation suffered because of the ascendance of Karl Marx who, it appeared, occupied much of the same ground but with greater authority. Time has seen the influence of Marx, outside the universities and among those few still convinced by the sweep of his ideas, decline catastrophically. The great states, most particularly Russia and China, which shaped themselves around his theories, have collapsed into the arms of a Western capitalism whose two chief props – the Industrial Revolution and free trade capitalism – owe a great debt to Smith. Smith's impact on the formation of economic policy and on its progress has been and remains prodigious. As often, if not invariably, happened with the other books I have selected, his work appeared at precisely the time it could become the template of a new age of thought.

Adam Smith was born in 1723 in Kirkcaldy, Fife, Scotland, and brought up by his widowed mother. We are told that as a child he was kidnapped by gypsies but rescued by his uncle. That seems to have cured him of any taste for drama. His future was dominated by immersion in books and mostly solitary study. He concentrated on mathematics and moral philosophy at Glasgow University and continued his studies at Oxford for another seven years. He never married. He is described as a shy man, sometimes quite spectacularly absent-minded – he fell into a pit of tar as he was walking, thinking, down the street; he would walk fifteen miles along country lanes after getting up, still in his dressing gown, working out some problem; he brewed his bread and butter instead of tea. After his mother died a maiden cousin looked after him.

In 1751 he was appointed to the chair of Logic and Moral

Philosophy at the University of Glasgow where he lectured on theology, ethics and jurisprudence. Despite or perhaps because of his extremely nervous public manner, faltering speech and weakness for lengthy digressions (which could have been not only endearing but welcome to students still largely taught by rote) he achieved fame as a lecturer and attracted students from as far afield as Russia. His method of composition was perambulatory, in his study, where he would walk up and down dictating to his secretary, and again pursuing impromptu hunches. A near-contemporary, Jean-Baptiste Say, described *The Wealth of Nations* as 'a vast chaos of just ideas, pell-mell with pieces of positive knowledge'. His mind was said to be an immense library, his memory phenomenal.

The only interruption to this monkish, learned life was the unexpected bonus of a Grand Tour. In 1763 he was appointed tutor to the young Duke of Buccleugh, whom he accompanied first to Paris where he met several of the leading intellectuals, the *'philosophes'*. In Paris for almost a year, he discussed political economy with Turgot and Necker, among others. It is thought that it was the physician to Madame de Pompadour who taught him the doctrine of the physiocrats. This was a loosely associated group of intellectuals who were working on new theories as to what really constituted a nation's wealth. They were coming to the conclusion that what made a nation rich was not the amount of bullion within the land (as had been thought from antiquity), but the productivity of its farms and agricultural industries. Smith was intrigued by these new and radical ideas. He was to build on them, though he would deviate from them quite essentially after twenty-five years of thought and study.

Back in London and Edinburgh he continued with his studies and his rewarding friendships. He read widely, loved poetry and could recite long excerpts in Latin, Greek, French and Italian, as well as in English. The philosopher David Hume was a close friend and influence. He was a clubman in both cities and enjoyed the

Adam Smith: 'It is not from the benevolence of the butcher, the brewer or the baker that we expect our dinner, but from their regard for their own interest.'

conversation of Edmund Burke, Samuel Johnson and Edward Gibbon. He was a compulsive book collector and amassed a huge personal library of works on history, science, astronomy, philosophy, physics and poetry.

At the age of thirty-six he published his college lectures in a volume called *The Theory of Moral Sentiments*. This brought him immediate fame. It was this which prompted the then equivalent of the Chancellor of the Exchequer to engage him as a tutor for the Grand Tour on which, after Paris, he went on to Geneva to meet Voltaire. Wherever he went he collected and catalogued ideas, opinions and information, not unlike Charles Darwin, building up a personally tailored encyclopaedia, consulting others of many disciplines, patient, determined, with the unbending aim of substantiating theory with evidence.

Having gathered his forces, it took Smith ten years to dictate the book. At the time the science of political economy did not exist. In *The Wealth of Nations*, Smith used analytical tools logically to investigate his subject, making deductions from observations of history, seeing patterns and mechanisms in the communal relations between individuals and nations, adducing principles. The scientific method exemplified and honed by Newton had struck deep. But Smith's observations and conclusions were also based on his conviction that man was a moral and social animal, not just one driven by appetite. Science must go hand in hand with sympathy for the human condition – overlooked by some of his more zealous disciples and disbelieved by some of his more severe critics.

The book was well received nationally and internationally but one distinguished and powerful reader above all may be said to have amplified Smith's message. Through this man's political power and that of a country which was to head the Industrial Revolution, *The Wealth of Nations* came to catalyse not only Britain's prevailing thought on economic theory but also its prevailing practice. The younger Pitt, who was to become George III's prime minister (in which position he would also help Wilberforce), became an early convert to and proselytiser of Smith's theory of free trade. The book was given the seal of the government.

Smith died in 1790, widely admired by scholars and, largely through Pitt, widely read and of influence in government circles. There were those suspicious of him because of his friendship with Hume and rumours of his influence on the French Revolution, but he died well appreciated. His influence expanded swiftly. Within twenty years of his death, one writer described him as 'after Napoleon the greatest monarch in Europe'. In 1846, the crucial and defining abolition of the Corn Laws was effected by disciples of Smith. At the 1984 Republican convention, delegates wore badges with his image on them as they cheered Ronald Reagan. Tony Blair uses Smith's arguments to criticise and reform the European Common Agricultural Policy. He continues to be a shaping intellect.

In summarising Smith's work I am principally indebted to Alan Krueger, Emma Rothschild and Jones and Skinner.

As Smith himself considered *The Theory of Moral Sentiments* (1759) to be a precursor of *The Wealth of Nations* it is worth looking at that book first. Smith did not regard himself as an economist but a philosopher and it could be argued that this, his first book, most clearly demonstrates his overall moral philosophy.

The book is an investigation of how moral judgements can be explained if we are driven primarily by self-interest. Smith said that all of us have the capacity to feel for others; out of sympathy will come justice and benevolence. We judge ourselves constantly and work towards pleasing others by our good conduct. Smith saw morality as a matter which began in imagination – to imagine the other person was to begin to sympathise with him/her – and he saw wealth creation too as a capacity bred by imagination – imagining ourselves becoming wealthier; 'it is this deception', he wrote, 'which rouses and keeps in motion the industry of mankind.' He then moved on to more controversial territory.

'The rich,' he wrote,

> consume little more than the poor and in spite of their natural selfishness and rapacity, though they mean only their own conveniency . . . they divide with the poor the produce of all their improvements. They are led by an invisible hand to make the same distribution of the necessities of life which would have been made had the earth been divided into equal portions among its inhabitants . . . thus without intending it, without knowing it [the rich] advance the interests of society.

This rather degenerated into the phrase 'the trickle-down effect' in the Britain and America of the 1980s and was much derided. If, though, by 'the rich' we mean those who create the true wealth of nations, Smith's apologists could argue that owing partly to the effect of his work, since the end of the eighteenth century when a marked rise in the standards of living and in population began, after millennia of either stagnation or very small growth, it was concentrations of often liquid wealth which drove the upsurge. Since 1820, standards of living have doubled every fifty-eight years, world population has increased by 600 per cent and millions of those whose ancestors were once paupers live like those whose ancestors were once princes.

Yet there is room for criticism here and it has never gone away. Did Smith fully attend to the reality of the lives of those at the bottom of the heap? Did his allocation of duties of the state cover wide enough ground with strong enough injunctions? Smith's central conviction, that self-interest would lead to the noblest actions, has been challenged continuously. But he was firm. Since people look after their own affairs better than anyone else, leave them as free as possible to do so and the result will be increased wealth which will benefit everyone. This, simplistically phrased, is typical of the Scottish Enlightenment in that it blends an optimistic reading of human nature with a reading which sees self-interest as the dynamo of individuals and of society. Straddling those two forces he predicated the greatness of capitalism.

He thought capitalism was a higher stage of human society than had been reached hitherto. He also believed it could be improved. It broke the back of the long history of slaves, serfs and the subjugated toiling for those who had successfully set themselves, it sometimes appeared immovably, above the mass. It broke the idea of a life fixed in one rut – like father, like son, with, for the majority, low life expectancy, no advance, no progress since time immemorial and for ever. This had been the history, often declared the fate, of the mass of mankind and Smith saw a way to change it radically. It was his great good fortune that along with the man came the technology which, pointed in the right (i.e. Adam Smith's) direction, would change the world.

The economic society of the past was wrong, he thought, and could be overturned. If we believe that in the hard-faced area of economics a book is less of an instrument, more of an ornament, it is worth recording the words of the later and hugely influential economist, John Maynard Keynes, who wrote, 'Practical men, who believe themselves to be quite exempt from intellectual influences, are usually the slaves of some defunct economist . . . who hear voices in the air, are distilling their frenzy from some academic scribbler of a few years back.'

Central to the philosophy of *The Wealth of Nations* was the belief that the human drive to self-betterment is innate. As a view of humanity, that was fatally qualified in the twentieth century. Self-betterment had very little to do with the Holocaust, the pogroms, the Gulag, the roll-calls of genocide, terrorism and oppression. Yet Smith's view of life has transferred profitably into the marketplace.

'It is not', he wrote, 'from the benevolence of the butcher, the brewer or the baker that we expect our dinner, but from their regard for their own interest. We address ourselves not to their humanity but to their self-love, and never talk to them of our own necessities but of their own advantages.' This has been key ever since, from the butcher and the baker to the privatisations of BT and BA – though often it is argued that the Smithian view shuts out the weak and puts down the disadvantaged.

Smith extended the economic view of the French *philosophes* he had met in Paris. He thought their focus on agriculture was too limited. He came to believe that a nation's wealth lay in 'the exchangeable value of the annual produce of its lands and labour' or that the basis of any nation's wealth would lie in the extent to which it carried on trade.

The prevailing idea of the day, and one which Smith opposed root and branch, was mercantilism. Mercantilism was the economic theory that trade generates wealth and is stimulated by the accumulation of profitable balances, which a government should encourage by means of protectionism.

Smith saw mercantilism as a protection racket, supported by guilds, nationally regulated apprenticeships and private companies such as the East India Company. He saw this as fatally restricted compared with capitalism, which was a liberating way of spreading wealth throughout society. It was all relative, he believed, and although the wealth of a prince far exceeded that of a poor man on one of his estates, yet through the more efficient distribution of wealth that poor man would gain in wealth and lift himself above comparably 'poor men' in countries untouched by capitalism. It may seem commonplace now to say that wealth is the result of the productive labour of the nation's people and the cause of wealth is trade, but at a time when wealth was piles of gold and silver and trade was wholly protectionist, this was revolutionary talk.

the dealers, by raifing their profits above what they naturally would CHAP. be, to levy, for their own benefit, an abfuid tax upon the reft of XI. their fellow citizens. The propofal of any new law or regulation of commerce which comes from this order, ought always to be liftened to with great precaution, and ought never to be adopted till after having been long and carefully examined, not only with the moft fcrupulous, but with the moft fufpicious attention. It comes from an order of men, whofe intereft is never exactly the fame with that of the publick, who have generally an intereft to deceive and even to opprefs the publick, and who accordingly have, upon many occafions, both deceived and oppreffed it.

Years XII.	Price of the Quarter of Wheat each Year.			Average of the different Prices of the fame Year.			The average Price of each Year in Money of the prefent Times.		
	£.	s.	d.	£.	s.	d.	£.	s.	d.
1202	—	12	—	—	—	—	1	16	—
	—	12	—						
1205	—	13	4	—	13	5	2	—	3
	—	15	—						
1223	—	12	—	—	—	—	1	16	—
1237	—	3	4	—	—	—	—	10	—
1243	—	2	—	—	—	—	—	6	—
1244	—	2	—	—	—	—	—	6	—
1246	—	16	—	—	—	—	2	8	—
1247	—	13	4	—	—	—	2	—	—
1257	1	4	—	—	—	—	3	12	—
	1	—	—						
1258	—	15	—	—	17	—	2	11	—
	—	16	—						
1270	4	16	—	5	12	—	16	16	—
	6	8	—						
1286	—	2	8	—	9	4	1	8	—
	—	16	—						
						Total,	35	9	3
						Average Price,	2	19	1¼

The theory Smith opposed had a win-lose dynamic. Pre-Smith, the seller 'won' by making the profit; the buyer 'lost' by parting with his money. In the mercantilist system, wealth was the amount of bullion or the number of coins you had. Smith argued and proved that trade was and, properly conducted, should be seen as a 'win-win' certainty. The seller got the money but the buyer got the goods he wanted and – this is crucial – at a cheaper price than if he tried to produce them himself. He used the example of claret, a familiar French wine with well-heeled bibulous Scots of his day. He argued that with good greenhouses and the right equipment it would be possible to grow wine in Scotland. Therefore no money would go across the water to France. Yet this would be ridiculous since it could be proved that it was far cheaper to buy the claret from France, where grape growing was easier, cheaper and more efficient, and use the money this 'saved' to invest elsewhere. Even better, he argued, when competition intensified between different vendors of claret, the wine could be purchased even more cheaply and even more money could be 'saved' for future investment.

Like Darwin, Smith would often work from the specific to the general: in this case from a family to a nation. 'It is a maxim of every prudent master of a family', he wrote, 'never to attempt to make at home what it would cost him more to make than to buy. And so, what is prudence in the conduct of every family can scarcely be folly in that of a great Kingdom.' Margaret Thatcher's references to the practice of her father in the shop in Grantham have a finer pedigree than many realised at the time.

Madsen Pirie from the Adam Smith Institute addressed the current trade difficulties over Chinese textiles to illustrate the transference of Smith's homely example on to the international stage. In old mercantilism, intellectually demolished by Smith, a country's wealth consisted of what it could hold on to, what was at that time the amount of gold and silver in its coffers. The power gained by one state is inevitably associated with the power lost by another, and the phrase 'the balance of trade' described how good a nation was at protecting its treasure. In that context, the increasing influx of cheap Chinese textiles at the beginning of the twenty-first century would be a cause for great concern. It ought not to be if we follow Smith's rules, argues Pirie. In fact, despite Smith and despite the passing of the theory of mercantilism, it still is an anxiety.

There are, I think, at least two reasons for this. First, there is something in the human psyche which cannot but believe that if you gain as a result of me paying, then you are the richer and I am the poorer – especially on the international stage. As with much other science, the true workings involved here are counter-intuitive. Because the second reason we employ in order to cling to mercantilism is the evidence before our senses. When cotton mills close for ever in Yorkshire and Lancashire, and whole towns become ghost towns; when the 12 million sari makers of India with their tested and ancient methods begin to be mown down by the machine-made saris of the Chinese; when goods from the East pour into the West and threaten what seemed impregnable fortresses of manufacture and then after a short siege capture and destroy them, then there is a 'natural' instinct to say – protect your own bullion, keep the gold and silver even if it is expressed in other less dramatic materials: how can this invasion be other than debilitating?

This is the fear and the moan heard on all sides today in the affluent West. What will happen to us when all our manufacturing is undercut? What will we become if we are not a country which makes things? Especially in Britain with our recent imperial record of manufacture when this dot of an island commanded 35 per cent of world trade, we see the loss of manufacture as the ebbing of our lifeblood and just as it would have been incomprehensible to medieval princes that they could wage war – the favourite occupation of many of them – without gold and silver in their treasury, so it is very difficult for many contemporary Britons to feel that they can manage a profitable peace without the dark satanic mills and mines and factory floors.

But Smith says this is wrong. And Pirie, one of his many current representatives on earth, points out that lobbying for tariffs, as the British and others are doing, is counter-productive. This is not Smith's way. Smith says buyers in Britain and elsewhere will get cheaper goods, Chinese labourers will get money they would not otherwise get, and British manufacturers undercut by the mass production skills of the Chinese (first patented in Britain) can move into making the more upmarket goods that, thanks to the Chinese, the British customer now has the money to buy. Except that to many at the sharp end it feels like the end of their world (which in some cases it is), and anyway, what is to stop the Chinese competing upmarket and further upmarket, undercutting upmarket as they have downmarket? Nevertheless, Smith is firm. His observation is that 'trade which, without force or constraint, is naturally and regularly carried out between any two places, is always advantageous to both.'

Through observations such as this, Pirie maintains, Smith's directive has had the most beneficial impact on the physical human condition of any teaching in history. It has made possible a generation of wealth which has transformed human existence in nations that have broadly adopted his free trade policies. Smith also maintained that free trade was a help in securing international peace; and there is what is sometimes called the McDonald's Theory, which holds that no two nations which follow broadly the same Anglo-Saxon economic model have ever gone to war with each other. (Britain versus Germany twice in the twentieth century could test that a little.)

In his argument to seek out the root of the wealth of nations, Smith argues for the 'Labour Theory of Value', although he realises that it cannot account for everything and acknowledges that the 'market price' will depend on supply and demand among other

The Bread Riot at the entrance to the House of Commons.
The Infamous Corn Laws were repealed in 1846.

factors. But the labour theory of value is central to his model and he argues that 'the value of any commodity to the person who possesses it and who means not to use or consume it himself, but to exchange it for other commodities, is equal to the quantity of labour which it entitles him to purchase or command. Labour, therefore, is the real measure of the exchangeable value of all commodities.' There is, as he acknowledges, much else, but Smith's core assertion has never been seriously challenged.

In his theory of the 'invisible hand', more recently reintroduced as the 'trickle-down effect' – and often dismissed as being a non-event – Smith takes his notion of the benevolence of self-interest into an area not too far removed from Richard Dawkins's 'selfish gene': arguing that the promotion of self-interest is a sure way to promote the greater general interest. Of the rich investor he writes, 'by pursuing his own interest he frequently promotes that of the society more effectually than when he really intends to promote it. I have never known much good done by those who affected to trade for the public good. It is an affectation, indeed, not very common among merchants and very few words need to be employed in dissuading them from it.'

Smith gets three cheers from fully committed disciples for a passage which follows the above, in which he pours scorn on the attempt of the state to invest for the public good. 'The statesman who would attempt to direct private people in what manner they ought to employ their capital, would not only load himself with a most unnecessary attention, but assume an authority which could safely be trusted, not only to no single person, but to no council or senate whatsoever, and which nowhere would be so dangerous as in the hands of a man who had folly and presumption enough to fancy himself fit to exercise it.' It was a doctrine repeated by von Hayek in his effective attack on the socialist command economy whether found as he saw it in the brainwashed misguided East or in some still contaminated nooks in the West.

Smith applied this to the history of famines, or 'dearths' as he called them.

> Whoever examines, with attention, the history of the dearths and famines which have afflicted any part of Europe, during the course of the present or that of the two preceding centuries, of which we have pretty exact accounts, will find, I believe . . . that a famine has never arisen from any other cause but the violence of government attempting, by improper means, to remedy the inconveniences of dearth . . . When the government, in order to remedy the inconveniences of dearth, orders all the dealers to sell their corn at what it supposes a reasonable price, it either hinders them from bringing it to the market, which may sometimes produce a famine even in the beginning of a season; or if they bring it thither, it enables the people and thereby encourages them to consume it so fast as must necessarily produce a famine before the end of the season.

During the Irish famine in the 1840s, this passage was interpreted, or misinterpreted, as Smith's apologists would claim, as being advice against giving any aid at all. And there are many who would argue, from the dozens of famines in Africa alone over the last quarter of a century, that this Smith doctrine leaves out far too much. The idea that left to their own devices people and systems will work out a decent standard of living is thought by Smith's opponents to be near-moonshine. Other major factors, they argue, from drought to genocide, play an important part. Yet the idea that the only way forward for sub-Saharan Africa is to be given the opportunity to free-trade their way out of their difficulties is strongly held and carries conviction.

Like Charles Darwin, Adam Smith was a great classifier and although he did not 'invent' the division of labour he was the first to observe it, classify it and in the context of his book point to its potential. This 'speculation' has been key to the roaring commercial successes of capitalism, burning through old practices first in the West and the USA and now on fire in China and Korea and India. Smith recognised the downside and suggested that an antidote could be government provision of lifelong subsidised education – a suggestion dismissed by Marx as a 'homeopathic dose'.

So we come to what many consider the very heart of the medicine, the free market. The decisive power is wielded by the customer. Smith believed that this would – as it did – enable risks to be taken, a marketplace to be established, and above all individual liberty to be exercised through individual choice.

The interpretation that some draw from this – that Smith's proposal is not much more than a licensed free-for-all with the strongest taking all – is anticipated by Smith. He believed that government regulation had a place here. In the crucial matter of monopolies, for instance, he observes, 'People of the same trade seldom meet, even for merriment and diversion, but the conversation ends in a conspiracy against the public, or in some contrivance to raise prices.' He hammers that home in a return to his basic belief in the power of the customer in this new state of wealth creation and distribution. 'The real and effectual discipline which is exercised over a workman', he writes, 'is not that of his corporation, but that of his customer. It is the fear of losing their employment which restrains his frauds and corrects his negligence. An exclusive corporation necessarily weakens the force of this discipline.' Yet there will be some who think that even in this crucial qualification Smith relies too much on a notion of the fundamental benevolence of mankind which is often found wanting.

It is almost a surprise, given the aura of free market which surrounds his reputation, that Adam Smith found an important role for government. It must, he said, enforce competition and punish all attempts to fix prices or restrict production. The government must provide national defence and although law, as he saw it, was heavily skewed towards protecting the property of the rich, he believed it ought to be enforced by governments for the stability of the state. He thought government should be responsible for transport infrastructure (save canals, which he thought could operate efficiently in private hands). Education should be guaranteed by the state even though it could be delivered through private institutions. He supported a form of graduated income tax: 'The subjects of every state ought to contribute towards the support of the government, as nearly as possible, in proportion to their respective abilities: that is, in proportion to their revenue which they respectively enjoy under the protection of the state.'

With remarkable speed this book, whose full title was *An Inquiry into the Nature and Causes of the Wealth of Nations*, became the blueprint for a whole new world of economics. Some of Smith's lesser suggestions were taken up immediately: an adjustment on malt tax, for instance, which followed his suggestion that more revenue could be raised were tax lowered. And almost immediately, as has been said, it reached the highest in the land, who took it to heart and put it to work.

The Wealth of Nations' greatness has never been disputed. Timing, though, played a part in its impact. It was read by men, especially Pitt the Younger, who became Chancellor of the Exchequer in his early twenties and prime minister at twenty-five, who were intellectual, widely educated and about to be at the helm of a country lifted high on the oceans of prosperity by wave after wave of commerce, swelling up from the depths of a country hoisted to manufacturing supremacy by the power of the Industrial Revolution. They saw in Smith an explanation, a solution and a philosophy. England especially was primed for it. Set to become the workshop of the world, the first great capitalist state, Smith gave it its laws. Perhaps a book such as this needs only two or three readers in the beginning. Provided they are sufficiently potent, rather like disciples, the words will be turned into deeds. Pitt was Smith's St Peter.

But he was by no means the only one. Almost instantly Smith

reached an intellectual elite. A few years before the outbreak of the French Revolution, Lord Shelburne wrote, 'I owe to a journey I made with Mr Smith from Edinburgh to London, the difference between light and darkness through the best part of my life.' Lord Granville, effectively Pitt's Chancellor of the Exchequer, read the book. A letter written to Pitt in 1800 shows how thoroughly he had taken on board Smith's views: 'I am confident that provisions, like every other article of commerce, if left to themselves, will and must find their own level, and that every attempt to disturb that level by artificial contrivances has a necessary tendency to increase the evil it seeks to remedy.' Smith was early called in as a government adviser and, we are told, treated with great respect and deference by the prime minister and the cabinet.

The American and French revolutions and the wars with France pushed economic reform down the agenda but Smith's ideas had rooted themselves deeply. Two years after his death, in 1792, Pitt ascribed Britain's industry and energy to Adam Smith, that author 'whose extensive Knowledge of detail, and depth of philosophical research will, I believe, furnish the best solution to every question connected with the history of commerce, or with the systems of political economy'.

The accolades have continued. Some years after Pitt's encomium, the historian Henry Mackenzie wrote:

> the publication of an author, in whose mind, beyond that of any writer of his time, was genius chastened by wisdom, and wisdom enlightened by knowledge, had changed in a great measure the opinions of many on the subject of commercial restrictions, and shown how much was to be gained by restoring to trade its natural freedom . . . France and England felt in a particular manner the justice of his doctrines, and it was an article in the peace of 1783, that the two countries should take measures for setting a commercial treaty between them.

*A commemorative plate for Queen Victoria's
Golden Jubilee – also celebrates the success of Britain's trade.*

The greatest test case for Smith's ideas, and that which could be said to have sealed the reputation of his theories, was the issue of the Corn Laws. In 1815, after Waterloo and the end of what had been, in effect, several centuries of war with France, Parliament, bereft of Pitt, introduced the Corn Laws, which decreed that agricultural produce should not be imported into Britain unless the domestic price rose to a very high figure. In effect it became an embargo: wholly contrary to Smith's teaching.

It took many years for the disciples of Smith to overthrow this regressive reappearance of mercantilism. In the 1820s the merchants of London petitioned Parliament to let them buy in the cheapest market and sell in the dearest. In 1823 William Huskisson became president of the Board of Trade and pushed reforms in the direction of free trade. The old embargo on foreign corn was replaced by a sliding scale of import duties; the Navigation Acts, a vital part of the old mercantilist system, were reduced in scope. But despite the Anti-Corn Law League, set up in 1815, the Corn Laws held firm – the emblem of all Smith stood against.

Eventually, after a disastrous harvest and economic depression, the Corn Laws were repealed in 1846 and the legislation became effective by the end of the decade. The protectionists had been routed by men whose motives were mixed, who moved through different economic and political conditions, who were often at the mercy of events, but who had in common a faith in *The Wealth of Nations*. The Smithian Victorians now ran riot in the markets of the world. What was accomplished here is thought by some to be a beacon of capitalism; by others the licensing of unprecedented rapacity. Marxism grew out of the free trade system. But Smith's prophecies worked through and 'won'. Professor Julian Le Grand of the LSE (and adviser to Tony Blair) describes the Marx–Smith contest thus: 'Marx may have been influential, but he was also wrong. Smith had the magic combination of being influential and right.'

Maynard Keynes probed Smith's principles and appeared to find weaknesses in the ruins of war in the first half of the twentieth century. For example, Smith held that an over-supply of labour would lead to a fall in wages, resulting in investment elsewhere, leading to more jobs and consequently no unemployment. The 1930s depression contradicted that. Yet in the longer run it seems that Keynes was addressing a local issue and Smith's model swung back into favour comparatively quickly with economists, especially Friedrich von Hayek and Milton Friedman, who pointed out that, in sum, it was not the market that had failed but governments and unions. In the 1980s a cover for *Time* magazine had the headline 'Can Capitalism Survive?' and there on the cover was a picture of Adam Smith, out of his mouth coming the bubble caption: 'Don't give up on me yet, folks!' Folks didn't, especially Reagan and Thatcher, and their example has been followed all over the world. Keynesianism is still present, but its influence is ebbing away as Smith now once again comes centre stage.

Professor Le Grand sees Smith's ideas now being pushed into the welfare state section of the British economy, as fiercely resisted as were the Smithian arguments against the Corn Laws. He sees this as the employment of self-interest for the public good and comes back to the simple sentence 'It is not from the benevolence of the butcher, the brewer or the baker that we expect our dinner, but from their regard for their own interest.'

Smith's ideas have spread far from their place of origin. In Peru, for example, the economist Hernando de Soto set out to overthrow what he saw as the rigid and stifling mercantilism of the Peruvian economy using Smith's ideas as his master plan. In his important book *The Other Path* he argued that Peru and other South American countries remained poor because they had not taken on board the lessons in *The Wealth of Nations*. The poor, he argued, stayed poor not through indolence or lack of materials, but because of their extra-legal status which excluded them from security, investment

A photograph of Professor Michael Faraday holding a
bar magnet, October 1857.

To light Manhattan at night power stations still use the same principles employed by Faraday's first electric generator in 1831.

Electro-magnetism, discovered by Faraday, is fundamental to the success of many modern inventions: this is the Maglev train at Frankfurt airport.

After Richard Arkwright's death he left 'Manufactories the increase of which is greater than that of most German principalities'.

China 2005: Arkwright's inventions revolutionised the manufacture of textiles throughout the world.

King James I of England agreed a new bible should be commissioned: six teams
of devout scholars took nearly six years to finish the initial translation.

Statesmen have often used the King James Bible to great effect. In Martin Luther King's famous 'I have a dream' speech at the Lincoln Memorial on 28 August 1963, he quoted directly from Isaiah.

At President Kennedy's inauguration he also quoted from Isaiah: 'Undo the heavy burdens and let the oppressed go free'.

Winston Churchill often used phrases from the King James Bible in his speeches and writings.

The influence of Adam Smith's *The Wealth of Nations* is still felt more than 200 years after its first publication.

'All the world's a stage': the reconstructed Globe Theatre in London maintains the traditions of Elizabethan performance.

Kurosawa's *Throne of Blood*, his 1957 film adaptation of *Macbeth*, demonstrates the global influence of Shakespeare's drama.

Shakespeare has influenced artists as well as writers: King Lear and the Fool portrayed by French artist Louis Boulanger in 1836.

William Shakespeare: 'A happie imitator of Nature ... a most gentle expressor of it'.

and proper ownership of the capital they generated. His book was an enormous success, ironically making him an assassination target for the Marxist terrorist group Shining Path, which had been doing well out of the frustrations of the poor until de Soto's work incorporated them in the legal system.

In Africa, Botswana, which has embraced Smith, is recognised as having one of the fairest governments on the continent, and throughout Asia the abandonment of restrictive practices and protectionism has led to a phenomenal bubble of prosperity. India, for instance, went from being one of the poorest countries in the world to becoming a potential superpower after the government reacted to the financial crisis and near-collapse of 1991 by cutting forty years of bureaucratic control, an exercise which took them seven hours! And Hong Kong, of course, is exemplary Smith. The man given credit for this was its British financial secretary, Sir John Cowperthwaite, a zealous free-trader who put his ideas into practice in this forlorn outpost of half a million people.

Milton Friedman summarises the results of Cowperthwaite's reforms:

> In 1960 . . . the average per capita income in Hong Kong was 28 per cent that of Great Britain; by 1996 it had risen to 137 per cent of that in Britain. In short, from 1960 to 1996 Hong Kong's per capita income rose from being about one quarter of Britain's to more than a third larger than Britain's. It's easy to state these figures. It is more difficult to realise their significance. Compare Britain, the birthplace of the Industrial Revolution, the nineteenth-century economic superpower on whose Empire the sun never set, with Hong Kong, a spit of land, overcrowded, with no reserves except for a great harbour. Yet within four decades the residents of this spit of overcrowded land had achieved a level of income one third higher than that enjoyed by the residents of its former mother country.

And now Shanghai has followed suit.

And all this is down to the employment of laws and principles gathered together by a scholarly bachelor working his way through mountains of notes in the justice-seeking, benevolent and open-minded spirit of the Scottish Enlightenment.

Adam Smith's friend, Dugald Stewart, selected the following passage as one of the most important of all Smith's writings:

> Little else is required to carry a state to the highest degree of opulence from the lowest barbarism, but peace, easy taxes, and a tolerable administration of justice: all the rest being brought about by the natural course of things. All governments which thwart the natural course, which force things into another channel, or which endeavour to arrest the progress of society at a particular point, are unnatural, and to support themselves are obliged to be oppressive and tyrannical.

TIMELINE
AN INQUIRY INTO THE NATURE AND
CAUSES OF THE WEALTH OF NATIONS

1776   Adam Smith publishes *An Inquiry into the Nature and Causes of the Wealth of Nations*

1783   William Pitt the Younger becomes prime minister; he achieves a number of economic reforms along Smith's lines

1790   Adam Smith dies

1815   The Corn Laws come into force, much to the anger of Smith's supporters

1817   David Ricardo, a strong opponent of the Corn Laws, publishes *The Principles of Political Economy*

1819   Peterloo Massacre of Corn Law protesters

1837   Joseph Hume, Francis Place and John Roebuck form the Anti-Corn Law Association in London

1839   Cobden is instrumental in establishing a new, centralised Anti-Corn Law League

1845   Potato failure in Europe and starvation in Ireland due to the disastrous intervention of British economic policy

1846   The Corn Laws are repealed, thanks to the protests of Smith's disciples

1867–   Volume I of Marx's *Das Kapital* is published, followed by Volume II in
94   1885 and Volume III in 1894

1914   British national debt rises tenfold due to the First World War

1920s   Government attempts to cut back spending to balance its budget and a severe recession results

1923   Calvin Coolidge, committed to non-interventionist government, becomes president of the USA

1929   Staunch individualist Herbert Hoover succeeds Coolidge as president
Wall Street Crash

1936   John Mynard Keynes publishes his influential book, *The General Theory of Employment, Interest and Money*
Tripartite Agreement between Britain, France and the USA aims to stabilise exchange rates

1939   Britain adopts a Keynesian approach to the economy, borrowing larger sums than ever before

1944   Bretton Woods agreement establishes a system of convertible currencies, fixed exchange rates and free trade
Plans for an international trade organisation fail, but they pave the way for the General Agreement on Tariffs and Trade

1971   Bretton Woods agreement breaks down

1973   Britain, Denmark and Ireland join the European Community
Massive oil price rises worsen Britian's balance of payments deficit

1976   Financial crisis causes the British government to abandon Keynesian policies and adopt monetarism instead

1977   The Adam Smith Institute, the UK's leading innovator of free-market policies, is founded

1979   Margaret Thatcher is elected prime minister and begins the process of a return to Smith's ideas
Chancellor Geoffrey Howe abolishes exchange controls

1981   Ronald Reagan beomes US president, claiming Smith's book as the justification for his economic plans

1983   The British economy achieves the third highest productivity growth among the G7

1985   The EEC agrees to a Single European Act aiming to create a unified economic area

1986   Peruvian economist Hernando de Soto publishes *El Otro Sendero* (*The Other Path*) in which he blames mercantilism for the economic troubles of much of South America
The Big Bang – Thatcher opens the UK stock market to foreign and domestic trade

1989   Communism collapses in Eastern Europe and it begins restructuring command economies along market lines

1990   Britain joins the Exchange Rate Mechanism (ERM)

1991   The USSR is dissolved and Communism falls in Russia
The post-colonial Indian economy begins to relax controls on foreign exchange and imports

1992   Britain leaves ERM, causing a fall in interest rates which helps to revive the economy
The European single market comes into effect with no barriers to capital, labour, goods or services
Under Thatcher's economic policies, the real income of British families has risen 37 per cent since 1979

1996   In Hong Kong, per capita income begins to rise from being around a quarter of Britain's income to over a third larger

2000   Hernando de Soto publishes *The Mystery of Capital: Why Capitalism Triumphs in the West and Fails Everywhere Else*, an analysis of the Third World's problems

THE FIRST FOLIO

1623

by

William Shakespeare

Mr. WILLIAM

SHAKESPEARES

COMEDIES,
HISTORIES, &
TRAGEDIES.

Published according to the True Originall Copies.

Martin Droeshout sculpsit London.

LONDON
Printed by Isaac Iaggard, and Ed. Blount. 1623.

One of the people I spoke to when I was thinking about this book was my friend the novelist Howard Jacobson. He was dismayed that the list held no novelists. 'I'm a novelist, you're a novelist, we love novels, novels changed my life and novels changed your life, good novels change lives every day; a list without a novel? Without one, not one, novel?' A mild paraphrase: Howard on song can be rather more emphatic than that.

I defended the list I had drawn up. I said that I wanted books that I could prove had changed, rootedly, the lives of people all over the land – people on trains, people at airports, people in clubs and pubs, women who were still campaigning for equality and enjoying the long-awaited acknowledgement of their right to orgasm, men who week in week out played, watched, celebrated and discussed a game so beautifully and simply constructed it remains a masterpiece of socio-leisure architecture, those who hold religious truths to be self-evident and those whose conscious and unconscious lives have been readjusted by the revelations from the Galapagos Islands, the industrialists and financiers who ride and lubricate international capitalism calling on the market and free trade as its two true parents, those whose lives are devoted to seeking freedoms which were given such a lead in the abolition of the slave trade, those who go to the moon, put on the light, send a fax, vote in a democratic country, fight for their rights; those whose daily lives and the reach of whose minds and ambitions have been transformed by books which set off a shot that rang around the world. Or words to that effect. So where, I had asked myself, in preparing this list, was *Middlemarch? Bleak House? Women in Love?* And for any passionate fiction reader, a list of novels could go on until the end of the book.

Yet that was one of the difficulties. Though *Middlemarch* might well have changed the life and thought of Howard Jacobson, and others, it is not as easy to quantify as an electric light or flying to the moon. Where can we weigh the good done by *Middlemarch*, where quantify the benefit to the world at large, where find a plausible proof that it can have a claim to have changed the world? And yet . . . Like most of you reading this book, I grew up and am still, I hope, growing up partly through books. I can remember so many books that touched and, for a while, changed my life. Schoolboy tales of square-jawed, honest, Christian and true Tom Browns made me pull myself together for an hour or two while still in short trousers; the romance of Robin Hood or the Three Musketeers had me making a bow out of two yards of cane bought at the ironmonger's and fashioning a sword from any likely slim branch of a tree which could be hacked off. On it went and on it goes still. Did the reading of Proust enlarge my sense of the possibilities of memory in life and in fiction? I hope so. Do the sentences of Samuel Beckett still ring down there in the helpful caverns of literary memory, the majestic lives of Dickens change the landscape of enjoyment and of a fictional world of a real city? I hope so . . . and on it goes still.

Every one of you will have a different list. Some can be books rarely remembered now and modest even when they were first published, but books which somehow made us recognise what we more largely could be and changed us. But I find it difficult to take a single book, or even, giving all the benefits possible, a body of work by D. H. Lawrence, for instance, and track through, as I have been able to do, I hope, with the other books, the ways in which they met the grand challenge of changing the world out there. Changing a single world, yes. And yes, those small fields of influence can and sometimes do grow in power over the years so that *The Waste Land*, which first fell largely on barren soil, became in my generation an accessible quarry of modernist mantras. But nevertheless, to hold to the argument about a book which flooded the world with newness and observable change, it was reluctantly my conclusion that to take a novel would be a testament of hope rather than a statement of what actually happens. Fiction on the whole when it changes lives, even as dramatically as *Young Werther*, changes the life of an individual, and that is its great strength. For this conclusion I plead guilty and stand condemned by fellow novelists. But the door is not altogether closed.

There is Shakespeare.

Shakespeare can stand for the innumerable writers of literary imagination who have given so much delight, and changed, if only for moments, the inner life. Shakespeare represents the many individual writers whose work has changed the lives of so many individual readers or, in his case, readers and viewers and listeners.

But there can also, I think, be made out a case for Shakespeare's First Folio, published in 1623, being a book which has indeed changed the world. It changed the English-speaking world, in its first few centuries of life, and it still does. But now the worlds of the fifty or more languages into which he is translated, regularly retranslated, played and read aloud, have also been changed. Professor Harold Bloom, the renowned American scholar, whose lifelong studies of and devotion to Shakespeare have been Herculean, passionately believes that, 'We can feel positively embarrassed and ashamed when we realise that our feelings are in fact shaped by William Shakespeare'. That is a claim of the highest and boldest order. But claims for Shakespeare, from his own day, have been scarcely less ambitious. His friend and contemporary, Ben Jonson, said that Shakespeare was 'not for an age but for all time'.

Since then the greatest critics, Dr Johnson, William Hazlitt, Coleridge, Sir Frank Kermode, have added their acclaim, while there is no writer in the world of any real distinction who will not doff the cap to Shakespeare and, more than that, regard him with 'awe', the word most often used by Harold Bloom.

His world reputation, and influence in many languages, through the plays, the three hundred films, the innumerable radio programmes, through professional and amateur productions, is unrivalled. And it is forever reburnished in England in the recently reconstructed (through the passion of an American – Sam Wanamaker) Globe Theatre, Shakespeare's theatre, beside the Thames in London, and the Royal Shakespeare Company in Stratford-upon-Avon, which in 2006 will mount all thirty-seven of his plays.

That reputation is there through the work and the work is there because, seven years after Shakespeare's death, the First Folio of his works was published. 'The First Folio', Harold Bloom has said, 'is equal, if not greater, in both its importance and its influence on Western culture, as the Tyndale or King James Bibles. Not even Chaucer's Canterbury Tales or Dickens' complete novels can match it.'

Anthony James West, in *The Shakespeare First Folio: The History of the Book*, gives a comprehensive account of this remarkable, fortunate and in some ways wholly unexpected publication. Playwrights rarely published their plays in those times. Ben Jonson was one to have done so, in 1616, and he was ridiculed for his pretentiousness. Plays were popular culture. Of his poems Shakespeare took great care. His plays he simply left behind when he decided to quit the stage and return to live the life of a comfortably-off gentleman in Stratford-upon-Avon. It is owing to the devotion of two friends of his that the First Folio was published and owing to them that eighteen of Shakespeare's plays (including *Macbeth, Twelfth Night, Antony and Cleopatra* and *The Tempest*) were preserved at all. Others were scattered around in abbreviated and blemished quarto editions: but they were only 50 per cent of his work for the stage.

A

PLEASANT

Conceited Comedie

CALLED,

Loues labors loſt.

As it vvas preſented before her Highnes
this laſt Chriſtmas.

Newly correᶜted and augmented
By *W. Shakeſpere.*

Imprinted at London by *W.W.*
for *Cutbert Burby.*
1598.

Shakespeare's plays were first printed as small, cheap, disposable pamphlets.

We owe a very great debt to John Hemynges and Henry Condell, members of Shakespeare's company and mentioned in his will as 'my Fellows, John Hemynges, Richard Burbage and Henry Condell', to whom he left 26s. 8d. each 'to buy them Ringes'. The two men have a memorial in Love Lane in the City of London. Their true memorial is the First Folio which they entered on the Stationer's Register on 8 November 1623.

When they started on this labour of love they had eighteen of Shakespeare's plays in quarto format: small, cheap, better than nothing, but deeply untrustworthy. They were disposable pamphlets, sold by street vendors as a programme guide. The quarto version of *Hamlet*, for example, is two hours shorter than the original and 'To be or not to be, that is the question' appeared as 'To be or not to be, aye, there's the point'. Hemynges and Condell were sticklers for textual accuracy. They went back to Shakespeare's original texts, which had been kept for sound business reasons – his plays were a commercial goldmine – by the company manager. They say in their preface that whereas 'before you were abused with diverse stolen, and surreptitious copies, maimed and deformed by the frauds and stealths of injurious impostors, now, even these are offered to your view cured, and perfect of their limbs, and all the rest absolute in their numbers as he conceived them'.

It is astonishing to us, today, with our lust for the original, the unique, the hand of the artist visible, that they did not keep Shakespeare's original pages. What was important was the preservation of the work in the monument of the Folio edition. Yet they left us with this remark on the plays as written in Shakespeare's hand: 'As he was a happie imitator of Nature, [he] was a most gentle expresser of it. His mind and hand went together, and what he thought he uttered with that easiness that we have scarce received from him a blot on his papers.' The unblotted page, the uncrossed-out line, the unimpaired; this incomparable epitaph has something transcendent about it.

The publication consisted of about nine hundred pages. It held thirty-six of his plays (*Troilus and Cressida* was the missing play: it proved too difficult to buy until a few years later; they paid about £50 per play) and was entitled *Mr William Shakespeare's Comedies, Histories and Tragedies*. There was a copper-engraved picture of Shakespeare by Martin Droeshout. Given the tenacity and loyalty of Hemynges and Condell it is a fair bet that this is a good or at least an acceptable likeness. The Folio was printed in London, near St Paul's, on handmade paper, in pica Roman type, and in two columns on both sides of the leaves. It is still today very easy, even comfortable, to read, and awe-inspiring to hold. William Prynne, a puritan who was disturbed by the corrupting influence of plays and players, was dismayed that 'Shakespeare's Plaies are printed in the best Crowne paper, far better than most Bibles'. About five hundred copies were published and a bound copy cost £1. Today? At the very least £100. It was indeed bigger than most bibles, a statement of stature as much as a publication of plays, intended to be, as it became, both a monument and the unpolluted source of the Shakespearean reputation. It was published as a classic and reprinted within ten years and ever since. Its editors urged readers to 'read and read [it] again'.

Though never out of print and always quoted, Shakespeare the book in the century of his death, the century of civil war and Restoration, was superseded first by the Bible which was plundered for the competing ideologies which led to the execution of King Charles I and the elevation of the Lord Protector, Cromwell, and then by the influence of the French on the prevailing taste for comedy brought back across the water by the restored monarch Charles II. It was in the eighteenth century that Shakespeare began to attain the beginnings of his great greatness.

Between 1733 and 1752, performances of his plays increased mightily, spurred on by the genius of and the fashion set by one of the commanding legends of the day, the actor and manager David

LEAR. MACBETH.

RICHARD III.^d HAMLET.

Mr GARRICK in Four of his Principal Tragic Characters.

David Garrick made his reputation as an interpreter of Shakespeare's great tragic roles.

Garrick. In 1736 a Shakespeare's Ladies' Club was formed 'with the specific aim of persuading the theatre managers to put on more Shakespeare'. In 1741 his monument was erected in Westminster Abbey; in 1751 the Professor of Poetry at Oxford, William Hawkins, gave the first lectures on Shakespeare at an English university; in 1769 Stratford-upon-Avon put on a Shakespeare Jubilee, presided over by Garrick and reported throughout Europe. And so the Shakespeare tourist industry was born. In 1776 the first complete translation of Shakespeare appeared in French, in 1795 the first complete edition printed in America was published and there were references to his work in every other form of literature.

Thomas Carlyle spoke for nineteenth-century Britain when he wrote, 'this king, Shakespeare, does he not shine, in crowned sovereignty, over us all.' Victor Hugo spoke for France when he wrote, 'After God, Shakespeare created the most', Goethe for Germany when he conceded that the German translation of Shakespeare was the best poetry and prose in the German language. Emerson for America and certainly for Harold Bloom when he wrote that Shakespeare 'invented the text of modern life'.

There is a Globe Theatre in Tokyo, a library devoted to Shakespeare on Capitol Hill in Washington DC which holds 179 copies of the First Folio. *Hamlet* is required reading for every fifteen-year-old in Bulgaria and somewhere, every day, from Nepal to Nigeria, from India to Iraq, from China to the Czech Republic, there is in train a performance of Shakespeare.

It is worth pausing a while to look at the quality of the admiration as well as admiring its width. David Garrick, widely called a genius in his time, who had been a pupil of Dr Johnson in his brief career as a teacher, basked in Shakespearean triumph on the London stage drawing crowds as big, almost, as those that were pulled into the Globe in Shakespeare's day (the Globe could hold over three thousand, and it has been calculated that *Titus Andronicus*, for instance, was seen by half the adult male population of

London – population then about 250,000). At the same time as Garrick's triumph on the stage, Dr Johnson established Shakespeare on the page. Fresh from his own triumph in writing the first defining English dictionary and fully registering English as a literary language largely through quotations, many of which came from Shakespeare, Johnson turned his gaze on to Shakespeare himself and after his edition of 1765 it became impossible for any scholar of reputation to regard Shakespeare with anything but reverence. Johnson made him the linchpin of English literature: a judgement both endorsed and extended in our day by Harold Bloom, who says, 'Shakespeare sets the standards and the limits of literature' and 'Shakespeare is the central figure of the Western Canon . . . Shakespeare remains the most original writer we will ever know.'

Johnson, in his edition of Shakespeare in 1765, puts him alongside the classical authors, Homer and Virgil. He is severe in his defence of the integrity of Shakespeare's works even when it troubles his mind. For example, in the eighteenth century it had become the convention, according to Professor John Mullan, that *King Lear* be performed in a 'cleaned up' and sting-drawn version put together by Nahum Tate. In Tate's script, Lear does not die, his daughter Cordelia is not murdered; indeed she marries Edgar, wronged son of the Duke of Gloucester, and presumably lives happily ever after. As Mullan points out, the original version troubled Johnson who 'fervently believed that literature should teach people to love virtue and wherever possible it should show virtue triumphant'. *King Lear* does the opposite of that and with unparalleled force. Yet Johnson steels himself and declares Shakespeare's version superior to that of Tate 'despite the fact that it offended his moral sensibilities'. (Of *King Lear*, Harold Bloom says, 'the greatest of all representations in Shakespeare is that of King Lear. Shakespeare seems to have personally broken through into an order of representation that we just don't know how to catch up with.')

In the preface to his edition, Johnson takes Shakespeare's side against those who criticised him for diverting from the principles of the classical unities, patented in Ancient Greece and well observed in what was thought then the leader of taste and sensibility, France. Pope, in his edition of Shakespeare, had chopped out those sections he thought insufficiently correct or elegant or polite. There was in Pope a distinct feeling that he was a poet on an equal footing with Shakespeare. Johnson, who had his own poetic reputation, was under no such delusion. He wrote:

Shakespeare's plays are not in the rigorous and critical sense either comedies or tragedies, but compositions of a distinct kind; exhibiting the real state of sublunary nature, which partakes of good and evil, joy and sorrow, mingled with endless variety of proportion and innumerable modes of combination; and expressing the case of the world, in which the loss of one is the gain of another; in which at the same time the reveller is hasting to the wine, and the mourner burying his friend; in which the indignity of one is defeated by the frolic of another; and many mischiefs and many benefits are done and hindered without design.

Johnson's edition, Mullan says, 'instigates a real field shift in critical opinion'. A shift which has gone even farther in the 240 years since the edition appeared.

Dr Johnson's authority took Shakespeare on to another plane even above that on which his friend, colleague, rival and protégé, Ben Jonson, had set him in the First Folio itself in an introduction still thought to be one of the finest appreciations of Shakespeare. It could be said that Shakespeare had succeeded where, according to Socrates, the Ancients had not. For none of them, Socrates observed, had combined tragedy and comedy. Shakespeare, wrote Ben Jonson, was greater than Aeschylus, Sophocles and Euripides in tragedy and Aristophanes, Terence and Plautus in comedy. Moreover, by combining them, as, later, Dr Johnson observed, he had bridged the

Socratic gap. Ben Jonson was extremely proud of his deceased colleague and wrote in terms he might have hesitated to use when Shakespeare was alive: 'Triumph, my Britain, thou hast one to show / To whom all scenes of Europe homage owe.'

In the early sixteenth century the English language was thought of as a poor cousin to the glory of France and the might of Spain and the magnificence of Italy, let alone the pillars of Latin and Ancient Greek. But just a few years before Shakespeare arrived in London, at the beginning of the 1590s, Sir Philip Sidney, the aristocrat poet, scholar and diplomat, who died a hero's death young on the battlefield, had said, 'English hath it equally with any other tongue in the world'. It mattered to the English to be on fighting terms with France, which was at least five times more populous, with Spain, which had put out the greatest armada the world had seen only to have it defeated by Drake and favourably foul weather, and Italy, seen through Dante and Petrarch as unassailably superior. England was embattled, its queen the object of assassination plots, yet its commerce was about to boom, its first empire to plant itself on foreign soils, its intellectuals to take a lead in what would become modern ways of thought. It mattered that out there was also a champion of words, a defender of the faith in language of majesty.

Shakespeare arrived on cue. The comparatively little we know about his life is well known. He was born in Stratford-upon-Avon in 1564. It was a town of 1,500 people, quite large for the time. As the son of a respected local merchant (his father was perhaps a butcher, certainly a glover — there are more than seventy accurate descriptions of gloves in Shakespeare's works and many butchering references in the early plays) he would have the freedom of the place and meet all classes and conditions of men and women, one of whom, Anne Hathaway, he married, possibly a shotgun arrangement (she was some years older than him) when he was eighteen. He had been to the local grammar school until the age of sixteen, where he would have been taught Latin and Greek. The history of the

Romans and the mythologies of the Greeks weave through his work. Ovid's *Metamorphoses* was a clear influence from school, as was Montaigne. Professor Bloom thinks that Chaucer was one of his very greatest influences and besides Chaucer, Tyndale – through the bibles of the time. This is an opinion which delights me as I think Tyndale's influence on the language and culture of the English-speaking world has been most unfairly neglected.

In London Shakespeare took on the making of sonnets to compete with the university wits, some of whom scorned his lack of academic marination at Oxford. He out-sonneted all of them and those sonnets, with his other poems, were, unlike the plays, the money-making, people-pleasing plays, printed and published in his lifetime. The poem was the thing and Shakespeare was happy to enter the lists. But the brightest wordsmiths were being pulled into the new booming theatres, five or six in London, the rage of the day both for the courtly leaders of fashion and the semi-literate, often illiterate, groundlings who stood and saw in the plays of Shakespeare people like themselves, just as the fashionable young men of the day saw actors living out lives they could well have lived, and indeed some of their named ancestors had lived.

For besides bringing together comedy and tragedy and all the strands so definitively listed by Dr Johnson, Shakespeare brought together language from low life as well as from high life. The high learning, elegance and wit of the sonnets were not abandoned; in fact as the plays unfolded, the grandeur of his lines, prose and verse, grew to be a mighty organ of English: but he also embraced the rough, slang-ridden, rude and bawdy language of the streets, perhaps even the very streets of Southwark where the Rose Theatre (his first venue) and the Globe were situated. Streets outside the walls of the City of London (which had great advantages in terms of escaping censorship), streets rife with prostitutes and their pimps, with rogues, pickpockets, sailors of many nationalities, mendicants, corner preachers, hawkers, drunks, low life.

A 1673 depiction of a playhouse
populated by a selection of Elizabethan characters.

His success as a playwright and actor-manager is well enough recorded and he returned to Stratford, his wife and family, whom one presumes he had visited or they him regularly or sometimes along the way (otherwise Stratford would not have acted as such a homing lure to a man at the peak of his powers) and there died in his mid-fifties.

It is by his words and his characters that we know him. His vocabulary, four centuries ago, since when the English dictionary has increased in size almost incredibly, is still regarded as the fullest of any writer. He had a vocabulary of at least twenty-one thousand different words – possibly, when the combinations and different uses of these words are added, about thirty thousand words. Most people who speak English rub along on about two thousand words for their daily use. The King James Bible of 1611 used about ten thousand different words. Even educated people today, pumped up with new words from science and industry, from new countries, newly discovered plants, insects, animals, will not have a working vocabulary above ten thousand words.

The English language at the end of the sixteenth century was in flux: a word more accurate than 'flux' might be 'turmoil'. Sailors and traders had brought words from over fifty other languages into the national word-hoard. The fifth-century Germanic influence still remained the rock of the language, the earthworks, the ur-words, the basic building blocks. There had been an influx of Old Norse with the Viking raids of the ninth and tenth centuries and then the waterfall of Norman French and other French dialects that brought tens of thousands of Romance words into English in the three or four centuries after 1066. They found associates in the Latin which had come back into the islands with the Roman Church. It was as if tectonic plates of language had shifted and clashed in the British Isles and out of this came volcanoes of vocabulary, spurtings of fiery paragraphs, hurled out on a breath and into the common air.

Shakespeare was the Krakatoa. He 'out-Heroded Herod'. 'Uncle me no uncle,' he said, and apart from witty conjunctions – he paired 'ill' with 'tuned', 'baby' with 'eyes', 'smooth' with 'faced', 'puppy' with 'dog' and hundreds more – well over two thousand of our words are first recorded in his plays, and these are very often words which have joined the bedrock.

He was the master of the memorable. 'What the dickens' has nothing to do with Charles but makes its first appearance in *The Merry Wives of Windsor*, as does 'as good luck would have it'. 'It beggar'd all description' and 'salad days' came from *Antony and Cleopatra*. There are so many, but as 'brevity is the soul of wit' I won't 'play fast and loose' or refuse to 'budge an inch', but 'in one fell swoop' let this paragraph like 'all our yesterdays' vanish into 'thin air'. It could be 'never ending'.

Phrases such as these are in the blood of the language and in that sense course through our history. From *Hamlet* alone we receive, among scores of others, 'the play's the thing'; 'in my mind's eye'; 'though this be madness yet there's method in it'. We can be 'cruel only to be kind'; 'hold the mirror up to nature' but 'more in sorrow than in anger'; 'the rest is silence'.

The best-known line in the world is 'To be or not to be, that is the question', and it is here that we touch on another inheritance, that of the creation of a fictional character so strong and branded on the mind that the character becomes a reference point in our lives. Hamlet is all young people working through a philosophy of life which takes account of the sudden realisation that it is dark as well as light, brutal as well as loving, inexplicable as well as comprehensible. Hamlet is for all nations, performed with equal conviction in many languages, a character claimed and recognised on every continent.

In the great soliloquies are dramatic twists and developments in a state of mind which, Harold Bloom argues, has no limits, is apparently infinite in its curiosity, its self-questioning and insights, its tests of the currency of existence. Freud, a deep reader, in

English, of Shakespeare, reworks him in his notion of the unconscious. He reads our minds in the plays, in the archetypical jealousy
of Othello, the consuming erotic volatility of Cleopatra, the fatal
adolescent passions of Romeo and Juliet, the evil of Iago, the
incomparably flawed merriment and vivacity of Falstaff. They are
characters we see around us today and we see them through
Shakespeare's invention. Invention in the sense of discovery. He
discovered before and more lastingly than Freud the deepest springs
of nature through character, and we see ourselves clearly through his
creations.

Emerson wrote:

> What point of novels, of manners, of economy, of philosophy, of
> religion, of taste, of the conduct of life, has he not settled? What
> mystery has he not signified his knowledge of? What office or
> function or district of man's work has he not remembered? . . .
> What maiden not found him finer than her delicacy? . . . What
> sage has he not outseen?

It is from a like appreciation that Professor Bloom argues that
Shakespeare in effect invented, discovered, what it is to be most
fully human today.

He was ravenous for the new. He used new words which had
appeared from the middle to the end of the sixteenth century –
words like 'multitudinous', 'emulate', 'demonstrate', 'dislocate',
'initiate', 'meditate', 'eventful', 'horrid', 'modest' and 'vest'. He
was very fond of making up compound words as we have already
seen – 'bare-pick't', 'half-blown' – it is difficult to resist quoting
them. There are, however – for this relief much thanks – words in
Shakespeare which are gone from use, probably permanently:
'questrist', for instance, or 'abruption', 'perisive' and his longest
word, which means with honour, 'honorificabilitudinatibus'.

John Barton, the scholar and author, who worked with the Royal

Shakespeare Company in Stratford-upon-Avon for almost half a century, told me the following, which apart from anything else explains why his plays could draw the applause of both the court and the groundlings. 'It is the monosyllables that are the bedrock and life of the language,' he said.

> And I believe that is so with Shakespeare. The high words, the high phrases he sets up to them bring them down to the simple ones that explain them. Like 'making the multitudinous seas incarnadine, making the green one red'. First there is the high language and then the specific clear definition. At the heart of Shakespeare, listening to it for acting, the great lines, often the most poetic, are the monosyllables. Deep feeling probably comes out in monosyllables. He teemed with word invention but in some way the living power of the language comes from the interplay of the two.

Here is not only an example of Shakespeare again driving at least two horses simultaneously – as he does tragedy and comedy, the heroic and the comic, the magical and the mechanical – but a hint of something even deeper, I think. It is now believed that language may have originated, or begun to form, more than 170,000 years ago as a sort of musical sound, a melody with gestures and the simplest monosyllabic expressions. That is, deep inside us as are the key monosyllables – 'the', 'there', 'and', 'then', and a couple of hundred others which are the rivets of the language. But over the millennia language has developed into a sophisticated multi-purpose instrument often better read than said. For some matters only from the solitude and silence of concentrated reading can the fullest benefits come. And just as many enjoy the acted Shakespeare and see his characters as his gift to us, whether transferred to Japan in a film such as *Throne of Blood* which recovers and revisits *Macbeth*, or acted in a school hall where swashbuckling adolescents of today easily assume the roles of the Capulets and the Montagues, so others

– Charles Lamb was the first to record this – much prefer to read Shakespeare. The argument is that there is so much in it which even the finest actor will have to speak without pause where a pause, perhaps a pause for an hour or so, is what is needed to think through how much the words mean.

One way in which Shakespeare has changed the world is by enriching the landscape of artists who followed him. All of us have more scope because of his language – there are thirty-three thousand quotations from Shakespeare in the *Oxford English Dictionary* – and all of us are enlarged by Hamlet, Falstaff, Cleopatra, Iago, who give character and accuracy to riots of passion often otherwise hard to describe or explain. But in the culture itself we see him here, we see him there, we see the Swan of Avon everywhere, from the musical *Kiss Me Kate* to Tom Stoppard's *Rosencrantz and Guildenstern Are Dead* to any of the hundreds of film, radio and television versions ever increasing in number and variety.

As English became a world language – partly because of Shakespeare himself – so his reputation spread. Not only did he influence Walter Scott at home, but Goethe, Stendhal and Hugo and Dostoevsky abroad; in music pre-eminently Berlioz and Verdi; Fuseli in painting, Freud in psychoanalysis. He has become an international reference point in culture and so through others drinking at his well he constantly refreshes the world. There is a Prison Shakespeare project which takes his plays into prisons and declares that 'Shakespeare's language and the social and essential literacy it inspires in others make prisoners realise that it is "their own shared birthright".'

Throughout Eastern Europe and the Soviet Union in the days of authoritarianism, Shakespeare was often adopted by the state, his plays used in the name of the ruling socialist-realist ideology. As often as not, though, so open are the plays to multiple interpretations, so free are they from ideology, the productions showed the opposite of the state's intentions. Thus, as Jonathan Bate has pointed out, theatregoers could see in *Hamlet* in the corrupt court of Claudius with its Polonian surveillance apparatus an allegory of the courts of Brezhnev, Ceausescu and Zhivkov. Though not in thrall to any ideology, not even the Christianity which must have informed Shakespeare's youth, Shakespeare's is the only work of fiction widely regarded as 'secular scripture', with Hamlet, after Jesus, the most cited figure in Western consciousness. 'There is something in Shakespeare which transcends beyond even his own language,' says Professor Bloom. 'Conceptually, I think that far more than great philosophers or scientists, his is the best mind of which we have evidence anywhere.'

None of which would have been possible without that First Folio, sold, bound, for £1 in 1623. The most recent sale in 2001 was for $6,166,000 at Christie's New York.

It is worth quoting Harold Bloom one final time as we move towards the end not only of this chapter but of all twelve of the books which I have argued changed the world. For this, the First Folio, Bloom makes claims which surpass that for all the other eleven books considered in this volume, claims which reach as profoundly as possible into the human mind. 'Shakespeare invented us and continues to contain us,' he writes. 'I sometimes suspect that we really do not listen to one another because Shakespeare's friends and lovers never quite hear what the other is saying, which is part of the ironical truth that Shakespeare largely invented.' He adds, '. . . Shakespeare's influence began almost immediately and has prevailed these four centuries since he died. If there ever has been a universal literary art, that art is Shakespeare's, an art that seemed nature to his contemporaries and that has become nature for us.'

'All the world's a stage,' Shakespeare wrote, and after writing this chapter I realise that although his influence can never be proved as unambiguously as the influence of Newton, Faraday, Smith, Darwin, Stopes and the others, it can nevertheless be seen and

A CATALOGVE

of the feuerall Comedies, Hiftories, and Tragedies contained in this Volume.

Two of Shakespeare's fellow actors, John Hemynges and Henry Condell,
were responsible for collating his work into what became the First Folio.

experienced. Our imaginations, when they feed on the lessons and insights to be drawn from the dead, make little if any distinction between Socrates and Hamlet, between Achilles and Henry V, between the Borgias and Iago: they have been enrolled equally in the pantheon of internal gods. And for the language, the signs, the marks and sounds and things which connect us and can lighten the steepest darkness of our conceptions and condition, it is to Shakespeare we turn, out of his mouth we speak time and again, acknowledging often without noticing the magic of his art, without which all the rest, and all in this book, would be silent. As Theseus says at the end of *A Midsummer Night's Dream*:

> And as imagination bodies forth
> The forms of things unknown, the poet's pen
> Turns them to shapes and gives to airy nothing
> A local habitation and a name.

TIMELINE
THE FIRST FOLIO

1623   The First Folio becomes the first collected edition of Shakespeare's plays

1632   Shakespeare's Second Folio is published

1642   The Globe Theatre is closed by the Puritans

1660   Margaret Hughes becomes the first woman to perform in a Shakespeare play. Her performance as Desdemona in *Othello* also marks the first woman to act on the English stage

1664   Shakespeare's Third Folio is published

1685   Shakespeare's Forth Folio is published

1736   Shakespeare's Ladies' Club is formed, calling on managers to put on more Shakespeare

1741   A monument to Shakespeare is erected in Westminster Abbey

1750s Shakespeare's plays are performed for the first time amongst American colonists

1751   The Professor of Poetry at Oxford, William Hawkins, delivers the first academic lectures on Shakespeare in an English university

1769   A 'Shakespeare Jubilee' is put on at Stratford-upon-Avon and reported in newspapers throughout Europe

1776   The first complete translation of Shakespeare in French emerges

1795   The first edition of Shakespeare's full works is printed in America

1864   The world's first Shakespeare Society is founded in Germany: Die Deutsche Shakespeare-Gesellschaft (DSG)

1879   The Shakespeare Memorial Theatre in Stratford opens with *Much Ado About Nothing*

1899   A simple photographic recording of a section of the stage production of *King John* becomes the first documented film of a Shakespeare play in any country

1909   A. W. Pollard publishes *Shakespeare's Folios and Quartos*, beginning an investigation of the publishing contradictions in Shakespeare's day and a more thorough examination of the quartos and folios themselves

1925   A Royal Charter is granted to the Shakespeare Memorial Theatre

1928   The complete works of Shakespeare are translated into Japanese by Tsubouchi Shoyo

1932   Following destruction by fire, the new Shakespeare Memorial Theatre is opened by the Prince of Wales on Shakespeare's birthday – 23 April

        The Folger Shakespeare Library, a world-class research centre devoted to Shakespeare, opens on Capitol Hill, Washington DC

1937   *As You Like It* becomes the first straight adaptation of a Shakespeare play in film, with sound

1944   Laurence Olivier's ground-breaking film version of *Henry V* is released

1961   Sir Peter Hall forms the Royal Shakespeare Company and the Shakespeare Memorial Theatre is renamed The Royal Shakespeare Theatre

1970   Shakespeare's head appears on £20 notes

1978   The BBC Shakespeare Project, an ambitious attempt at bringing Shakespeare to the small screen, begins with *Romeo and Juliet*

1988   The Globe Theatre, Tokyo, is opened to showcase local and international productions of Shakespeare plays

1997   The New Globe Theatre is officially opened

1998   The London Shakespeare Workout: Prison Project is launched allowing actors and film-makers to work alongside offenders and ex-offenders to explore and develop skills of self-expression and boost confidence through Shakespeare's language

1999   BBC Radio 4's *Today* programme votes William Shakespeare 'Man of the Millennium'

ACKNOWLEDGEMENTS

To write a book such as this needs many hands on deck. I have been very fortunate to work, on the television series of the same name which I have written and presented, with several colleagues from the Arts and Features Department of ITV. Our work together has been invaluable for the book.

The script editor, Jonathan Levi, has been outstandingly helpful for both the book and the series. The producer/directors of the films – Robert Bee, David Thomas, Daniel Wiles and, once again, Jonathan Levi – were a pleasure to work with in the necessary selection, editing and focusing of so much available material. The aim was to try to follow the example of Faraday and make these books accessible, while not letting go of the kernel of the matter. All of us were further enriched by the contributions of Associate Producer Suzannah Wander and researchers Tom Lane and Hannah Whittingham who became swept up as we were in this enterprise. To all of them, many thanks.

What follows is a chapter-by-chapter acknowledgement of the key works drawn on and very supportive conversations held with a range of academics who (and this was a relief!) were sympathetic to the book's aims. To them, for distilling what was often a lifetime's experience into a brief hour, I am very grateful.

I have tried to be accurate and if faults are spotted then I take all responsibility. Working with the people mentioned above and below has been a great pleasure and an education.

Principia Mathematica (1687) by Isaac Newton

KEY TEXTS

I. Bernard Cohen *A Guide to Newton's Principia*; I. Bernard Cohen and Anne Whitman *Isaac Newton: The Principia*; James Gleick *Isaac Newton*; Jane Jakeman *Isaac Newton: A Beginner's Guide*; Andrew Motte's translation of *The Principia*; Jenny Uglow *The Lunar Men*.

CONVERSATIONS

Rob Iliffe (the Newton Project online); Dr Peter Mandelbrote (Director of Studies and Research Fellow, Peterhouse College, Cambridge, also the Newton Project online); Adam Perkins (Newton expert and Manuscript/Rare Books Archivist, University Library, Cambridge) – a great deal of help both on the phone and in person; Professor Simon Schaffer (Faculty of History, Cambridge University); professor Jim Al Khalili (Head of Theoretical Nuclear Physics group, University of Surrey).

Married Love (1918) by Marie Stopes

KEY TEXTS

Peter Eaton and Marilyn Warwick *Marie Stopes: A Checklist of Her Writings;* June Rose *Marie Stopes and the Sexual Revolution*; Ross McKibbin 'Introduction' in the Oxford text of *Married Love*.

CONVERSATIONS

Royal Society of Literature; Dr Lesley Hall (the Wellcome Trust).

Magna Carta (1215) by Members of the English Ruling Classes

KEY TEXTS

Danny Danziger and John Gillingham *1215: The Year of Magna Carta*.

CONVERSATIONS

Tony Benn and various people from the think-tank Liberty.

The Rule Book of Association Football (1863) by A Group of Former English Public School Men

KEY TEXTS

James Walvin *The People's Game: the history of football revisited*; Phaidon *Magnum Football* (stills); Simon Kuper *Football Against the Enemy*.

CONVERSATIONS

Mark Bushell (National Football Museum); David Barber (FA statistician); Fiona Bettles (Uppingham School); Rusty MacLean (Rugby School); Professor Robert Colls (School of Historical Studies, University of Leicester).

On The Origin of Species (1859) by Charles Darwin

KEY TEXTS

Janet Browne *Charles Darwin: The Power of Place*; Cyril Aydon *Charles Darwin*; James A. Secord *Victorian Sensation*; Steve Jones *Darwin's Ghost: The Origin of the Species Updated*.

CONVERSATIONS

Janet Browne; Adam Perkins (Darwin Archivist at Cambridge University); Professor Jim Secord (Department of History and Philosophy of Science, University of Cambridge); Professor Simon Schaffer (Department of History, University of Cambridge); Professor David Kohn (Drew University, Madison, New Jersey); Dr Jo Cooper (Bird Curator, Walter Rothschild Museum).

On the Abolition of the Slave Trade (1789) by William Wilberforce in Parliament, immediately reprinted in several versions

KEY TEXTS

David J. Vaughan *Statesman and Saint*; James Walvin *Black Ivory: a history of British Slavery*; S. I. Martin *Britain's Slave Trade*; Kevin Belmonte *Hero For Humanity: a biography of William Wilberforce*; Adam Hochschild *Bury The Chains*.

CONVERSATIONS

Dr Brycchan Carey (abolition expert – also interviewed in TV programme); Professor David Richardson (WISE, Hull – also interviewed in TV programme).

A Vindication of the Rights of Woman (1792) by Mary Wollstonecraft

KEY TEXTS

A Vindication of the Rights of Woman edited by Miriam Brody with a revised introduction and notes; Caroline Franklin *Mary Wollstonecraft: A Literary Life*; Lyndall Gordon *Vindication: A Life of Mary Wollstonecraft*; Vivien Jones 'Mary Wollstonecraft and the Literature of Advice and Instruction' in The *Cambridge Companion to Mary Wollstonecraft* edited by Claudia Johnson; Janet M. Todd *Mary Wollstonecraft: A Revolutionary Life*; also a number of references and links within Germaine Greer's *The Female Eunuch*.

CONVERSATIONS

Dr William Foster (expert on American gender history, Assistant Professor of History, Redlands, California); Vivien Jones (Professor of Eighteenth-century Gender and Culture, School of English, University of Leeds); Beverly Kemp (Woman's Library, London); Professor Mary Beth Norton (Pittsburgh Professor, Cambridge University); Janet M. Todd (Professor of English Literature at the University of East Anglia); Lyndall Gordon (Fellow of the Royal Society of Literature and Senior Research Fellow at St Hilda's College, Oxford).

Experimental Researches on Electricity (3 volumes, 1839, 1844, 1855) by Michael Faraday

KEY TEXTS

Iwan Rhys Morus *Michael Faraday and the Electrical Century*; Dent and Dutton *Experimental Researches on Electricity*; James Hamilton *Faraday: The Life*.

CONVERSATIONS

Professor Frank James (expert on Faraday, Royal Institution); Peter Day (editor of *The Philosopher's Tree: A Selection of Michael Faraday's Writings*, Michael Faraday and Fullerian Professor of Chemistry, Royal Institution).

Patent Specification for Arkwright's Spinning Machine (1769) by Richard Arkwright

KEY TEXTS

S. D. Chapman *The Cotton Industry in the Industrial Revolution*; Richard L. Hill *Richard Arkwright and Cotton Spinning*; Steven King and Geoffrey Timmins *Making Sense of the Industrial Revolution – English Economy and Society 1700-1850*; Philip Ardagh *Wow!: Discoveries, Inventions, Ideas and Events that Changed the World*.

CONVERSATIONS

Geoffrey Timmins (University of Central Lancashire, author of *Making Sense of the Industrial Revolution*); Professor Karel Williams (co-director of the ESRC Research Centre on Socio-Cultural Change); Jenny Uglow (author of *The Lunar Men*); Professor M. J. Daunton (Faculty of History/HPS, Cambridge University); Alun C. Davies (tutor of Open University course 'Cities and Technologies').

The King James Bible (1611) by William Tyndale and Fifty-four Scholars Appointed by the King

KEY TEXTS

Ward Allen *Translating for King James*; Benson Bobrick *The Making of the English Bible*; Adam Nicolson *Power and Glory: Jacobean England and the Making of the King James Bible*; *The Adventure of English* series 1, episode 3.

CONVERSATIONS

Adam Nicolson; Dr Peter Ruckman (Independent Fundamentalist Baptist Church); various members of the Gideon Society International, USA.

An Inquiry Into the Nature and Causes of the Wealth of Nations (1776) by Adam Smith

KEY TEXTS

The Wealth of Nations, edited and with introduction by Alan B. Krueger; Emma Rothschild, *Economic Sentiments: Adam Smith, Condorcet and the Enlightenment*; Jones and Skinner (eds) *Adam Smith Reviewed*; Hernando de Soto *The Other Path*; Hernando de Soto *The Mystery of Capital*.

CONVERSATIONS

Madsen Pirie (the Adam Smith Institute); Professor Julian Le Grand (the LSE).

The First Folio (1623) by William Shakespeare

KEY TEXTS

Anthony James West *The Shakespeare First Folio: The History of the Book*; Michael Wood *In Search of Shakespeare*; Andrew Gurr *Playgoing in Shakespeare's London*; Peter Blayney *The First Folio of Shakespeare*; Harold Bloom *The Anxiety of Influence*; Harold Bloom *The Western Canon*; Harold Bloom *Shakespeare and the Invention of the Human Being*; Jane Martineau et al. *Shakespeare in Art*; Peter Ackroyd *Shakespeare: the Biography;* Professor Frank Kermode *Shakespeare's Language*.

CONVERSATIONS
Dr Jonathan Bate; Professor Harold Bloom; Dr Gail Paster (Folger Institute, Washington DC – also interviewed in TV programme); Dr Moira Goff (British Library); Clive Hurst (Bodleian Library); Dr Simon Palfrey (Liverpool University).

Picture Acknowledgements

Photo insert pages 1–24
© Alamy/allOver photography:18 bottom. © The British Library:6 (Cott.NeroD.VIIf5v), 17 (10804.f6). © Corbis:13 top Wally McNamee, 19 bottom Ryan Pyle, 21 top Flip Schulke. © Corbis/Bettmann:4, 15top, 16, 21 bottom. Corbis/Hulton Deutsch:15 bottom. © Corbis/Reuters:13 bottom Rebecca Cook. © Corbis/Sygma:2 bottom. © Corbis/Zefa:2 top Larry Williams. © Getty Images:18 top Jeff Spielman, 21 bottom left and 22 Time Life Pictures. © The Kobal Collection/TOHO:23 bottom left. Musée de la Ville de Paris, Musée du Petit-Palais/photo Giraudon/ Bridgeman Art Library:23 bottom right. © National Museums of Liverpool/Walker Art Gallery:14. © The National Portrait Gallery, London:20, 24. © The Natural History Museum, London:10. © Reuters: 9 George Esiri. © Science Museum, London/Science & Society Picture Library:1, 19 top. © Science Photo Library:3 top European Space Agency, 3 bottom Bluestone, 11 A.Barrington Brown, 11 bottom Klaus Guldbrandsen. © The Shakespeare Globe Trust: 23 top John Tramper. © Marie Stopes International: 5

bottom. © Topfoto.co.uk: 7 top and bottom, 8. © Wellcome Library, London: 5 top. © Wilberforce House, Hull City Museums and Art Galleries UK/photo Bridgeman Art Library: 12.

Illustrations within the text

© The British Library:66-67 (Cott.Aug II.106), 73 (Cott.-Claud.D.VI), 138 (*Punch* May 1861),171 (Captain Marcus Rainsford *An historical account of the Black Empire of Hayti*,1805), 263 (C.35.I.11), 267 (1.e.2), 270 (C.132.h.46), 289, 300, 319 (G11631),325 (C.34.I.14), 334 (C.11.h.23), 341 (G11631). By permission of the Syndics of Cambridge University Library:128 (Ms.DAR.121.p36) . © Corbis:228, 304. © Corbis/Archivo Iconografico SA:27. © Corbis/Bettmann:80, 168, 197, 281, 304. © Corbis/Hulton-Deutsch:43, 276. © Mary Evans Picture Library:108, 174, 186. 310. © Mary Evans Picture Library/The Women's Library: 181, 189, 200. © The Galton Institute, London:37. © Getty Images:77 Time Life Pictures. © Getty Images/Hulton Archive:97, 161, 294. © Imperial War Museum,-London:104. John Murray Archive:121. © Natural History Museum, London:133, 144. *The Parliamentary History of England from the Earliest Period to the Year 1803*, 1816 Vol.28 1789-1794:155. © popperfoto.com:112. Private Collections:21, 91, 328 photo Bridgeman Art Library. © The Royal Institution, London/photo Bridgeman Art Library:209, 214, 219, 223. © Science Museum, London/ Science & Society Picture Library:237, 241, 247, 252, 255. © Thompson/*Pearson's Magazine* August 1939:58. © The Master and Fellows of Trinity College, Cambridge:7, 14, 18. © Wellcome Library, London:49, 54.

INDEX